The
Young Writer's
Guide to
Getting
Published

Kathy **Henderson**

W
WRITER'S D

Cincinna
www.writersdi

Excerpts from "The Nauga Hunters" are reprinted with permission from Matthew Cheney. The story first appeared in *Merlyn's Pen*.

The poem "We Are a Thunderstorm" is © 1990 by Amity Gaige, from the book *We Are a Thunderstorm*. Reprinted by Landmark Editions, Inc.

The poem "Opossum," by Vicki May Larkin, is reprinted with permission from Vicki May Larkin.

The excerpt from *Genie of the Lamp* is reprinted with permission from Very Special Arts. *Genie of the Lamp*, by Beth Lewis, was the 1992 VSA winning entry.

Sample film and audio/video scripts are reprinted with permission from Richard L. Rockwell, WOAK Station Manager, Royal Oak School (Missouri).

Part opening illustrations prepared by Jennifer Bolten.

The Young Writer's Guide to Getting Published. © 2001 by Kathy Henderson. Manufactured in the United States of America. All rights reserved. No part of this book may be reproduced in any form or by any electronic or mechanical means including information storage and retrieval systems without permission in writing from the publisher, except by a reviewer, who may quote brief passages in a review. Published by Writer's Digest Books, an imprint of F&W Publications, Inc., 1507 Dana Avenue, Cincinnati, Ohio 45207. (800) 289-0963. Sixth edition.

Other fine Writer's Digest Books are available from your local bookstore or direct from the publisher.

Visit our Web site at http://www.writersdigest.com for information on more resources for writers.

To receive a free weekly e-mail newsletter delivering tips and updates about writing and about Writer's Digest products, go directly to our Web site at http://newsletters.fwpublications.com.

05 04 03 02 01   5 4 3 2 1

Library of Congress Cataloging-in-Publication Data

Henderson, Kathy
   The young writer's guide to getting published / Kathy Henderson.
      p.   cm.
   Rev. ed. of: The market guide for young writers. 6th ed. © 2001.
   Includes index.
   ISBN 1-58297-057-2 (alk. paper)
      1. Child authors. 2. Authorship—Handbooks, manuals, etc. 3. Authorship—Competitions. [1. Authorship—Handbooks, manuals, etc. 2. Authorship—Competitions. 3. Child authors.] I. Henderson, Kathy. Market guide for writers. II. Title.
PN171.C5H4   2001
808'.02'083—dc21   2001026176
                                                             CIP

Editor: Brad Crawford
Production coordinator: Mark Griffin
Cover designer: Chris Gliebe, Tin Box Studio, Cincinnati, OH

With kindness, love and appreciation

to my very special Mouse

ACKNOWLEDGMENTS

It would take another whole book to properly acknowledge all those who have helped this book become the anticipated and valuable guide that it is. I'm just as grateful now as I was while compiling information for the first edition fifteen years ago (imagine!) to generous friends and colleagues, as well as the many folks I've never met who nevertheless send me information and leads to new markets and contests, warnings about markets and contests, and advice to share with young writers and those who support them. Without this network the guide would have become too much of a burden for which to assume personal and professional responsibility. I'm grateful also to the hundreds of editors and contest sponsors, perhaps thousands worldwide, who provide such marvelous opportunities for young writers to share their talented work with others.

With this sixth edition, I am especially indebted to my current *Writer's Digest* editor, Brad Crawford, for his expert help and patience. I must also extend thanks to two of my previous editors for their input and continued support: Michelle Howry and Jack Heffron. A special "thank you and I'll miss you" to two dear industry friends: Mert Ransdell, who recently retired from WDB, for support of this project dating all the way back to the first self-published edition in 1986. And to Celia Pinson Iskandar, who died so young yet contributed so much as a young writer; Celia's mother, Maxine Pinson; as well as her father, sister and husband for the courage to look beyond their own grief and let Celia's spirit and love of writing shine on to inspire others.

With special thanks to:

Fiona Cull
Jessica Renee Leving
Corey S. Dweck
Kameel Stanley
Jonathan Cofsky
Megan R. Mattingly
Jessica Dunn

Rich Wallace
Gerry Mandel
Shirley Jo Moritz
Deborah Morris
Ronald A. Richardson
Rachel Hubbard
Danielle Dunn

ABOUT THE AUTHOR

 Kathy Henderson, originally from Detroit, has lived for the last thirty years in the upper "thumb" region of Michigan. After spending nearly twenty-five years living and working on a family dairy and cash crop farm, she now divides her time between writing, speaking and a business career in marketing and management. She's also active online, where among other things she serves as WizOp (forum manager) of the Building Your Business forum on CompuServe.

Her interest in helping young writers began in 1984 when her daughter's eleven-year-old Oklahoma pen pal wanted advice on how to market the two hundred short stories and three science fiction novels he had already written. In addition to *The Young Writer's Guide to Getting Published*, first published in 1986, Mrs. Henderson has written a dozen other books for young people. She is an active member of several national writers' organizations and enjoys the many visits she makes to schools, libraries and conferences around the country.

READER'S NOTE

The Young Writer's Guide to Getting Published was published in its five previous editions as *The Market Guide for Young Writers*. The text contains occasional references to previous editions using the old title, but make no mistake: It's the same book.

TABLE OF CONTENTS

PART ONE

Chapter One
BEFORE YOU BEGIN

Chapter Two
ARE YOU READY TO MARKET?

FROM THE AUTHOR

Dear Reader,

Have you ever watched racehorses as they're standing in the starting gate? They're full of energy, chomping at the bit, ready to burst out full speed the moment the gate swings open.

They remind me of the eager young writers I meet through the letters they write me or at the schools I visit. They, like you, I imagine, are full of energy and excitement, eager to burst out onto the track that leads to publishing success. If you rush out unprepared, however, the race to the finish line could be a disappointing one.

I wrote this book as a training guide to help prepare you for the publishing tracks that excite you. Even if you are familiar with past editions, please take the time to read through part one before racing to the market and contest lists. While the basic advice remains the same, I've added new information that many of you have asked for. Plus, a whole new stable of successful young writers and dedicated editors and contest sponsors shares experiences and advice.

This sixth edition is extra special as it was published on the fifteenth anniversary of the original book that I self-published so long ago. So many changes have occurred in my life, and in each edition, since then. Many of you reading this were not even born yet! But one thing has remained constant over the years: Talented young writers continue to find publishing success because of the many editors and contest sponsors who provide opportunities, encouragement and recognition.

Happy Writing!
Kathy Henderson

FOREWORD

Once when I was in the fourth grade, our class was getting ready for Thanksgiving. I'm sure we heard stories about the Pilgrims and the Wampanoag Indians who befriended them. I can't really remember. In fact, even when I search my memory, I can't remember the name of a single classmate. I can only remember one thing about the entire fourth grade.

That one thing is a picture I drew of a turkey. The teacher hung it up high over the chalkboard. In front of the whole class, she said, "Look how good Kent's turkey is."

I felt very proud at the time. Somehow that sense of accomplishment has stayed with me for almost forty years. The good feeling I had in being recognized for my creative work has been a lasting influence on me, and on my career.

I think there must be no better feeling than one that comes from the sense of creating something yourself. It may be a picture of a turkey, a rabbit made from clay, or a story or poem.

Writing gives me great joy. I believe it is so with you also.

Over the years I've had the fun of seeing the poems and stories of thousands of young people. Some of these stories interested me as a reader more than others. A few we picked to publish in *Highlights*. There is one thing that I always remember when I read these—the writer's sense of accomplishment; the pleasure he or she gained through the experience of writing.

Writing is more than the activity of putting one word down after another. You cannot write without thinking. Good, clear writing is a sign of good, clear thought.

The process of writing helps you think. It helps you reflect on ideas and explore your thoughts. You can first try your ideas and words out on yourself. Then you can share them with others.

This book is about sharing your ideas and thoughts. It's about a good way to share a little bit of yourself with others. Your audience may at first be friends and family. After a while, you may want a larger audience for that bit of yourself.

The author of this book has been writing for a long time. She came to want a larger audience early on in her writing. She had felt the satisfaction and joy of writing, and she felt a strong wish to share with others.

We can imagine that Kathy Henderson found a number of ways to share her work.

Remembering the joy of sharing—as well as the difficulty of finding out how to share—prompted Kathy to write this book.

This edition is the result of a desire to refine and improve the information given in earlier volumes. By helping countless young writers, Kathy has given back some of the joy writing has given her.

In this book you will meet a number of young writers. Notice how much they are like you. You will meet here, too, a number of editors. Notice they seem like people with whom you could sit down and talk.

There is sound advice in this book—lots of tips on getting started, helpful pointers about the writing process and a host of ways to give yourself the encouragement. Rejection, a part of every writer's life, is explored in a sensible way.

The up-to-date listings of where to send your writing are the best I've seen, by far. Their completeness gives you a broad choice of publications and a wide number of contests. Those publications and contests listed here will allow you to find your audience. They will allow you to share your thoughts and talents.

This is a book to be used. On its pages lie the hard-won wisdom of an author who has learned how to share the joy of writing with others.

Kathy Henderson is offering young writers like you valuable knowledge about writing. By using the information in this book you can increase that sense of personal accomplishment gained through writing.

Kent Brown, editor
Highlights for Children

PART ONE

Chapter One

Before You Begin

Welcome back, readers of past editions, and a hearty hello to new ones!

Since 1986, when the first edition was published, there have been many changes in the publishing world. But in the last few years, more than during any other time in publishing history, there have also been some major changes in the way writers approach getting published, in the growing variety and number of publishing opportunities and in the actual submission process. I say "some" because a lot has not changed.

Writing—good writing—and getting it accepted for publication still takes skill, talent, hard work and perseverance. Finding literary success and riches as a published writer is still far from guaranteed. Being in the right place at the right time with the right manuscript still depends a lot on the type of planned luck that comes from watching for opportunities and being prepared to take advantage of them. Publishing scams still exist and, worse, are often harder to spot and avoid. Writing and trying to get published can still generate the most exhilarating experiences, as well the most disappointing ones.

The personal computer has made it much easier for writers to self-publish their work. It's also now much easier and cheaper to edit and publish the work of others, especially in the growing e-publishing business. The popularity of the Internet and World Wide Web has contributed to the growing number of publishing opportunities available to all writers. Unfortunately, those same advancements have also made it more costly and difficult to sell some forms of traditionally published materials.

I was sad to learn that David Melton of Landmark Editions in Kansas City, Missouri, has stopped sponsoring one of the best, most prestigious and financially rewarding book contests for young writers. Mr. Melton says sales of *Written & Illustrated by . . .* award-winning books have dropped too low to continue them. Teachers and students are now focusing more on expanding their use of technology including accessing the Internet, with its growing number of student-focused writing and publishing opportunities.

But whether it's on the Internet or in more traditional forms of publishing, each month the work of dozens of young writers appears in publications all around the world. To do what these people have done, you don't need to be at the top of your class in reading or writing or be labeled "gifted" or "talented." You don't need to know somebody in the business or have lots of money or years of experience. You don't need to live in an unusual place or lead an unusual life. And you don't need any fancy equipment. As many young writers have proven already, you don't even need to wait until you are older to try.

There are only two specific things you do need to know beforehand: *who* publishes the type of material you like to write and *how* to prepare your finished story, poem, article, play or script before submitting it. *The Young Writer's Guide to Getting Published* has that special information, plus a lot more to help you become a *published* young writer.

This chapter provides an overview of the marketing process. Combined with chapter four (the proper way to format and mail manuscripts) and chapters eight and nine (the names and requirements of markets and contests open to submissions from young writers), you'll have all the basic information needed to start submitting. If you have prior marketing experience, these chapters will refresh your memory and bring you up to date on who is currently publishing what.

If you aren't sure what marketing your writing means, or if you already know what it means but aren't sure you're ready to try it, skip these first two chapters for now and start with chapter three. Then come back and join us.

WHAT'S NEW IN THIS EDITION

I encourage all readers, including those familiar with past editions, to take the time to read through this edition in its entirety. In addition to the updated markets and contests and new profiles of editors, contest sponsors and young writers, this edition contains new and expanded information in many other areas. More important, from the standpoint of helping you prepare and market your manuscripts, I've focused more on what it means to be a writer and why it's important to continually improve your writing skills, plus how to research, study and evaluate opportunities. In particular look for

- more about submitting novels and other book-length manuscripts
- detailed formatting directions, plus examples for plays and scripts
- examples of properly formatted poems
- examples of query and cover letters
- expanded information about the growing opportunities and changes in electronic "online" (e-publishing) communications, markets and contests
- more answers to the questions young writers ask most
- detailed information on how to study markets and their guidelines
- advice about markets and contests to avoid
- additional resources about writing and marketing
- insight to help you evaluate and develop your writing and marketing skills
- more than forty new market and contest listings
- more information about now-famous people who were first published as young writers
- special author's tips, like the one on page 5, sprinkled throughout the book that will alert you to recommended resources, additional information, warnings and reminders

The market and contest lists in this book are the result of a special survey of editors and contest sponsors across the world. Their enthusiastic responses made it possible to compile a promising list of publications and contests that are especially receptive

Author's Tip:

If you are serious about writing and plan to make it a career, I recommend that you read *The Young Person's Guide to Becoming a Writer* by Janet E. Grant. This practical book will help you develop your talent, explore your options, find help and chart a course for success.

---

to submissions from young writers. Many listings have specific sections, whole issues written or whole Web sites devoted to writings by young people. Other listings, such as those with mainly adult readers, encourage young writers and consider their work especially in the areas of essays, opinions, profiles and personal experience. Contests may be specifically for young writers or may have separate categories for them. A few markets and contests have no age preferences or restrictions; however, they recognize that some young writers produce work as good as or better than many of the adult submissions. Remember, however, that only the markets and contests responding to my survey and agreeing to be listed are included. The main criteria is that they will seriously consider, for awards and/or publication, submissions made by young writers.

Why are so many editors interested in hearing from you? The answer is simple: Many of them were once young writers too! One editor expressed the feeling shared by many others when she wrote, "Your guide is a great idea. I only wish it had been available eight or ten years ago for me."

MORE ABOUT THE LISTINGS

Many of these markets not only publish material from young writers but offer payment as well. Others offer free copies of issues containing the writer's work instead of payment. Sometimes they offer both. Online (or e-publishing) opportunities are almost entirely just that—online. If your submission is accepted, it will most often appear directly and only on the associated Web site.

As you search through the listings, pay special attention to entries marked with an asterisk (*), or star. Markets and contests bearing this symbol represent especially good opportunities for young people. They have special issues, columns or departments featuring young writers' work and, therefore, are likely to accept more material than will other markets. If you are a very young writer (twelve and under) or are especially eager to get published, these are your best opportunities. If you are thirteen or older and have little writing or marketing experience, concentrate your efforts on starred markets and contests. Consider other listings only after carefully studying the requirements and objectively evaluating the quality and maturity of your manuscript. Don't think these opportunities aren't challenging. Many are among the most highly respected publications in their fields. However, your work has the best chance of success here. Submitting to other markets and contests now would be like trying to stuff Cinderella's stepsister's big foot into her tiny glass slipper. Highly unlikely!

The listings also contain symbols to help you evaluate and compare opportunities. For instance, a checkmark (✔) indicates a listing new to this edition, although it is not necessarily a recently established publication or contest. The maple leaf (✤) identifies Canadian markets and contests. Listings based outside the United States and Canada or that are especially global in nature are preceded by a globe icon (🌐).

The double cross (‡) indicates markets and contests to be considered only by more mature young writers (fourteen and older) or by very determined and experienced younger writers. Watch also for a special author's note at the bottom of some of these opportunities. These markets and contests are often highly specialized and maintain very sophisticated editorial preferences. Manuscript acceptance here can be very difficult to achieve even for adult writers. Still, the editors and sponsors of these markets and contests are willing to consider manuscripts by young writers. Consider your options and your work carefully before trying these markets. Submitting inappropriate material is a waste of time and energy for both you and the publication.

A few starred (*) listings will also have a double cross (‡). This means that they offer young writers special opportunities;

however, competition is exceptionally tough. The high number of submissions a market receives compared to the space reserved to print or display them sometimes increases competition. An editor who receives one thousand submissions monthly with space to print only ten yearly will have to reject the majority of the manuscripts received. Thus, well-written and correctly submitted manuscripts often get rejected.

DOLLARS AND SENSE

A few markets insist that writers become subscribers before they will consider their work for publication. In addition, many contests require an entry fee. A dollar sign ($) will alert you to these listings. Entry fees for most contests are minimal and are normally used to defray the costs of the contest, including payment for prizes and/or publication of winning entries. Many of these contests are also marked with an asterisk (*), meaning that despite the entry cost, they are still good places for young writers to consider. A few contests require more substantial entry fees, often five dollars or more.

Do not disqualify a market or contest from your submission list just because it has an entry fee or insists that only subscribers or club members may submit material. Take into account the following factors as well:

- Who is sponsoring this contest?
- Is the entry fee reasonable?
- How are the fees used?
- How much competition will my entry or submission face?
- Will I be competing with others my own age or with similar experience?
- Do I need to subscribe first, or will the price of a subscription or membership be deducted from my payment if my work is accepted for publication?
- Would I enjoy being a member of this writers organization?
- Have I studied the contest's rules or the market's guidelines carefully to determine if my planned submission would be appropriate?
- Are there any extra benefits that make the entry fee worth-

---

Author's Tip: Warning!

Beware of publishers and contests that ask you to pay to see your work printed or to collect your prize. Read all rules, acceptances, evaluations and award notices *carefully*. *Never* pay to have accepted manuscripts published or to collect awards from contests.

---

while? For example, does the contest or market offer writers professional critiques of their entries for no or little additional cost?

- Do I know other people who have entered this contest? What was their experience?
- Can I afford the fee?
- Are there other markets or contests that would be better for me to try first?

Remember that there is always some cost involved in submitting to markets and contests, even if it's just paper, envelopes and postage—one to send your manuscript and another (known as an SASE or self-addressed, stamped envelope) to have it returned if not accepted. Entry and subscription fees are additional. No matter how minor the cost, make sure your material is well written and appropriate to make the submission cost a worthwhile risk.

OPPORTUNITIES THAT SEEM TOO GOOD

If you enjoy writing, the prospect of being published or winning an award can be very exciting. Unfortunately, there are some publishers and contests that attract amateur writers with promises of publication and large cash awards, trophies or other prizes for a fee. You may receive information from such publishers and contests through the mail (or e-mail) or see ads for them in magazines and newspapers. You may not realize that a publication or contest expects *you* to pay to have your work published until *after* you have submitted your manuscript. This situation is similar to subsidy or vanity publishing, which is discussed below.

Be aware also that some literary consultants or agents—

Author's Tip:

Many authors enjoy receiving letters from their readers. I know that I do. However, due to our busy schedules, we can't always respond as quickly as we'd like. Often we are asked for information that is inappropriate or impossible for us to give. For advice on writing to published authors, please see page 105.

working independently or in conjunction with a publisher or contest—offer free evaluations and publishing advice in exchange for a "reading fee." A reading fee may be one price, such as $150 for a book manuscript, or may be charged on a per page basis according to the type of work submitted.

If you want advice or help with a manuscript, look for less expensive, and often more productive, solutions. Find out if there is a writers group that meets in your school or neighborhood. Ask for references from teachers, librarians or bookstore clerks, who can recommend books to read or may know of an experienced writer willing to work with you. Many organizations, such as the National Writers Association, include manuscript help as part of the yearly dues or for a reasonable fee. Some writers exchange manuscripts with each other through the mail, with each writer supplying a return envelope and postage. E-mail now makes exchanging manuscripts even cheaper and easier. However, many writers, myself included, still prefer to read and comment on paper copies. Printing out e-mailed manuscripts can be an unwanted expense for the receiver. Be sure to agree on the preferred format before you exchange manuscripts.

SUBSIDY PUBLISHERS (VANITY PRESSES)

Subsidy book publishers (also known as vanity presses) are publishers that invite you to submit your manuscript, accept it for publication, *then* tell you how much it will cost you. They often offer free information such as how-to-get-published booklets or other valuable-sounding gifts. Their ads may say that you can obtain a free, professional evaluation of your manuscript without obligation. Sometimes they cite famous authors whom they claim to have worked with in the past.

The Internet's growing popularity has created a new breed of questionable subsidy-style publishers. Yes, legitimate e-publishing exists. Even Stephen King has used this medium. But please realize that the explanations and warnings that follow apply equally to traditional and Internet-based subsidy publishing. Also remember that there are some important differences between self-publishing and subsidy publishing.

Subsidy publishers typically respond to submissions in one of two ways. First, they may praise your work and you as a writer, claiming you have the talent of a potential best-selling author. They can't wait to sign you as a client and help you get your work published. They promise that it will all happen quickly. Second, they may claim your work has merit, but it isn't quite good enough to publish, yet. They will then say that with their expert editorial help and publishing guidance, they can help you produce a published book. Whatever their pitch, the catch is the same: *You* must provide all or most of the funds to publish your book. In other words, when *you* send them enough money, they will print your book. They may or may not help you sell or distribute it. If they do, a significant amount of time may pass before you receive your share of the sales.

Selling your new book to readers is another matter entirely. Despite their promises, subsidy publishers have little incentive to market your book because you have already covered their costs, plus a handsome profit. Likewise, it may not matter to them if your book is well written or just your ego on display. Since their primary purpose is to get you, the writer, to pay for your book's publication, they may not be objective about the merits of your manuscript.

Internet-based subsidy publishers also respond to submissions as described above. The results, although handled completely through the speed and ease of cyberspace, remain essentially the same: The e-publisher charges you a fee for the privilege of uploading your book to its Web site, where others who are interested in reading it can download the text to their computers. Whether or not you, as author, receive any payment based on the number of times your book is downloaded, depends entirely on the contractual terms of each e-publisher. Please, please, read all of the terms and conditions carefully before participating in this type of venture.

If you're a fan of the "Little House on the Prairie" television series, you may remember Charles Ingalls falling into the vanity publishing trap when he submitted his father's autobiography to a publisher. Grandpa Ingalls wanted so much to have his book published. Charles, after reading the publisher's praise and not wanting to disappoint his father, sent the money he had saved for a badly needed new plow to get the book published. At first everyone celebrated the publishing success of Grandpa Ingalls. Before long, though, everyone realized that it was a hollow victory. Grandpa Ingalls, in particular, was embarrassed and disillusioned especially after bragging about his writing ability and publishing success.

CONTESTS WITH HIDDEN COSTS

Similar tactics are used by some contests. The initial entry fee may seem quite reasonable, perhaps only a dollar or two, or, no entry fee is required at all. Sometimes, an entry fee will be referred to as "nominal" or "modest" even though they expect you to pay twenty-five dollars to fifty dollars or even more to enter your work. Like subsidy book publishers, they may offer free information for a self-addressed, stamped envelope (SASE). Typically, their ads boast thousands of dollars in annual prizes plus publication of winning entries in anthologies.

An e-publishing twist is getting the writer to share personal information such as an e-mail and regular address, plus hobbies and interests. This information is then exchanged or sold to other companies, resulting in many unwanted offers in your e-mail and regular mailboxes.

You will be delighted when an official-looking letter arrives proclaiming you a winner. But your heart will sink when you realize that to see your masterpiece in print, you must first buy a copy of the anthology in which it will appear. It's not uncommon for a single copy to cost sixty dollars or more. I've also seen letters from contests that only awarded prizes (cash and/or trophies) to

---

Author's Tip:

....

Webster's New World Dictionary defines honorarium as "a payment as to a professional person for services on which no fee
is set or legally obtainable." Honorariums (gifts or money)
are often given to speakers as a token of appreciation from the
sponsoring organization. Reputable contests *do not* require
winners to pay anything in order to collect their awards.

"winning" contestants who paid to attend the awards banquet.
Others may offer a certificate verifying your winning entry, then
offer to mount it for "free" on a beautiful plaque that will only
cost you fifty dollars for engraving and shipping.

Here is a portion of an actual award letter sent to an unsus-
pecting friend of mine. (For legal reasons, references to the organization's identity have been omitted.)

Dear _____ Entrant:

CONGRATULATIONS! The judging has been com-
pleted in your category/categories, and one or more of your
entries has been selected for a _____ award.

The entries this year were exceptional in all categories,
and yours was/were among the best.

The honorarium for each category award is $110. Your
total *contribution* [italics mine] is $220. Each category winner
is [*sic*] of beautiful Gold, Silver, or Bronze _____ statuette.

PLEASE REMIT YOUR HONORARIUM ALONG
WITH THE PROPER FORM/FORMS BY DECEMBER
31, 1992.

Again, congratulations for being a _____ winner!

Accompanying this awards letter was a sheet claiming: "Most
recipients of the _____ award wish to order additional duplicate
statuettes and certificates for other individuals who have contributed to the creative and productive aspects of the winning entry."
The price for each duplicate statuette was even *higher* than the
first one, plus, they wanted fifteen dollars for a duplicate
certificate!

Author's Tip:

Here are two excellent Web sites that feature additional information and updated listings about "vanity" anthologies, "worst poetry" contests and other questionable publishing opportunities: http://www.sfwa.org/beware/contests.html and http://www.wind.wind.org/endall.htm.

"What turnip truck did they fall off of?" asked my friend incredulously. Although she did not collect her award, the contest sponsors most likely didn't care because before they declared her a winner, they had already collected sixty dollars in fees for the two essays she had entered.

Such publication and contest offers, before their true nature is exposed, are particularly enticing to beginning writers eager to see their names in print or writers frustrated by a continual stream of rejection slips. (Even experienced adults get fooled occasionally. The friend mentioned on page 12 is an experienced adult editor.) There is nothing illegal about such offers. But, to me, they take unfair advantage of writers' dreams of success by getting them to believe that this is how the publishing business traditionally works. Worse, they usually charge writers much more than it would cost them to take their manuscripts to a local print shop and have them typeset, printed and bound into book form, known as self-publishing.

THE SELF-PUBLISHING DIFFERENCE

Many poets, writing clubs or other community groups self-publish collections of their work, primarily to share with family and friends. This is similar to students publishing a yearbook, school magazine or classroom anthology. They may sell a few dozen copies; some even make a profit. The difference is that when people self-publish their work, they understand their responsibilities from the beginning and have control over the cost. For instance, they choose the number of printed copies, the type of paper used and binding. No one is making exaggerated claims of fame and fortune. (I hope!)

Author's Tip:
....

Young Author Day books, which many elementary students write, illustrate and help bind, are an excellent example of worthwhile self-publishing projects.

EGO ALERT!

The worst thing about subsidy publishers and vanity presses is that they inflate writers' egos using flattery that has no connection to the truth. Like Grandpa Ingalls, some writers think it's an honest appraisal of their talent or potential as a writer. And, like him, they declare themselves failures when they learn the truth about the circumstances. What they don't realize is that they haven't learned anything objective about their talent or potential at all! After such an experience, some good writers will abandon writing entirely, thinking they can't succeed; others charge blindly ahead, believing they are great writers whose work needs no improvement.

Don't become victims of such misguided assumptions and sales tactics. This is not how reputable publishers and contests operate. In any case, when in doubt, check it out with someone more experienced.

In compiling this guide, I have taken great care to avoid listing such questionable opportunities. Please write to me immediately if you receive a request for money to collect an award or to guarantee publication of your work from any of the listings included in this book or any others of which you are aware. Send a detailed letter and include photocopies, if possible, of any correspondence you have received to the address listed at the bottom of page 240.

ADVICE TO THOSE WHO SELF-PUBLISH

As pointed out earlier, self-publishing can be a fun, inexpensive and worthwhile experience especially for students or community groups. Unfortunately, too many writers waste time and money self-publishing their work as a way to avoid the editing process, assuming that it would destroy the quality or creativity of their

---

Author's Tip:

....

Draw & Write Your Own Picture Book, by Emily Hearn and Mark Thurman, is an excellent reference book that even younger students can read and follow. Teachers (K–12) and older students will find more detailed advice from David Melton's *Written & Illustrated by . . .*

---

work. As can happen when you work with subsidy publishing and vanity presses, this may lead to questions about the credibility, integrity and quality of your work or your writing ability later on.

If you insist on self-publishing larger works, such as books or newsletters, do so in a responsible manner. Although you may do your own editing following advice found in many excellent reference books, it is much wiser to enlist the help of a professional editor. Find someone whose judgment you respect but who can bring objectivity and perspective to the task. Rewriting, revising and polishing are key steps to producing quality work. Producing a quality product should be the goal of any publisher.

The Complete Guide to Self-Publishing, by Tom and Marilyn Ross, is an excellent resource for those wanting to know everything about writing, publishing, promoting and selling their own books.

GAINING A COMPETITIVE EDGE

Unfortunately, no one can guarantee that all writers, regardless of age, will find a willing, reputable market for their work. There are, however, several things you can do to give your material an edge against the competition. These basic principles (covered in chapter three) are followed by professional writers. Bear in mind that although other people may help you, you alone are responsible for the final content and condition of your submitted manuscripts.

GETTING DOWN TO BUSINESS

If your parents have ever paid good money for music lessons, you've probably heard them say a million times, "Go practice." Off you trot to your piano, tuba, drum or violin to hammer, blow,

---

Author's Tip:
....
Have trouble thinking up new ideas? Can't tell a good idea from a bad one? Check out *Where Do You Get Your Ideas?* by Sandy Asher.

---

rap or stroke the notes of the scale. All the while, your mom's taken refuge in the garage and out of earshot, and your dad is in the kitchen trying in vain to tap his foot to your beat.

But hand your mom or dad a little story or poem you just wrote from the top of your head and out come the "oohs" and "ahs" and "Neanderthal is sooooo talented. He's a natural born writer." No one ever tells you, "Go practice your writing."

Until now.

I'm telling you, "Go practice your writing." Give that budding talent a chance to bloom and grow. You'll be amazed at what a little daily stretching of the mind and fingers will do for the quality of your writing. Quality writing gets published. Practice also keeps the idea mill churning.

FOR YOUR EYES ONLY

Keep a notebook handy for writing down special thoughts or feelings. Jot down descriptions of places you visit. What makes them different from other places you've seen? Why do some places, like McDonald's or Kmart, look the same wherever you go? Try to describe your home for someone who is blind or deaf.

Learn to exercise your senses. What does your living room sofa *feel* like? Is it rough or smooth? Can you smell the kind of stuffing it has? Go through each room, recording how things feel, smell, sound, look and taste.

Study how people look. What do their expressions say about them? Have you ever been really close to a very old person? Did you ever notice the different medicines that seem to seep from their bodies? What does a baby smell and look like while in the process of messing a diaper? Don't just wrinkle your nose, *show* what he looks and smells like using word pictures. What comparisons can you make?

Record how people talk. Do they use slang or proper English? Do their clothes reflect the way they talk? Do they slur their words, and if they do, why? Is it a speech impediment or just laziness? Are they bashful and shy or boisterous and loud? If you could feel the voice of a big husky man, what would it feel like? Does he pound out his words like a jackhammer? Does his breath smell?

How does your teacher look when you first see her each morning? How does she look at the end of the day? Can you tell if the day has been good or bad?

Read, read, read. But avoid reading only what currently interests you. Read a variety of things—books, magazines, newspapers—even if you don't fully understand them. Sample topics and genres[1] you would normally skip.

While reading your favorite author's work can be a great help in learning to write well, postpone it while drafting your own stories, especially if you tend to be too critical of your own work. Besides deflating your confidence, it can hamper your originality and make it harder for you to finish the stories you start. In fact, some writers deliberately read a few pages of what they ordinarily consider boring material to motivate themselves to return to their own work.

A SECRET WEAPON ONLY YOU CAN USE

If I asked one hundred people to write a story based on the same idea, do you know what I'd get? One hundred different stories. That's because each of us is a unique individual; no two people are exactly the same.

Exercise your writing mind daily and your writing will grow stronger and more creative. You'll gain the confidence to risk writing stories only you can tell. You will develop what is natural for you, for the way words can be woven together in interesting, inspiring and informative ways. With practice, your writing will take on a special cadence, a distinct rhythm that flows with the

---

[1] Pronounced zhan ra, genre means kind or type. For instance, romance, western, realistic fiction, science fiction, fantasy, historical and how-to are examples of different genres.

Author's Tip:

....

To better understand how successful writers draw from their interests and experiences, read biographies and other thought-provoking works by or about well-known writers. My personal favorite is *Gates of Excellence* by Katherine Paterson, author of such wonderful books as *The Bridge to Terabithia*, *The Great Gilly Hopkins* and *Jacob Have I Loved*.

For help in developing your own writing style and habits, try *Writing From the Inside Out* by Charlotte Edwards, *Becoming a Writer* by Dorothea Brande, and *Word Painting* by Rebecca McClanahan. These books include stimulating exercises. Brande's book is especially useful for writers who lack self-confidence, have trouble finishing what they start or can't get started. McClanahan's book is especially useful in learning how, when and why to include specific sensory details in your writing.

---

tone of your writing. This is part of what's known as a writer's *style*. It makes your writing different from all other writing. Your style may vary with each new manuscript you create. It's important, however, to develop your own style from the inside out as you draw on your emotions, interests and experiences to create something new.

Style makes your writing special. And *your* style is the secret weapon only you can develop to become a successful writer.

THE POST POSITION

In horse racing, jockeys like to start from lane one, the post position, because it offers the shortest distance around the track to the finish line.

If there's a shortcut to getting published, it's taking time to find out what editors and contest judges want. So, before you burst out of the starting gate, set yourself up for the post position by reading chapter three, "The Basics of Getting Published," and chapter four, "How to Prepare Your Manuscript." For inspiration and insight, read chapter seven, plus get a look behind the scenes of several markets and contests in chapter eight.

Chapter Two

Are You Ready to Market?

When most people think *markets*, they think stores and shopping: buying groceries at A&P, perhaps, or a new pair of jeans at the mall. But when writers think *markets*, they are thinking of places to which they can send their manuscripts to hopefully be published.

The world is full of people who would like to be published. *Wouldn't it be great*, they think, *to see my name splashed across the cover of a best-selling book?* Or, *I bet people would pay big money to read how my great-grandfather sailed ships across the Atlantic.* Or, *Someday I'm going to write a story about the time I visited Uncle Ned and Aunt Fanny's farm and how I sat on some eggs in the chicken coop and tried to hatch them.*

Their ideas may be good, even great. The problem is they are would-be or wanna-be writers. They want to be published, but they don't want to write. They are not ready to market.

ARE YOU A WRITER?

Well . . . do you write? Do you capture your thoughts and imaginings on paper? *Yes?* Then you are a writer.

Sometimes it's very hard. It's like trying to catch dandelion puffs in a wispy net on a windy day or struggling to hit the baseball when it's the bottom of the ninth, there's a guy on third and your team is one run down. We get frustrated, angry and impatient forcing words that don't want to come out. Then we look at what we've written, expecting—*hoping*—to see something wonderful for all our hard work, and all that's there is a jumble of words that doesn't sound at all like the wonderful, perfect story we had planned in our heads.

Sometimes it's easier. Words seem to jump out of our minds and scamper straight down our fingertips to form tidy black images on paper. The story picture is clear, often better than we had imagined. Correct a misspelling here, cut an adjective there and, *poof*, we've created something interesting and well written.

Poetry. Short stories. Essays. Plays. Newspaper articles. It doesn't matter what you write, how well you write or how easy it is for you to pull the words from your head and have them land creatively on paper.

If you write, you are a writer.

BUT ARE YOU READY TO MARKET?

Some writers write a lot and hope that everything they write will be published. Some writers write only when inspired. They usually don't create as many marketable manuscripts as more active writers who are determined to get published. Just the same, they hope that their work will be published.

There are also people who write for themselves. They may enter a contest occasionally or send a poem they wrote to a friend, or they may not want to share their work at all. They don't care if they get published. They may not even *want* to be published. (They may even be afraid to let others read their work. I know. I feel that way sometimes.) And that's OK. It should be their choice to make.

Unfortunately, in school you don't always have a choice. Your teacher assigns a writing project. She's going to read what you wrote or you won't get a grade. Reading your essay or book report to the class may be mandatory. You have to do it. You are a part of a process writing class where students must read and critique each other's work. Then, as the last step in the process, everyone's work gets published in some form and is usually distributed to parents and other students to read. It might even be printed in the local newspaper.

However, when it comes to work you've written on your own, just because you wanted to, you have a choice about sharing it with others. No one should ever force you to enter it in a contest or submit it to a market if you don't want to. It doesn't matter why you don't want to share it. *It's perfectly OK to write just for yourself.* Even though you're not ready to market your work now, you may change your mind later. I suggest you read chapter seven. You may find just the encouragement and inspiration you need to give marketing a try. And, take time to read through all the how-to market information that follows to get an idea of what it's all about.

IN WHAT CATEGORY DO YOU BELONG?

Not all young writers are beginners, and not all beginning writers are young. There are some very accomplished and successfully published young writers. And, then there's Dennis Volmer, considered one of the youngest writers (age six) to have had a book published under a professional royalty contract. There are many others, some with enough writing and marketing experience that they're far beyond the beginner stage, even though they still have much to learn and many more situations to experience.

Some folks began writing or trying to publish when they were great-grandparents. One woman in our local writers club was ninety-three when she entered our contest for the first time. She'd been writing her whole life. She was a beginner at marketing.

I never planned on becoming a writer. It happened quite by accident one day when I read an editorial in our rural weekly newspaper. It made me *so* angry that I sat right down and wrote a letter to the editor to complain. After the editor read my letter, he did a most surprising thing: He called and said, "I like the way you write. Would you consider writing 'The Farmer's Wife' column for us?" Suddenly, not only was I going to be a writer but a published writer. I was a real beginner even though I was already married and had a child. I knew nothing about getting published or preparing a manuscript. Plus, the only writing I'd ever really done was for school assignments or diary entries that read like weather reports. You know the kind: It snowed today. The temperature was 32°. Mom drove me to school. Hardly publishable material!

Stephen King, one of the world's most famous and successful

writers, has been writing since he was a child. At one time he and a friend even published their own "magazine," which they wrote, photocopied and stapled together, then sold to kids at school, charging as much as a quarter. The school eventually made them stop selling their magazine, but King didn't stop writing. Stephen King may have been young and inexperienced, but compared to me he was hardly a beginner. He wrote regularly and seriously practiced his writing craft. (Note: Read one of King's early short stories in chapter six.)

CHECK YOUR WRITING AND MARKETING ATTITUDE

How serious are you about your writing? Do you work at it every day? How do you feel about editing? Do you always review your work with the idea that it could be improved? Are you willing to rewrite, revise, cut and polish your manuscript until every word has a purpose that moves the piece smoothly from beginning to end?

Do you put yourself—observations, imagination, feelings, emotions, opinions, fears and joys—into your work so that you write pieces that mean something special to you? Do you include something of value for the reader, something he or she can relate to?

Robert D. Sutherland, editor and publisher of *The Pikestaff Forum*, said this in a note he wanted to share with young writers:

Authors of poetry and fictional stories should write to please themselves first; one has to be true to one's vision and express oneself honestly for the work to "live" and for the labor of creating it to be enjoyable and fun. But authors should remember that if they submit their work to be *published* (which means making it available to a broad audience), they have certain responsibilities to their readers too.

If one says, "Here, read my work," that work had better be worth a reader's time. In other words, it should provide something worthwhile, useful or valuable (including enjoyment) for the reader to take away. If it does not, if it is too personal to the writer, or too obscure, or too trivial or silly, the readers will feel their time wasted. Therefore, writers had better submit for publication only their *very best*, and that which will have value for others. Writers should *not* indulge themselves at their readers' expense.

That's good advice for writers of nonfiction too.

SEND ONLY YOUR VERY BEST WORK

Revise and rewrite until what you submit is the best you can do. Revise and rewrite until each paragraph, sentence and word says exactly what you mean it to say. Make this type of editing plus the drafting of new manuscripts a regular part of your practice or training routine. Like a skater repeatedly etching figures onto the ice, a musician practicing to perfect the way he plays a certain tune or an athlete working to develop both body and game skills, your writing will improve with practice and fine-tuning.

Ask an adult, perhaps a teacher, a parent or a more experienced writer, to read your manuscript and offer constructive criticism. Listen carefully to their comments, then decide whether you agree or disagree with their advice. Sometimes hearing someone else's opinion will help you view your material in a new way; yet always remember that *you* are the creator. You must be the final judge of your work's readiness for submission. In the end, follow the advice you agree with and politely disregard the rest.

Listen to your material read aloud. Recite your work into a cassette recorder, then play back the tape while you follow a written version. This often makes it easier to note construction glitches and awkward words or phrases. If you do the reading, read what you have *actually written*. Also, read it as though you were seeing it for the first time. Don't add a lot of voice inflections as a dramatic actor might. You're looking for places that may need editing, not auditioning for a part in a play! (Play and script manuscripts benefit from a different form of testing. See the Appendix for more details.)

It's very easy to read what you think you have written or intended to write. However, your actual words, not your reading of them, must provide all the drama, action and emotion. Readers should be able to visualize your settings, feel and see with your

---

Author's Tip:

....

For help planning and editing fiction stories, read *Wild Words! How to Train Them to Tell Stories* by Sandy Asher.

Older students may also enjoy my personal favorites by author Gary Provost: *Make Every Word Count* and *Make Your Words Work*.

---

characters as if they were with them in the story. *Show*, don't tell your story. This applies to poetry and nonfiction work as well. If you must explain what you mean, then your job as a writer isn't finished.

Put your writing away, out of sight, for a day or two (even a week or more for longer works) before editing it. You'll be amazed at how mistakes you didn't notice before will suddenly jump out at you like they were waving little red flags. Granted, you may not always have time to let writing assignments from school "cool" before turning them in; but take time before submitting a manuscript to an outside market or contest.

MORE ABOUT REWRITING AND REVISING

Rewriting and revising refer to the types of editing you do to improve your manuscript *content*. Many people use the terms interchangeably. To me, however, rewriting refers to rewording a particular sentence or paragraph so it says exactly what I mean, using the best and least words possible. I don't change the meaning, just how I present it. I substitute more precise (active) nouns and verbs for weak adjectives and adverbs. I fiddle with sentence structure and word placement.

When I revise something, I make bigger changes, like reordering whole sections of a story or article. I may change my mind about the kind of statement I'm making, start over with a slightly different topic, add a new scene, twist a plot, create a whole new story opening or ending, add or subtract characters, deliberately lengthen or shorten the manuscript. Sometimes you can revise a previously published manuscript to resubmit to a different market or contest.

POLISH AND PROOFREAD

Correct all grammar, punctuation and spelling mistakes in your final copy before mailing it out. If, while evaluating your work, you discover it doesn't seem quite right, rewrite and revise it. Polishing, on the other hand, prompts you to view the work as a whole, making sure all parts fit snugly together like a completed jigsaw puzzle. Look for missing or misplaced parts. As you reread it, forget that you are its author. Be as objective and truthful as possible. (This is not an easy task when editing your own work!) Here are just a few questions to ask yourself:

- Is there a strong beginning that flows smoothly into the middle section, which in turn stimulates the reader and leads him into the climax and ending?
- Do characters sound and act like real people? Could a reader predict how they might realistically behave in a different setting?
- Can you imagine a setting that would make your characters uncomfortable? Happy? Excited?
- What is the main conflict or problem that the main character faces? What point have you tried to illustrate?
- Have you tied up all loose ends, supported your premise using word illustrations (facts and images) with which readers can easily identify?
- If you have a market or contest already in mind, does the length fall within the word limits set?

Many times the various aspects of the editing process overlap. You might notice and correct problems associated with the questions above during the initial rewriting and revising stage. Or you might get so involved working on small parts of a manuscript during rewriting and revision that you overlook problems that affect the overall presentation. It's like the adage: You can't see the forest for the trees.

The good thing about proofreading is that you don't have to do it until your manuscript is ready for its final presentation. After all, why bother correcting a misspelled word in a first draft when you might cut it in a second, third or fourth draft? Don't stop to fix typographical errors, look up correct spellings and fret over

---

Author's Tip:

....

There are many good how-to-write books on the market that identify and discuss in detail the various parts of a story, poem, article, etc., and how to seamlessly weave them together. Studying these will help you improve both your writing and editing skills. *Writing for Children and Teenagers*, by Lee Wyndham, contains detailed information suitable for young writers ages twelve and up, especially those interested in writing fiction. Teen writers working on adult topics will also find this book useful.

For honing your nonfiction writing and editing skills, I recommend *Words' Worth*, by Terri Brooks, in addition to the Gary Provost books mentioned earlier.

For final polishing and proofreading, there is no better addition to any writer's personal reference library than *The Elements of Style*, by William Strunk, Jr. and E.B. White.

---

just the right word or phrase while you're trying to be creative. It's too easy to lose your creative momentum. The purpose of the first draft is to get the basic idea down on paper, much like painters first sketch in pencil the basic elements of the picture they plan to paint. Add the flourishes and details later.

Many manuscripts can be improved if writers put more time and effort into their editing. Yet, be aware that a manuscript can also be ruined by too much editing. Like writing, editing skills improve with practice.

After a thorough polishing, you'll need to go over the material again, looking for technical mistakes such as misspellings or errors in punctuation and grammar. For instance, match your nouns and verb tenses correctly. If the manuscript is already in standard format, look for typographical errors. Misspelled words are easily overlooked because you thought you knew how to spell them. Our mind assumes the word is correct, so our eyes skim over the word rather than see the mistake.

Write or type a fresh copy of your manuscript after any major editing session. Computers and word processors make this a simple task. Incidentally, although computers and word processors allow you to edit directly on screen, most writers find it easier to work on a printed copy (commonly referred to as a *hard* copy).

LEARNING TO EDIT

Hone your editing skills by reversing the creation process and rereading favorite books, stories, poems, articles, etc. After enjoying the work's overall impression, try taking it apart. Why did the author choose this way to begin instead of that way? Identify where the beginning ends and the middle begins. Look for specific words that evoke the five senses: seeing, hearing, tasting, smelling, touching. How do the characters' words and actions help you imagine them as real people? Try to rewrite a passage using your own words. Is your version as effective as the original work? Can you identify specific things the author used early in the story to plant certain ideas in the reader's mind and point to things that happen later? What happened during the most crucial point in the story? How did the main character react? What if the main character had acted differently?

This dismantling process works equally well for nonfiction and poetry. For another perspective, try this process on works you didn't enjoy. Determine exactly what turned you off. For instance, did you have trouble identifying with the main characters? If yes, was it because of the writing (story construction, word choice, plot directions, etc.) or because you weren't interested in this type of story? Was the story too predictable, meaningless, absurd?

BECOMING A SUCCESSFULLY PUBLISHED WRITER

The level at which you are now, as well as your chances for publishing success, depend not so much on your age or experience as on your attitude. Writers who are determined to publish usually succeed. They may be serious about pursuing a writing career or just enjoy it as a hobby. Occasionally, getting published occurs by happy accident, like it did for me. (But don't count on continued success this way. The odds of it happening again are probably worse than winning the grand prize in the Publisher's Clearing House sweepstakes.) Most often, and especially for the most rewarding results, getting published takes dedication, persistence, patience, lots of hard work, good writing, plus a willingness to learn who is publishing what.

MORE ABOUT YOU

Do you believe in yourself? Are you willing to risk rejection? Are you anxious to improve? Will you spend the time it takes to learn what editors want to see in the manuscripts they receive? If you can honestly answer yes to these questions, you are ready to travel the writing and publishing road.

Think about what is in store for you. What writing and publishing goals do you have? How do you plan to reach them? How much time are you willing to devote? From whom can you get help? Five years from now, what will you have written? In ten years? Twenty?

Other questions will help you identify what kinds of writing to pursue. Ask yourself, What am I interested in? What are my hobbies? What types of writing do I like to read? What sort of writing turns me off? What's my opinion of the world today? If I could go anywhere, where would I go? If I could be anything, what would I be? Who do I admire most? What traits do I look for in a friend? What do my enemies have in common? How are they different?

Jot down your answers to these and other questions that make your mind search for answers. Explore them in journal or diary entries. Often we really don't know what we think until we see our thoughts spelled out on paper. Refer to these answers later as you decide what to write about and as you research which markets and contests to enter.

From time to time reevaluate your responses. Have you reached your short-term goals? Are you closer to your long-term ones? Is it time to set new ones? How has your outlook changed? What experiences have had the most influence on you?

As mentioned in the first author's tip in chapter one, Janet E. Grant's book, *The Young Person's Guide to Becoming A Writer*, is an excellent book for serious young writers. Through a series of exercises, forms and "food for thought" narratives, Ms. Grant helps young writers develop their talents. She demonstrates how to experiment with different writing techniques, how to develop character sketches and how to work in different genres. More importantly, Ms. Grant (once a young writer herself) shows you how to personally and objectively evaluate your own writing skills, as well as brainstorm and set goals. It's almost like having an accomplished professional writer as a personal mentor.

Writing is exercising the brain and pouring the sweat out on paper. The more thinking you do, the more you'll find to write about. The more you write, the more work you'll have to publish.

Chapter Three

The Basics of Getting Published

Have you ever played Pin the Tail on the Donkey? It can be pretty hard to get that tail to stick in just the right place while wearing a blindfold. Yet, a lot of writers try to get published in much the same way. They grope their way around, hoping their manuscript will land in the right place. Writing and marketing can be both fun and challenging, but if you approach it as a professional writer would instead of like a game, your chances of getting published will improve dramatically.

Acting in a professional manner and trying to write like an adult are not the same thing. Trying to write like an adult is one of the worst things a young writer can do. One of the best things you have going for you is your youth. Write to express your feelings and your ideas; don't try to mimic what you think an adult writer might do. Believe in yourself. Tell the stories you need to tell, and tell them in your own way.

Acting professionally also has nothing to do with age. It means behaving in a courteous, responsible way. It's learning what's expected and taking the time to provide it. Your interest in reading this book indicates that you're not only eager to get published, but want to do it right.

This chapter and the next explain the right things to do. If I didn't think you were smart enough and ambitious enough to do them, I wouldn't have spent so much time and trouble sharing them with you. And if there weren't a lot of editors and contest sponsors who believed you could do it and do it well, the last half of this book would be pretty empty. Here, then, are the basics of getting published.

Author's Tip:

Many beginning writers have a hard time understanding both the creative development and the visible changes their manuscripts go through from draft to polished, properly formatted manuscript to final printed page. In 1992, a marvelous paperback book was published that not only describes in detail how one writer got an idea and transformed it into a book, but includes reproductions of handwritten notes, drafts in various stages, comments from editors requesting changes and copies of printed pages before and after final editing.

The book is titled *James A. Michener's Writer's Handbook: Explorations in Writing and Publishing*. Even the youngest writers will find it interesting and learn from it.

LOOK SHARP—PREPARE IT LIKE A PRO

Prepare your finished manuscript following the standard formats described in chapter four. Proofread again, making any corrections before submitting your work.

Occasionally, editors or contests will want, or allow, manuscripts formatted in a slightly different way. For example, while most editors insist that manuscripts be typed, a few will accept handwritten work. Some contests do not want judges to know the entrant's personal information, so they ask for the author's name and address to appear on the entry form but not on the manuscript itself. The preferred format for individual poems, plays or scripts also varies between certain markets and contests. Under most circumstances, editors and contests will expect to see manuscripts prepared using standard formats.

If you have made only one or two small mistakes per page on a final draft, neatly correct them. To make them as inconspicuous as possible, use a lead pencil or black ink pen. (Editors generally will use colored pens or pencils to indicate where corrections or edits are needed.) Acceptable handmade corrections include

- Indicating that two letters or words have been reversed. words Two
- Drawing a thin line through a word or short line that should

be deleted. [~~word~~]

- Correcting a misspelled word by drawing a line through it and printing it correctly in neat letters directly above or in the nearest margin. [~~corect~~] *correct*
- Using a small arrow to indicate a missing word or two; add the word by printing it neatly as you would when correcting a spelling error. [add ∧word]   *the*
- Using the paragraph symbol (¶) to indicate where a new paragraph should be started.
- Placing a forward slash (/) between two words that have run together.

If you find more mistakes or if your page has a sloppy appearance, make a fresh copy, *then check it again.* This is for your benefit. Editors cannot meet with you personally and have no idea whether or not you are a good writer; therefore, the first impression they get will be from your manuscript's overall appearance. By sending a neatly prepared and properly formatted manuscript, you will be telling editors and contest judges that you care enough about what you write to give it the best chance of acceptance.

Think of yourself as a busy editor out to buy a new pair of shoes. Where would you expect to find the best quality? In a store where the shoes are soiled, mismatched and thrown in a jumble on a display table for you to sort out? Or in a store where the shoes are neat, clean and paired together for easy selection?

Make it easy for editors and judges to read your material. They will respect the time and effort you have taken. When the choice is between two manuscripts of close or equal merit, the one that looks better will always win.

SIMULTANEOUS SUBMISSIONS

Submit one manuscript at a time to a market or contest. In other words, do not submit the same manuscript for consideration elsewhere until you have received an answer from the first. Mailing the same manuscript to more than one place at a time is called *multiple* or *simultaneous submission*. Editors become extremely annoyed if a manuscript they have the spent time and trouble reading is accepted elsewhere before they have had a chance to make their decision. Many guidelines specifically state: *No simultaneous submissions accepted.* Although some adult writers occasionally make simultaneous submissions, my advice to young writers is to always stick with the one-to-one rule.

Occasionally writers are encouraged to submit several poems together to a single editor or contest. This is not a violation of the "one manuscript to one market at a time" rule because you are not asking two people to consider the same material at the same time. Again, read individual guidelines for details.

You may, of course, send different manuscripts out to different markets and contests. In fact, writers are encouraged to have several things "in the mail" at the same time. More about that later.

STUDYING AND COMPARING OPPORTUNITIES

Sending your very best work will not help you get published if you submit it to the wrong place. But how can you be sure which is the *right* place?

The answer, unfortunately, is you can't if the right place means the place where your manuscript is guaranteed to be accepted.

There are ways, however, to determine appropriate places for you to try, places where a particular manuscript has a good chance of being seriously considered. Remember: An appropriate market or contest for one manuscript may not be an appropriate place to send the next one. And one that is good for your friend may not be the best place for you.

Studying and comparing market opportunities is a multistep process that needs to be redone from time to time because the publishing field does not remain the same year after year. New opportunities present themselves while others fade and die away. The Internet's growing popularity makes this even more true now than ever before. A few markets and contests last, getting bigger and branching out, but even they go through changes. Editors come and go, staffs move to new locations, editorial policy changes are made, regular departments and special columns are added or deleted, they may decide to publish more fiction or less poetry or—best of all—raise the rates they pay writers for their manuscripts.

HOW TO CHOOSE OPPORTUNITIES

First determine which markets and contests are the most appropriate for you. Understand which ones accept submissions from someone your age, writing ability or experience, location and interests. Also decide which markets are of most interest to you.

Part of this work has been done for you. Of the many thousands of markets and contests open to freelance writers (a writer who does not regularly work as an employee for the publisher), only those interested in receiving submissions from young people (age eighteen and under) have been included in this book. However, not all of these opportunities are appropriate for each reader. As you read through the listings, make a list of or checkmark those that sound appropriate for you.

Try not to become overly enthusiastic at this point. Because you are naturally creative, dozens of new ideas for articles, stories and books will suddenly burst like kernels of hot popcorn in your head as you read through the listings. (Tip: Keep paper and pencil handy to jot down new ideas so you won't forget them.) Be selective. Try to pick from five to fifteen markets and/or contests that seem to want the same types of manuscripts you have already completed or plan to write.

You may want to make two lists, one with opportunities that look good for a specific manuscript and another of markets that pique your interest or seem especially suited to you.

Next, send for the writer's guidelines and/or contest rules from each place on your list, or access the guidelines via the Internet. If possible, request a sample copy or borrow one from the library. When available, read samples directly online. You don't need to request materials from everyone at once, but make requests from at least five so you'll have a variety to study and compare. Enclose a self-addressed, stamped business (#10) envelope (commonly referred to as SASE) or whatever the listing requires with your request.

For online opportunities, I prefer printing out the guidelines for the markets and contests that I think are most promising to

Author's Tip:

If you have friends or classmates[1] who are also interested in getting published, share the chore of collecting sample copies and writer's guidelines. Whether you do it alone or with others, keep a master list of what you have already requested and received. Note on the list the date you received the guidelines and the issue of the sample copy. Send for updated material every year or so.

me. Store these alphabetically by site in a ring binder or file folders. Create a special folder to bookmark the pages in your browser software. Choose a method that makes it as convenient as possible to retrieve the information for further use.

When the guidelines and samples arrive, read them thoroughly. Study each individually to get a feel for the type of material they publish. Read *everything*: featured pieces, author blurbs, letters to the editor, editor and/or publisher's messages, tables of contents, even the advertisements. Watch for announcements of special contests or invitations to send your writing. Just as no two writers are the same, neither are any two markets or contests the same. There are always some differences no matter how similar they may look at first.

Ask yourself the following questions:

- Is this what I expected?
- Did I misinterpret the information contained in the listing?
- Do I still think this is an appropriate place to send my work?
- Can I tell how much competition I would have submitting here?
- Would I be proud to have my manuscript published here?
- What benefits are there for me in getting published here?
- What new ideas for writing occur to me as I read this?

---

[1] Collecting, studying and comparing publishing opportunities is a valuable experience that helps young people develop both their creative and critical thinking skills. Teachers should encourage students to actively participate rather than compiling the information for them.

In addition to studying and comparing opportunities, take a good, objective look at any manuscript you are planning to submit. Make a list of its identifying features. For instance:

- Is it a short story, poem, script, essay, etc.?
- What is its genre and subject matter? Is it mystery, adventure, humor, science fiction, etc.? Could it also be sports-related, outdoorsy, about school or church?
- If there is a main character, how old is he or she? What interests does he or she show in the story? What happens in the story?
- What is the setting for your piece?
- To what age reader would it most appeal? (Someone your own age, younger, older?)
- Do you have illustrations or photographs that would be appropriate to submit with it?
- How long is it?
- Has it ever been published before?
- How well written is it? (Do you think it is one of your very best pieces? Or is it just pretty good?)

Now comes the hard part. Considering all that you know about your manuscript and appropriate markets and contests, ask yourself two questions:

1. At which one or two places would my manuscript have the *best* chance of being accepted?

2. Which one or two represent the *highest quality* or *most prestigious places* (a well-known publication, one that offers payment or one of particular interest to you) that are appropriate for my manuscript? Remember: Your chance of acceptance in these markets may be lower because the editors receive many submissions, publish only a few pieces like yours in each issue, say that they are very selective, or reject it for some other reason (perhaps it's an adult market).

If you are very lucky, the answers to these two questions will be the same. Most likely, however, you'll have the names of four different opportunities. Do you submit to the easier one or go for the biggest reward first? That's a choice you will have to make yourself for each manuscript you want to submit. I know many writers who have almost everything they submit accepted the first or second time out, but they always pick the easiest markets.

Personally, I prefer being rejected by the best and working my way down my list. (*Actually, I prefer getting accepted by the best!*) You'll have to decide for yourself. The important thing is to pick several solid possibilities. If it isn't accepted by your first choice, immediately send it out to the next choice on your list.

If it gets rejected by all four, begin a new list. While you're at it, reevaluate your manuscript's merits. Could it use a little rewriting or more polishing before you tackle that second list of appropriate opportunities? Did you receive any useful comments on it? (See the section "Some Words About Rejection" on page 48, for some tips on dealing with rejection and evaluating editors' comments.)

LOCAL, REGIONAL AND SPECIAL OPPORTUNITIES

Some of the best and most appropriate markets and contests for young writers are in your own neighborhoods, cities and states or relate to a special interest or circumstance. In every edition of the guide, I list several opportunities representative of what can be found in many areas around the country. The America & Me Essay Contest, sponsored by the Michigan Farm Bureau, for instance, is limited to students in Michigan; but every state has some type of writers group that publishes a magazine or newsletter or sponsors either regular or occasional writing contests.

Don't overlook writing a letter to the editor, editorials, guest opinion pieces and feature or filler stories about people and events of interest in your community. Many writers overlook writing nonfiction pieces, yet they are easier to get published and usually pay. This is especially true of magazines, which may publish only one or two poems or short stories but ten or more columns, tips, articles, how-to's and other types of nonfiction in each issue. Obviously, the more of something they publish, the better the chances of getting that something accepted.

Your local newspaper is also a great place to get a job as a stringer reporter or columnist. Newspapers, especially smaller dailies and weeklies, are always short-staffed. My local paper (and

---

Author's Tip:

....

Writers interested in targeting easier nonfiction markets should read Connie Emerson's book, *The 30-Minute Writer, How to Write and Sell Short Pieces*. It includes dozens of tips and ideas for writing personal essays, humor, opinion pieces, reviews, anecdotes, miniprofiles and more.

The Internet is also full of excellent publishing opportunities for new writers. However, I don't think seeing your work displayed on a computer screen will ever match the exhilaration of seeing your work published on real paper.

---

the one where I was first published) is constantly looking for young writers interested in covering school sports and community events.

Whether you reply to an ad or go in on your own, be prepared to answer any questions the editor might ask you. (You may want to do a practice interview with a parent or friend acting the part of the editor.) Try to anticipate the editor's reaction, any objections that might be raised. What will you answer if you're asked what you want in return? Are you looking for a paid job? (This is most likely a set fee—in 1971, when I started, I got two dollars for each weekly column published—so don't count on getting rich. On an up note, my column did run above Erma Bombeck's.) Or are you willing to work for the opportunity to be published and to learn more about the business? (Tip: If you apply to a nonprofit organization, be prepared to donate your services. At a regular business, however, first try for a paying position, even if it's a tiny amount. Part-time reporters may be paid minimum wage for time on the job but may not be paid for the time it takes to actually write the article.) More likely, you'll be paid a set amount for each assignment you accept and complete.

Figure out in advance how you will present yourself: You need to show enthusiasm, dedication, persistence and that you can be trusted to meet deadlines. You must show that you are willing to accept criticism and to rewrite and polish when necessary. Editors also need to know that you won't get discouraged or ornery if your section or piece gets moved or cut altogether because the editor decided something else was more important. (You most likely will not be consulted on this.)

Have work samples with you, or mail a few of your best pieces with a query letter. Be very selective; they won't be as interested in how much you've written but whether you show real promise as a writer. For local interviews, take along a scrapbook binder with your pieces (published and/or unpublished). The editor may not have time to read through them immediately; however, leave a few photocopies of your best pieces behind.

Also try local radio and television stations, especially local cable and PBS stations, and the community relations directors at area hospitals or other civic-minded organizations. And, don't forget to get involved at school.

Special interest magazines and other periodicals also offer young writers excellent opportunities. Always be on the lookout for one-of-a-kind contests or invitations to submit material. A few years ago, for instance, The Learning Company, which makes computer software programs for children, and The Tandy Company, which made Tandy computers, sponsored a Silly Story Contest for students using one of The Learning Company's software programs. It was a fun, one-time contest that drew thousands of entries from eager young writers.

For special interest magazines, you will often be submitting your work with adults. If you target publications of high interest to you, such as a hobby, computer or pet market (anything that you read regularly), you can compete on equal footing. Many times, because you have learned the basics of getting published, you'll have a better chance than adult readers who don't know how to properly prepare a manuscript or edit.

Writer's Digest, The Writer and *ByLine* offer writers updated market and contest information in each month's issue. If you are very interested in writing, subscribe to one of these magazines. *ByLine* is the best choice for beginning and young writers, but I know writers as young as ten who regularly read *Writer's Digest*. Numerous writing-related Web sites, such as *Inkspot* and my *Young Writer Network*, also provide new and updated information.

Writing and marketing are ongoing processes. Keep several

Author's Tip:

If you've ever had a little brother or sister want to tag after you wherever you're going, then you know how an editor feels when receiving inappropriate submissions. The editor doesn't have any use for them, and after trying to explain this nicely a few times with no result, the editor gets frustrated and doesn't ever want to be asked again!

pieces in the mail (to different places, of course) so that if one comes limping home, you can still hope the best for the others. And don't stop writing while you wait to hear from an editor! Get started on a new project right away.

THE BIG "NO"

Editors sometimes reject even well-written material for a number of reasons. By far the biggest reason is something editors call *inappropriate submissions*. This means that that particular publication or contest never uses the type of material submitted. The manuscript's subject may be of little or no interest to that magazine's readers. It may be a short story when only nonfiction is used. It may be hundreds of words over the preferred length. The wording or topic may be too easy or too hard for the readers. The reasons are many; but, in general, they make a manuscript inappropriate for that particular publication.

Editors waste a lot of time and energy dealing with inappropriate submissions—time they could have spent reading and replying to your submission. In fact, so many inexperienced writers (old and young) submit inappropriate material that some editors will no longer consider unsolicited manuscripts. (*Unsolicited* means that the editor did not specifically ask to see the material before receiving it from the author. All of the markets and contests listed in this book will consider unsolicited material from young writers if submitted properly.)

To avoid making an inappropriate submission, study the market and contest information carefully. Send for (or download) and study the guidelines or tip sheets offered. Buy, send for or borrow a sample issue[2] if you are not familiar with the publication; then read it objectively to determine if your manuscript is appropriate.

Pay close attention to the "Editor's Remarks" and the "Sponsor's Remarks" sections in the listings. Here you will find special advice, from the editors of that publication or contest, about submitting material. If your manuscript does not closely match their requirements, look for a market that does or rewrite a manuscript to meet the guidelines of a specific market. This is often possible when a manuscript meets most of the requirements but the length is incorrect or when you haven't emphasized the right perspective or angle.

EXPECT TO BE EDITED

Once your work has been accepted by an editor (and even some contests), it will probably need further editing before being published. This happens to all writers no matter how carefully they have edited and polished their manuscripts before turning them in.

There are many reasons an editor may edit or make changes to your manuscript. It may have been too long for the available space, or the editor may have felt different wording would make your message easier to understand. This is true not just with books or magazine stories but with all types of work.

Editors have a responsibility (a large part of their job) to edit material when necessary. Thankfully, most editors will make only minor changes. Most of the time you'll discover that the editor's changes have made your manuscript better.

Occasionally, you may not like the editor's changes. If the piece has already been published, you cannot do anything but try to forget what happened and go on to your next project. If you absolutely hate the changes made, do not submit to that editor again. There are many other markets from which to choose.

View any changes from the editor's point of view. If you can't seem to get over it, break a few pencils or kick a few wastebaskets

---

[2] Occasionally, free or low-cost sample issues of a publication are not available. This is the exception, however. If at all possible, read one or more issues of a publication before submitting material to it.

until you calm down. Think long and hard before writing, calling or e-mailing an editor to complain. Consider this message from Dawn Brettschneider Korth, former editor of *Straight*:

> Please tell teens that it's normal to have your work edited. I've had complaints from teen writers when I changed *one word* of a poem—when it was misspelled and used incorrectly! A sixteen-year-old threatened to sue the company over a poem in which I reversed two lines to make his rhyme scheme consistent. Such scathing letters make editors reluctant to deal with inexperienced teen writers. All we want to do is help them.

WORKING WITH AN EDITOR

When editors feel that all or parts of a manuscript need to be rewritten or revised, they will often make suggestions and ask the writer to make them. If this happens, decide whether or not you think making the changes will improve your work. (Please note that even if you change a manuscript according to an editor's suggestions, you are not guaranteed that the revised work will be accepted.)

If you don't understand what you are being asked to do, or if you don't agree with all the suggestions, discuss your feelings with the editor by phone (if invited to), in a letter or by e-mail.

Explain why you think a suggested change is unnecessary and/ or make new suggestions. This give and take between writers and editors happens all the time. Don't be afraid of it. It's not very different from the way coaches work with their players. If you and the editor can't agree on what needs to be done, you can always decide not to have it published there. Most times you will be free to submit the manuscript elsewhere.

Any manuscript may be edited, even those submitted by famous authors. It is a necessary, though sometimes uncomfortable, part of the publishing process.

The more you know about writing, editing and publishing, the easier it will be to understand and work with an editor throughout the editing and publishing process.

KNOW YOUR RIGHTS AS AN AUTHOR

When you write something, by law you automatically become the copyright holder (owner) of that manuscript. If an editor agrees to publish your manuscript, she will "buy the rights" to it. Often magazines, newspapers and newsletters buy *first serial rights* or *one-time rights*, which gives them permission to publish your manuscript one time. The rights are then returned to you, and you may offer the same manuscript to another editor for *second* or *reprint* rights.

A number of publications and some contests buy *all rights*, which means that once you agree the publication can publish your manuscript (or artwork, photographs, etc.), the work becomes their property (they hold the copyright) and it is no longer yours. You may not send it to another market or contest. Even though you no longer own the copyright, you will be credited as the author if it is published.

For legal reasons (and often to make things simpler for staff members), many markets and contests that accept submissions from young people assume all rights to that material whether or not it is published. Some markets and contests state that policy in their listings. Even if it is not listed here, it will be spelled out on the guidelines or rules sheet or in a letter or contract sent to you when your work is accepted.

Professional writers and other adults seriously pursuing publication of their material are often advised *not* to sell all rights if at all possible. However, the situation is very different for young writers. Since many of the best opportunities for young writers are also the ones that insist on buying all rights, I personally think young people (and many beginning adult writers) have more to gain from being published by such markets than retaining copyright to their material. It is a decision that you and a trusted adult should make together. Consider the manuscript in question and the reputation of the market or contest with whom you are dealing. Also keep in mind that many markets that buy all rights will reassign them to the writer at a later date upon written request, particularly if the writer is planning to reprint the material in a noncompetitive way.

For example, I once sold all rights to my research and interview notes about farm accidents to a top-quality agricultural magazine. Later, when I wanted to reuse some of the material in a safety article targeted to high school students, I wrote to the editor, explained the situation and asked for reassignment of my rights. He was happy to comply. He had no further use for the material, and the market to which I was planning to submit was not in direct competition with his.

On the other hand, especially for teens, it never hurts to try negotiating with an editor. Suggest to the editor that you prefer to sell only first serial rights. Buying all rights saves some paperwork, but a publication that doesn't intend to reuse your manuscript will have no objection to buying first or even reprint rights instead.

Many publications are now asking for, or including in their all rights statements, e-publishing and worldwide rights. If your work has been accepted and you do not understand what rights the publisher is planning to assume, ask for clarification. Do this before the piece is published. Afterward it may be too late to object or have the copyright agreement changed. Ideally, you should understand what rights may be involved *before* submitting your work. Unfortunately, that isn't always possible because editors and writers may negotiate different rights for specific manuscripts.

(Incidentally, I had to ask Matthew Cheney for permission to reprint the part of his story that appears as a sample manuscript in the next chapter, even though the story had appeared in two separate issues of *Merlyn's Pen: The National Magazine of Student Writing*. However, I needed reprint permission from Landmark Editions to reprint one poem from Amity Gaige's book, *We are a Thunderstorm*, even though the book's copyright is registered in her name. Every situation is different. How did I know from whom to seek permission? I asked!)

Negotiating a book contract is more complicated and confusing than dealing with magazines and newspapers. There are many things to consider. Most publishing companies offer writers a *standard book contract*. Unfortunately, what is standard at one company is different at another. All writers should have any contract offered to them checked by a reputable literary

Author's Tip:

For young writers (and their parents and teachers) interested in learning more about contracts, I highly recommend *Negotiating a Book Contract: A Guide for Authors, Agents and Lawyers* by Mark L. Levine. This slim handbook takes you step-by-step through the negotiating process and explores in simple language what the various contract clauses, legal terms and publisher's offers mean.

Copyright issues and other legalities of publishing in online or other electronic forms are still being determined. Try to stay abreast of decisions and changes in this area by reading writing-related magazines or accessing the latest information available on reputable Web sites.

---

agent[3] or lawyer familiar with the publishing industry. Many writer's organizations offer contract information and/or trustworthy advice. (Note: Young writers are welcome to join the National Writers Association, which offers such services to members.)

A number of questions in chapter five, "Answers to Questions Young Writers Ask Most," deal with these and related issues.

The copyright of a message or library file of an online information service, such as CompuServe or America Online, is usually held by its author. The online service also holds a *compilation* copyright. You must obtain the author's permission to make further use or to distribute any portion of a message or file. In some cases, you may also need specific permission from the online service. Refer to the online service's terms of service (TOS) for more information about its online copyright issues.

Copyrights can be very confusing. More information about current copyright law is available by sending $3.75 with a request for "Copyright Office Circular 92," stock number 030-002-00168-3, to:

---

[3] Literary agents seldom represent young writers, and normally there is nothing a literary agent can or would be willing to do for an amateur writer that he can't do for himself.

Superintendent of Documents
U.S. Government Printing Office
Washington, DC 20401-9371

Forms and instructions for registering your copyright with the U.S. copyright office are available free by writing to:

Copyright Office
Library of Congress
Washington, DC 20559
Or call: (202) 707-9100

It now costs thirty dollars to register a copyright. Remember, however, you *do not* need to register your copyright. As soon as you put your thoughts down in some type of fixed form (on paper, audiotape, film, computer disk, etc.), your work is automatically protected by law. You are the legal copyright holder until you give it away. Neither ideas nor titles, however, are protected by copyright. (Note that copyright issues may differ in countries outside the United States. Again, when in doubt, read the guidelines or ask the editor for help in understanding copyright issues if you have work accepted for publication.)

CONTEST TIPS

Contests offer young writers some of the best opportunities to get published. You'll want to pay just as much attention to writing and editing your entry as you do with any manuscript you are planning to submit. But contests also require an extra amount of care so you don't sabotage your chances before you start. Keep the following additional guidelines in mind.

When entering writing contests, follow all the stated rules *exactly*. If a contest says you may submit only one poem, don't send two. Both may be disqualified, and you'll lose your entry fee without any possibility of winning.

If a contest states that entries must be typed, type them. A judge will not overlook the mistakes you make when entering a contest. Chances are the judge will never see your entry.

Most contests have someone who opens entries and reads them to see if the rules have been followed. Only those entries that follow all the rules will be sent on to the judge or judges.

Don't lose before you begin.

Entering writing contests can be an exciting and rewarding experience. Boost your chances of winning by following these additional tips and suggestions:

1. Send for a complete list of the contest rules, regulations and eligibility requirements. Rules and entry forms are often available via e-mail or on the contest Web sites. Unfortunately, the rules for every contest can't be listed in this book because of space limitations. Send a self-addressed, stamped envelope (SASE) to receive the rules or guidelines if they are not available on the Internet.

2. Follow all the rules exactly. This includes where your name, address and other information are to be placed; the number of entries you may submit; and how manuscripts are to be prepared. If the rules do not give specific guidelines for this information, follow the standard formats provided in this book for submitting manuscripts to an editor. For online contests, e-mail or upload your material in the requested computer file format.

3. Don't forget to include entry fees or required forms with your submission. Some contests for young people request that a parent, guardian or teacher include a *signed* statement verifying that the entry has been written entirely by the young person. Include this statement if required.

4. Don't limit yourself to contests designed just for young writers. Many talented young writers have placed in or won contests open to adults. However, you have the best chance of winning in contests that are for or have categories open to young people only, especially if they also have age groups; are specifically or exclusively sponsored for young people in your local, regional or statewide community; and focus on a topic of special interest and/or importance to you.

5. If possible, read the winning entries of an annual contest from the previous year or contest. Just as reading back issues of magazines will help you understand a publication's editorial preferences, so will studying past contest winners. Yet, don't let this stop you from entering something that may seem a little different.

For example, Amity Gaige won first place in the 1989 Written and Illustrated by . . . Awards contest for her submissions of poems and photographs, *We are a Thunderstorm*. That same year Adam Moore was named a Gold Award winner for his nonfiction book, *Broken Arrow Boy*, which recounted his experience recuperating from a serious accident. Though Adam did most of the writing and illustrating, his book also contained some material done by other people. Nearly all past submissions (and winners) of this contest were fiction stories with drawn illustrations, yet Amity and Adam won with entries that met all the contest requirements but were a little different.

Remember, too, that judges often change from year to year.

6. Don't be discouraged if you don't win. Most contests award prizes for only first, second and third place. Some also name a number of honorable mention winners. A judge, like you, has personal likes and dislikes. From many entries, a judge must choose only a few and will make the selection based on personal preference. Another judge or editor may like your work better.

SOME WORDS ABOUT REJECTION

To become a published young writer takes more than enthusiasm and talent. You must be aware of opportunities. You must study and follow the guidelines set by editors and contest sponsors. You must understand that while some manuscripts are rejected for poor writing, others are rejected for reasons not readily apparent to the writer. These include: (1) time needed to print an issue or post it on the Internet; (2) space available for displaying manuscripts; (3) the number of manuscripts received for consideration; (4) the number of manuscripts already accepted for publication; and (5) the personal preferences of the editors, staff and judges.

Rejection is disappointing. It hurts. But rejection must be put in perspective. The editor or judge has not rejected you personally. He simply picked another manuscript that better suited his needs at that moment—much like you might consider one pair of shoes over another of equal quality.

You should feel especially honored if an editor or judge sends back any constructive advice, comments or criticism about your manuscript.

Editors are busy people who deal with hundreds of manuscripts yearly. They cannot afford either the time or expense to write to you personally concerning your manuscript's rejection. Most times you will receive a generic, preprinted note known as the *form rejection slip*.

The wording on a form rejection is usually so vague it is difficult to tell exactly why a manuscript was rejected. There is, however, an unofficial code many editors use to signal writers that their manuscript has some merit. It is a busy editor's way of offering encouragement. The code goes something like this:

If an editor *signs* his name himself, then something in your manuscript caught his eye. It may be the flow of your words, your ability to make a point, your characterization within a story or something else. You are on the right track. Keep at it!

If an editor *jots a word or two of encouragement*, such as "good idea" or "nice try," he means your manuscript was better than most but perhaps lacked that certain spark that would have made it outstanding.

If an editor *writes a few words of advice or criticism*, such as "your characters are a little weak" or "the plot needs tightening up," he means your manuscript was good enough to be given careful consideration. With a little more effort, you may have a winner.

Of course, there are variations on this code. Some editors try hard to encourage promising young writers and will send a short, personal note rather than a rejection slip. Sometimes a rejection slip that simply says, "Sorry. This does not fit our needs at this time," means just that. They can't use it whether or not they like it.

Rather than dreading a bit of criticism, look forward to it. It is usually easier to pinpoint minor flaws in a well-written manuscript than in a poorly written one where the trouble is so spread out, it is hard to offer any meaningful help in a short note. An editor who offers encouragement, either by praise or constructive criticism, deserves your appreciation. Whether or not you make use of that advice is up to you.

You may be lucky enough to find yourself a published young writer with your first attempt. Then again, you may need to submit material many times before, finally, one of your manuscripts is selected for publication. If you have a strong desire to write, then never be discouraged. With practice your writing will get better and better, and so will your chances of being published.

SET THE RIGHT GOALS

Be careful not to set the wrong goals for yourself. A writer whose only goal is to be published will likely experience many more disappointments than will a writer who hopes to be published one day but whose goal is to enjoy writing and become a better writer.

Do not expect everything you write to win a contest or be accepted for publication. Consider how a musician prepares for a performance. He may continue to take lessons, trying out new pieces, practicing over and over again the pieces he has learned in the past. For his actual performance, he will not play every piece he has practiced. Instead he will pick and choose those he plays and enjoys the best. He also considers which pieces he feels the audience will like hearing.

As a writer, your audience is your reader; your performance, your manuscript. Pick and choose manuscripts you feel represent your best work. When choosing which markets and contests to submit to, consider what you have to offer that would interest the readers of those publications.

Chapter Four

How to Prepare
Your Manuscript

Next to the care you put into creating your work and the attention you pay to selecting an appropriate market, nothing is more important than how to present it to an editor or contest judge. Your manuscript should look crisp, clean and polished so the editor will concentrate on what you have written. This is especially important for teen writers targeting adult markets and contests.

Follow the specific guidelines requested by a particular market or contest if they differ from the standards, *especially for contests*. Otherwise, your work may be rejected no matter how good it is. Worse, some markets and contests won't return an inappropriate submission even if accompanied by an SASE. Inappropriate submissions made by e-mail or uploaded to Web-based publications and contests may not be acknowledged. And *no* market or contest will assume responsibility for unsolicited manuscripts or original artwork or photographs.

With so many variations in policy, it's impossible to give specific advice for preparing all types of manuscripts, artwork and photos in this guide. Following are the general guidelines and formats that most printed magazines and contests will accept. They are very easy to understand. (See page 59 for additional advice on formatting material that will be e-mailed or uploaded to an online service or the Internet.)

Do not use scented or colored paper; fancy typewriter type or decorative computer fonts; hand-drawn pictures in the margins; or special bindings, folders or covers for your manuscripts or mailing envelopes. *Please* don't concoct any tests for an editor to pass, such as placing pages upside down, backwards or out of order. Many insecure amateur writers do this, thinking that if a manuscript is rejected and returned to them with the pages still mixed up, it proves that the editor didn't even bother to read their submission.

These writers also prefer to think that editors are prejudiced against them or not smart enough to see what wonderful writers they are—anything to avoid admitting that their manuscript could be improved, that they chose an inappropriate market or that it just wasn't possible for the editor to use their work.

What they don't realize is that an annoyed editor will simply return a rejected manuscript in the same condition it arrived. Editors are delighted to discover new talent of any age, but they will shy away from working with writers who obviously do not trust them to do their jobs right.

Remember, there's nothing wrong with being a young, inexperienced writer; but if you are serious about getting published, you don't want to *look* like a young, inexperienced writer. Give your writing the best possible chance of attracting an editor's eye by following the formats outlined here. If you must overlook or bypass some of the guidelines, have a sound reason for doing so. This is one time where it's best to follow the logical side of your mind and not the creative side.

Of course, for very young writers who will be handprinting their material, the guidelines are less strict. In fact, a few markets and contests, such as *Stone Soup* and *Creative With Words*, want to receive a student's original handmade manuscripts and artwork. The majority of markets and contests, however, prefer to receive typewritten manuscripts. The original text and artwork (or photocopies of it) can be included with the typed version.

GUIDELINES FOR STANDARD FORMAT

Whether you handwrite or type[1], there are some specific things to keep in mind.

---

[1] Computers and word processors have become so commonplace, at least in the United States and Canada, that *typewritten manuscripts* refers to those created on any typewriter, word processor or computer. Listings that read *no computer printouts* or *no dot matrix* mean (1) they don't want to receive manuscripts printed on green-and-white-striped computer paper, and (2) they do not want to receive manuscripts printed with dot matrix printers that are not easily read. As long as your dot matrix printer prints with strong, black type, feel free to use it.

Write or type on only one side of a page. Leave wide margins of at least 1″ on all four sides of each sheet. Use only a standard typewriter pitch such as pica or a basic serif computer font that resembles typing (such as Courier or Times Roman) and that prints 10 or 12 cpi (characters per inch). Always print your final draft using a good, clean black ribbon in your typewriter or printer, or print using an inkjet or laser printer. If you still use a dot matrix printer, be sure the printout is not faded or hard to read. (For handwritten guidelines, see page 58.)

The text of all manuscripts should be double-spaced. To double-space, set the line spacing on your machine to number 2. For word processing software, set the line spacing to "2" or "double." This option is usually found on the paragraph format submenu. This will leave a full line of empty space between each line of type and make it easier for the editor to make notes.

For typed work, always use regular twenty-pound white bond paper. Never use erasable typing paper for a final manuscript. It smudges and smears too easily. For simple mistakes, use a light film of liquid correction fluid or the newer (and neater looking) liquid correction paper. If you need to correct or delete an entire sentence, try press-on correction tape available at office supply stores.

Pay attention to word length limits on fiction and nonfiction, and to line limits on poetry. If you send a manuscript with both writing and illustrations, include a second copy of the manuscript text prepared in the standard format.

Many typewriters and computers can justify (or make even) the right margin. However, editors prefer that manuscripts have a ragged margin on the right side. (Note: The pages of this book are justified. For an example of a ragged right margin see Figures 4-1 and 4-2.)

PAGE 1

You will use a slightly different format for the first page of your manuscript. (See Figure 4-1 on page 54.) At the top of your first page, starting at the left margin, single-space your name, address, city, state, zip or postal code and telephone number with the

Matthew Cheney   **word count** ⟶ About xxx words
00000 Street   **date** ⟶ September 1990
City, ST Zip Code
(000) 555-0000
SS# 000-00-0000

**Your name,
address, phone.
SS# here**

THE NAUGA HUNTERS ⟵ **title**
by
Matthew Cheney ⟵ **author**

start your story here

⟶ Hank, a thirteen-year-old boy with wispy brown hair and spindly legs, spotted his little brother sitting on the floor of the living room, watching a cartoon.

"Hey, Chucky, wanna go nauga hunting?" asked Hank.

"What's a nauga?" asked Chucky, turning away from the television.

"A nauga's a little thing—'bout the size of a cat—that has big long teeth and a red feather for a tail," explained Hank, with the appropriate hand movements.

"A featha for a tail?"

"Yup, And naugas can change color so we can't see 'em, 'cept for the tail; that don't change color."

Figure 4-1. Sample story format, page 1

last name | **keyword from title** | **page number**
Cheney✓   →NAUGA HUNTERS   →8

Hank stood up and jumped on his brother; they fell to the damp ground. His eyes were sparkling and his lips were unfirm. "Would I lie about that, you little . . ." His voice faded as he pulled his arm up to punch Chucky. Chucky was crying now. Hank stood up. "Forget it," he said. "Supper'll be almost ready." Chucky was still on the ground. "You comin?"

Chucky pulled himself up and brushed off his rear end. His face was streaked with tears. "Yup," he said softly.

"Well, hurry up. Then after supper maybe we can go hunt some more naugas. They ain't invisible at night."

"Thought you said they ain't real—like dragons."

"You *believed* me? Boy, maybe you are stupider than you look." He turned around and headed for home, his little brother trying to keep up.

THE END

Figure 4-2. Sample story format, all pages following opener

area code. *(For contest entries, check the appropriate location for this information.)*

On the next line, type your social security number. If you don't have a social security number, include your date of birth. Editors must have this information on file before paying writers for material. On some submissions it is appropriate to put the exact or approximate word length of your manuscript across from your name, next to the right margin. I also like to include the date I mailed my manuscript. You can easily add this before mailing by printing it neatly with a black pen. (Use the date you are mailing it, not the date you originally wrote it.)

A copyright notice is not really necessary, but you may include it. Copyright notices are most often placed on poetry submissions or on manuscripts being sent to small, literary magazines, newspapers or newsletters that are not copyrighted. This will encourage the editor to include your copyright notice when your poem or other manuscript is published. Remember: Most editors are not expecting to see copyright notices on submitted manuscripts.

With the exception of your first page, plan on twenty-six lines of double-spaced manuscript type on each page. If you find yourself always typing too close to the bottom of the page, lightly mark with a pencil where your last line of type should be; then erase the line later. Most word processing software programs have a feature that automatically counts the number of words in a document. You may need to adjust this number if text in headers and footers or other nonmanuscript words are included in the word count.

Type the same number of lines per page to easily estimate the number of words in your finished manuscript. With proper margins and twenty-six lines of type, you will average 250 words per page.

Drop about one-third of the way down the page and, using capital letters, type the title of your manuscript. Under the title, center the word "by," then center your name the way you wish it to read in print.

Switch your typewriter to double-space, drop down two lines and begin your story or article. Editors will use the empty space left on the top of your first page to write notes to the typesetter

---

Author's Tip:

Most word processing software allows you to type in the header information once and then automatically repeats it on each new page. Be sure the page numbers are correct and in the right location.

---

or copyeditor. Leave at least a 1″ margin at the bottom. When using a computer to write or prepare your final manuscript, change the formatting to double-space just before printing out the document.

If you wish to include a title page, type it exactly as you would the first page of your manuscript without including any of the story. It is not necessary to include a separate title page with a manuscript less than six to eight pages long.

PAGES 2, 3, 4 . . .

On each additional sheet, put your last name at the top left-hand corner, followed by a forward slash and a key word from your title, and place the page number at the far right side of the same line. The key title word may also be centered on the line. This is called a *header*. (See Figure 4-2 on page 55.) This will help an editor reorganize your pages if they are dropped or shuffled.

In book manuscripts with multiple chapters, I use both methods. Here's how the header for this page looked in my manuscript:

Henderson/YWGGP   Chapter 4   91

At the end of your manuscript, drop down two lines and center the words "The End." This may seem a little silly, but a busy editor or typesetter appreciates knowing where the end of your piece is. Journalists sometimes center the number thirty (-30-) instead of typing "The End." However, this symbol is not used very often anymore.

If you use a computer, you may want to note the file name

you used for your manuscript, especially if you are submitting the manuscript on a floppy disk or via electronic transmission.

Never staple or bind your manuscript in any way, unless required by market guidelines or contest rules. At the same time, however, use common sense. Hold together short manuscripts, such as a few poems, a short story of up to six pages, and articles of similar lengths, with a single paper clip. Consider using a binder style clip on bulkier manuscripts (twenty-five to fifty pages), such as a longer collection of poems or short stories or in-depth nonfiction articles or book proposals. Hold together larger manuscripts, such as a complete fiction novel, with two sturdy rubber bands, one going lengthwise, the other across the width.

Of course, you can hold together your file copies of manuscripts in whatever way you prefer. I often use a relatively new product called a Paper Gripper. It holds pages together with the ease of a paper clip and sturdiness of a staple, yet can easily be removed and either replaced or reused. I store my copy of large book-length manuscripts in a ring binder with sticky notes or tabbed divider pages between chapters.

HANDWRITTEN MATERIAL

If possible, type your manuscript or have someone type it for you. However, some editors who are willing to receive material from young people thirteen and under do not mind receiving handwritten or handprinted material as long as it is neat and legible.

Unless you have excellent cursive handwriting, print your manuscript. Check editors' guidelines for their preference. Use separate sheets of white, lined, loose-leaf paper for handwritten manuscripts. Use wide-ruled paper if you write big. If you use narrow-ruled paper, write on *every other line* so that the editor can easily read it and make any necessary notes.

To prepare your handwritten manuscript, use the same rules of format that apply to typewritten material.

Write on *only one side of the paper*. Number each sheet. *Never* use paper torn from a spiral-bound notebook. The pages stick together and edge bits fall off, making a mess.

Very young writers may use tablet paper with ruled lines. Remember: Write on only one side of the sheet.

For all writers, put your manuscript pages in order but leave them loose. Never bind or staple them together. (However, a teacher submitting several copies of her students' work may use a paper clip on each individual manuscript.)

To correct handwritten material, draw a line neatly through the mistake, then go on. If you make many mistakes on one page, rewrite the whole page.

Use the same guidelines for mailing handwritten manuscripts as with typewritten material. Follow the market tip sheet for submitting art or photographs.

COMPUTER UPLOADS

Formatting for manuscripts to be uploaded or e-mailed (that is, sent from your computer to another computer using a modem or direct cable) depends on three important factors: (1) the type of communications software that operates your modem, (2) the preferences and requirements of each computer system to which you want to send material, and (3) the software program you are using to e-mail or upload the manuscript.

In the early days of personal computers, manuscripts were saved and sent in standard ASCII or binary formats with hard carriage returns and line feeds inserted directly into the text. By using one of these two forms, almost anyone who had access to the same online system could download manuscripts, usually stored in library files, to their own computer, even if they had a different type of computer or software. For instance, someone with an IBM-compatible computer system could upload a manuscript that someone with an Apple, Amiga, Commodore or some other brand could download with little or no problem.

Nowadays, the issue of using a standardized or generic type of file format isn't as critical because many software programs can automatically convert files to a format they can use. However, some problems still exist, especially when an editor or writer is using either an outdated version or a brand-new version of a software program. When a market or contest accepts submissions by uploading, by e-mail or from an online form, follow the preferred file format guidelines. When e-mailing, check whether or not your manuscript should be sent as a file attachment or as part of the body of the text message itself. Due to concerns over contracting computer viruses, many editors will not open an unsolicited manuscript or message that comes as a file attachment. The editor may delete your e-mail without ever opening it.

(Remember that work uploaded to another computer system is still protected by copyright laws. You can download it for your own reading enjoyment, but you *cannot* sell it to others or use it as if it were your own.)

Before trying to upload a manuscript, find out how to format a file *in advance*. You will waste valuable time and money if you don't. On commercial information services such as CompuServe and America Online, complete directions, guidelines, as well as additional tips and advice can be found stored in a forum or community's special library files area. If you can't find the file format information, leave a message asking for advice. Also watch for special announcements displayed on-screen when you log on.

Although formatting manuscripts for uploading differs from formatting for traditional markets, follow the general advice given throughout this guide. Rewrite, revise and polish before sending a manuscript. Manually check and correct grammar, punctuation and spelling. Don't just rely on the spell checker or grammar feature in your software program. A spell checker won't catch a mistake in word choice if the wrong word is spelled correctly or is not in its dictionary.

POETRY

Poems may be single or double-spaced. You may type your poem as you wish it to appear, double-spacing between verses if necessary. The spacing you choose will often depend on how it looks on the page. (See Figures 4-3 and 4-4 for examples.)

Include your name, address and other information on each page. Type only one poem per page, centering the poem on the page. This is easy to format with a computer. If you are still using a typewriter, type the longest line of your poem first to determine the correct tab position. Here's a tip for those who have trouble centering poems on the page: Using clean, white paper, type your

Amity Gaige   Copyright 1990
0000 Street
City, ST Zip code
SS# 000-00-0000
Birthdate 00-00-00

WE ARE A THUNDERSTORM

Individually,
    we are single drops of rain,
    falling silently into the dust,
    offering scant promise
    of moisture to the thirsty land.

But, together,
    we can nourish the Earth
    and revive its hopes and dreams.

Together,
    we are a thunderstorm.

Figure 4-3. Sample poem

poem as you normally would, indenting one or two tab spaces at the beginning of each line. On a second sheet of paper, type your name and other information where it should appear. When you are finished, cut your poem neatly from the first sheet leaving as much white space as you can. Position your poem where it should be, and secure it lightly with one or two small strips of tape. Send clean photocopies of this master.

PLAYS AND SCRIPTS

The standard formats for preparing radio and theater scripts often differ from the written formats for stories, poems, articles and fillers. Check with your librarian or audiovisual teacher for help in locating a sample script. Study it carefully. Notice the differ-

Vicki Larkin   Copyright 1992
0000 Street
City, ST Zip code
SS# 000-00-0000
Birthdate 00-00-00

OPOSSUM

It would be awesome
    to have a pet opossum.
It would be fun
    to have just one.
"Do you think, Mary Lou,
    that I should get two?"
"It would appeal to me,
    if you would get three."
I'd like to open the door
    and have marching in, four.
The house would sure be alive,
    if I brought home five.
They could help pick up sticks,
    if I decided on six.
It would be heaven,
    if I had seven
It would be cause to celebrate
    if I stopped at eight.
It would be fine,
    with just nine.
I would really like ten
    but then again . . .
It might not be that awesome
    to take care of an opossum.

Figure 4-4. Sample poem

ences in typing dialogue, description and sound effects. Use the sample script as a reference when you type your play, radio, film or video script.

You can also find sample scripts in many language arts books. If you need more help, check with the drama teacher at your school or ask for advice from someone involved with your community theater. Also check the guidelines provided by the markets and contests for additional help.

When submitting a play or script to a magazine, leave the pages unbound and double-space each line of the text. A magazine will publish your work on the printed page, very much like a fiction short would be published. However, most theater groups and contests prefer scripts that are professionally formatted in proper play, script or audiovisual format and submitted in lightweight folders or grip binders. To allow for binding, set your left margin at 1½".

Since I know next to nothing about play and script writing, in the past I have asked Sandy Asher, writer-in-residence at Drury College and an award-winning children's book writer and playwright, to share some tips and resources. See the fifth edition.

Writers interested in submitting plays or scripts to professionally oriented markets and contests should consult a reference book such as *The Writer's Digest Guide to Manuscript Formats*, by Dian Dincin Buchman and Seli Groves. This book contains every single formatting detail you need to prepare a polished, professional-looking manuscript. Guidelines are also included for writing treatments, synopses, outlines, concepts and story lines. There is even information for pitching ideas to television and movie agents or producers. The following simplified formats are suitable for submissions to many local and regional markets and contests and to several of the listings contained in this guide. There are also many other writing reference books, as well as Web sites, that provide formatting advice and examples for every type of manuscript imaginable.

In Figure 4-5 (page 1 of Beth Lewis's 1992 award-winning play), notice how the set descriptions and actions of the performers are italicized. If you can't italicize type, use all caps.

Figure 4-6 shows the first page of *Hefty's*, a short (thirty-

GENIE OF THE LAMP

NARRATOR: The dictionary defines autism as "detachment from reality together with the relative and absolute predominance of the inner life . . . The reality of the autistic world may seem more valid than that of reality itself; the patients hold their fantasy world for the real, reality for an illusion . . ." In other words, "wishes and fears constitute the contents of autistic thinking . . ."

Lights dim and end scene 1.

ACT 1

Backdrops of buildings and lights in a big city. A man, woman and young teenage boy gather around a trash can from where a small fire is giving them warmth in an alley. They are bundled in ill-fitting clothes, torn and dirt-stained. The woman has a scarf over her head and tied under her chin. She also has on a pair of fingerless mittens and open toe shoes. The older man has on a ragged khaki army jacket, but no hat or gloves. He keeps his arms pressed to his side and leans close to the fire. The boy is wearing oversized pants and shoes, and a woman's winter coat that has fur on the collar and cuffs. He is seated on the bare ground near the can, is cradling an old metal teapot in his arms and is rocking back and forth. A female narrator stands center stage dressed in black. A spotlight as she speaks.

GRIFFIN: *(angrily)* Boy! How many times do I have to tell you to get up and warm yourself?

(The boy stares out blankly at the man and continues rocking.)

ANNIE: Now Griffin, don't yell! My head can't take it with you always yellin' all the time. Don't you see the boy's busy? Leave him be.

GRIFFIN: Busy! Why he ain't busy. That boy's never busy a day in his sorry old life. I swears it, Annie, sometimes I think you're just as nutty as Corey over here.

Figure 4-5. Simplified sample play format. Reprinted by permission of Very Special Arts; *Genie of the Lamp*, by Beth Lewis, 1992 VSA winning entry. In 1992, the VSA production role of Corey was played by a deaf actress who signed her role.

minute) film produced by Dick Rockwell, who wrote and produced the script. (He is also a station manager of WOAK, a cable TV channel at Dondero High School, Royal Oak, Michigan.) Notice how (1) the scenes are numbered for reference, (2) camera directions and set location are indicated in capital letters, (3) actions to be performed are typed, and (4) the speaking character's name is centered on the line and typed in all capitals. The dialogue is also indented from both margins. A footer lists the date of the draft, the title and the page number. The wide left margin leaves plenty of room for a binding. The two-column format shown in Figure 4-7 is standard for audiovisual scripts.

EXCEPTIONS: WHEN AND HOW TO BREAK THE RULES

There may be times when you want to send an editor material prepared in a special way. Just remember to include the written part of the manuscript on a separate sheet of paper following the standard format as best you can. If the editor then decides to publish your material, she will be able to give this copy to the production department to use.

Here are some examples where you might consider breaking the standard formats for submitting material:

Situation: You do beautiful calligraphy work and your manuscript tells teens how you make extra money by designing and selling personalized stationery.

You might: Prepare your manuscript following the standard formats, then include as your cover letter a short message written on a sheet of stationery that you have designed.

Situation: Your class has compiled a special collection of stories written and illustrated by the students. One of the students or your teacher has written an article about the project.

You might: Type the article using the standard formats plus include a free copy of your book for the editor to read.

Situation: You have a handicap that makes it difficult to type or write neatly.

1. FADE IN

2. EXT. JERRY'S BACKYARD—DAY

    LEGS pumping across an expansive luxuriously green lawn. JERRY sprints the final fifty yards of his run and stops.

    He leans forward, breathing heavily, placing both hands down on the top of an ancient sundial on a carved pedestal. Even his patio is elegant.

3. INT. JERRY'S LIVING ROOM—DAY

    LOUIS, the family's lifelong servant, anticipating Jerry's arrival, pushes aside the luminous draperies covering an enormous picture window.

4. EXT. BACKYARD—DAY

    Jerry catches his breath. He appears exhausted but purposeful. This is his day. He is preparing for the challenge of his life.

5. INT. LIVING ROOM—DAY

    Jerry enters, sweat dripping like champagne from his body. He is thirty-something, wearing a yuppie jogging outfit.

    Louis greets him by handing him a towel. This guy is waited on hand and foot. Does Louis wipe him too?!

    LOUIS
    Good run this morning, sir?

    JERRY
    Thanks Louis, I'll be reading in a few minutes.

6. INT. JERRY'S HOUSE BATHROOM—DAY

    JERRY—(VO)
    When I think back to that day at Hefty's, I recall that I was in the best shape of my life—physically, mentally, and gastronomically.

2/6/91   HEFTYS   1

Figure 4-6. Simplified sample film script formatted using Focal Point Tools '93. Reprinted by permission of Dick Rockwell.

VIDEO	AUDIO
A foggy day in London Town.	Fog horns echo through mist-shrouded streets. Carriage wheels clatter on cobblestone.
Sherlock Holmes runs down the steps of his Baker Street home. Watson follows furiously behind.	Footsteps . . . then . . . **WATSON:** HOLMES, WAIT YOU FORGOT YOUR UMBRELLA.
Holmes turns.	**HOLMES:** WHAT IS IT YOU SAY, YOU BLUBBERING IDIOT?

Figure 4-7. Simplified sample audiovisual script formatted using Focal Point Tools '93. Reprinted by permission of Dick Rockwell.

You might: Prepare your manuscript to the best of your ability. Include a cover letter telling a bit about yourself. Consider having someone else help you prepare your final copy.

Situation: For a holiday present, you typed some of your poems on special paper, then illustrated or decorated them yourself and hung them in pretty frames.

You might: Retype your poem on a separate sheet of paper using the standard format. Include this with a photograph of your framed poem or include an extra illustrated poem for the editor.

COVER LETTERS

If you wish to tell the editor something about yourself or add information about your story or article such as how you came to write it, you may do so on a separate sheet of paper called a *cover letter*. This letter is written like a regular personal or business letter with your name, address, telephone number and date at the top, plus the name and address of the publication to whom you are writing. If possible, locate the editor's name in a current issue of that publication. Begin the letter with "Dear Mr." or "Ms." followed by the editor's last name. If you don't know the editor's name, simply write "Dear Editor."

Make your cover letter as brief as possible, rarely more than one page. Always type cover letters using single-spacing. Use a regular business letter format. Unless a listing suggests otherwise, tell the editor only those things that relate directly to the manuscript you are sending. Though editors may want to know all about you, your family, your friends and your hobbies, they probably do not have time to read about you now. If editors want more information, they will request it. Remember: You are trying to interest the editor in your manuscript, not in you personally.

QUERY LETTERS

A writer sends a *query letter* to an editor to find out in advance whether the editor would be interested in receiving a manuscript about a certain topic. Most editors prefer that young writers send a complete manuscript, though older teens attempting to publish in adult publications may send query letters outlining their proposed article.

As with cover letters, keep query letters to one page and no more than two. *Always* type a query letter, and address it to a specific editor if at all possible. (You may need to call the publication for the name of the current editor. A receptionist or secretary can give you the information; do not ask to speak to the editor directly.) Include an SASE with your query letter so the editor may respond. If you have been published before, send one to three photocopies of your best pieces, especially if the article (or a portion of a book) is similar in style or genre.

In one or two paragraphs, briefly describe the article (or book) you have written or plan to write. Give a few pertinent details, especially facts about people interviewed or relevance to current topics. In another paragraph, briefly describe why you are interested in this piece and any pertinent credentials you have. Many writers find drafting a good query letter harder than writing the finished manuscript. That's another good reason young writers should concentrate on submitting completed manuscripts. Many of the resources mentioned in this book have sections on writing query letters.

It is highly unlikely for young writers to be represented by literary agents.[2] If you are a serious older teen with a full-length book manuscript, play or script, you may send a query letter to an agent asking if he or she would consider you as a new client. Be sure to enclose an SASE. You may send a short sample of previously published work. *Do not send your manuscript, a synopsis or outline with your query.* If an agent finds your project interesting, she will write to tell you exactly what you should send.

BOOK-LENGTH PROJECTS

Sometimes it seems that every young writer who contacts me wants to know the same two things: "How do I format and submit a novel or nonfiction book-length manuscript?" and "To which book publishers can I submit it?" Unfortunately, the reason I do not include many book publishers in this guide is that very few publishers, except for those sponsoring first-novel contests, are particularly interested in seeing book-length submissions from young people. I don't like to discourage anyone, but the odds of getting a book manuscript accepted are so low for young writers that it is not practical to spend a lot of time and space here providing details in writing and formatting book-length manuscripts and proposals. The advice I've given you so far, including using a standard format to prepare the final manuscript, applies equally to preparing a final book manuscript.

However, many times book publishers do not want to see a complete manuscript. Instead they request a full synopsis (including the ending!) and a sampling of several chapters, usually the first three. For advice on constructing a synopsis of a novel or a nonfiction book proposal, seek help from an experienced adult or consult a book or other reference material that specifically focuses on preparing book-length projects. Michael Larsen's *How to Write a Book Proposal* is just one of many excellent books

---

[2] The best method for a serious young writer to find a reputable agent is through the recommendation of an established author. Many writer's organizations maintain lists of agents.

that provides step-by-step instructions. You will find many of the books I've mentioned in the author's tips throughout this guide helpful as well.

To locate book publishers and what types of submissions they want to see, check *Writer's Market*, the *Children's Writer's & Illustrator's Market*, *Novel Writer's Market*, and *Literary Marketplace*.

These guides are targeted to adult writers, so you may need help in understanding the listings. However, unless publishers specifically state that they do not want submissions from young people, you can submit your manuscript to them. Understand that your manuscript will be competing for an editor's attention with submissions by older writers. Your manuscript will rarely, if ever, be given special consideration just because you are a talented young person.

Request the writer's guidelines just as we've already discussed for magazines. Instead of studying sample copies, request a copy of the publisher's current catalog for specific information about the books that company is currently publishing. Also go to the library or bookstore and skim the shelves for books similar in style, content, topic or that otherwise indicate that your manuscript may fit in well with a particular publisher's collection. Watch for published books that would compete with your new book, if published. When submitting a book proposal or in a cover letter accompanying a complete manuscript, point out competitive titles. Include why and how your novel or proposed book differs from previously published works.

(If you are successful having a book-length manuscript accepted, please write me with the details. I'd love to be among the first to say, "Congratulations!")

PACKAGING AND MAILING

If your manuscript is more than four pages long or if you are including artwork or photographs, use a large manila envelope to hold your material without folding it. When addressing your mailing envelope, use the editor's name whenever possible; for example:

Susie Kaufmann, Editor
Thumbprints

P.O. Box 428

Lexington, MI 48450

Locate the name of the current editor by checking the masthead, usually located near the front of the publication.

Protect artwork or photographs by placing them between pieces of cardboard. *Never* use a staple or paper clip on a photo. It will cause ridges in the photo and make it difficult to reproduce. *Never* write on the back of a photo with a pencil or hard-tipped pen. Put the information on an address label, then attach the label to the photo back. You can also write safely on the photo

---

Susie Kaufmann
P.O. Box 428
Lexington, MI 48450

Place
Stamp
Here

Gerry Mandel, Editor
Stone Soup
Children's Art Foundation
P.O. Box 83
Santa Cruz, CA 95063

Figure 4-8. Sample Mailing Envelope

Stone Soup
P.O. Box 83
Santa Cruz, CA 95063

Place
Stamp
Here

Susie Kaufmann
P.O. Box 428
Lexington, MI 48450

Figure 4-9. Sample SASE

Author's Tip:

....

Don't guess. Have your package—manuscript, plus letters, artwork, photographs and self-addressed, stamped envelope—weighed at the post office or on a reliable postal scale to determine the proper amount of postage. Do not seal your package until it has been weighed and the correct postage determined. You can then attach the correct amount of return postage to your SASE. *Do not use postal meter strips on SASEs.* If you frequently send the same size packages, make a chart to remind you of postage amounts.

---

back using a special grease pencil found in art and office supply stores. Or use a nonsmudge felt-tipped marker.

Affix the proper amount of postage to both your mailing envelope and the self-addressed, stamped envelope and/or postcard you put inside your mailing envelope with your manuscript.

SASE: SELF-ADDRESSED, STAMPED ENVELOPE

Use a second manila envelope for your self-addressed, stamped envelope (SASE). Fold it in half to fit inside the mailing envelope. Include enough postage for the return mailing.

Many editors will not return your material if you do not enclose a self-addressed, stamped envelope with the proper postage. Some editors will not even read a manuscript that is not accompanied by an SASE. Editors cannot afford to pay for the return of manuscripts from every writer who submits material. It would cost thousands of dollars each year! They would rather use the money to pay writers for work that is accepted for publication. A few listed markets state that they do not return material. Do not include a self-addressed, stamped envelope with your material when submitting manuscripts to these markets and contests.

As computers are becoming more accessible, fewer writers are including an SASE to return rejected manuscripts. If you prefer that an editor destroy rather than return your rejected manuscript, include those instructions in your cover letter.

If you are worried that your package may not reach an editor,

	Place Stamp Here
YOUR NAME YOUR ADDRESS CITY, STATE, ZIP CODE	

Fig. 4-10. Sample Front of Self-Addressed Postcard

(Title of your story) —————————————————

(Date you mailed it) —————————————————

(Who you mailed it to)

—————————————————————————

—————————————————————————
Received by

—————————————————————————
Date

Fig. 4-11. Sample Message Side of Postcard

if you want to assure your manuscript's arrival at a market that will not return it or if you do not want it returned, enclose a special self-addressed, stamped postcard. (See Figures 4-10 and 4-11.) Most editors will mark a postcard and return it to you.

MODEL RELEASE FORMS

Occasionally a publication or contest will ask that the author, artist or photographer provide a statement signed by the person granting an interview or photograph, to prove that he or she agreed to the project and understood how the material might be used (such as in a magazine). When the person signs the form, he or she is permitting publication of the material. Such a form is known as a *model release*. Sometimes a market will supply a copy of the model release form it prefers, or you can find examples of them in reference books. However, if only a simple form is needed, you can design one yourself.

On a clean sheet of paper, write your name, address, phone number, and the name, address and phone number of the person being interviewed, photographed or used as a model. Have that person write a sentence or two clearly showing that he or she understands that the information, photograph, etc., may be published or used for publicity purposes. (You can write up this statement ahead of time.) Have the person sign his or her name and that day's date. Sign your name too. If possible, have another person sign it as a witness.

If you are dealing with someone eighteen or younger, have a parent or guardian also sign the model release form.

You do not need to provide this form unless the market or contest requests it. You may not always know when a release is required; therefore have a model release form signed by anyone readily identifiable in a photograph you hope to have published or whose work you include in your manuscript. For instance, my publisher requires all persons contributing essays and photographs for the profile chapters to sign a copyright release form.

ARTWORK

While some larger, flexible pieces of artwork such as posters and illustrations may be sent rolled up in a special cardboard mailing tube, most markets and contests prefer that artwork be mailed *flat*. Don't fold or crease the artwork in any way.

Protect the surface of your art with a sheet of paper to prevent smudging or dirtying. To mail it, put your artwork between two pieces of sturdy cardboard cut slightly larger than the artwork itself. Secure with at least two rubber bands. Ordinary manila folders, large enough to hold your work, cardboard and extra papers such as entry forms or a manuscript, may be used. For pieces larger than 9" × 12", use a shipping envelope with a special lining made of plastic bubbles or other filling. These can be found at art and office supply stores, your local grocery store or department stores. For overly large artwork, make your own mailing envelope by measuring and cutting sheets of sturdy cardboard from a box (such as those televisions, bikes, or other things come in). Use strong, waterproof shipping tape on every exposed seam, as well as around the entire package to ensure that it does not open in transit. Most shipping services, including the U.S. Postal Service and United Parcel Service, will not accept packages wrapped in paper or tied with string.

Include your name, address and phone number on your artwork. (You'd be surprised at the number of artists and writers who forget!) Check the market or contest guideline sheets for the preferred location for this information. Some markets request it be put on the back, providing it doesn't bleed through or otherwise damage the picture front. Often there is a small corner to print the information so it doesn't interfere with the subject of the piece. This information is in addition to any personal signature that you include directly on your illustration or painting.

Some contests do not want personal information on the artwork itself. In this case, include the proper entry form with all the necessary information.

PHOTOGRAPHS

Some markets and contests insist, and most prefer, that you shoot with 35mm film at the lowest shutter speed possible, which will still give you a clean, unblurred image. According to a survey done by professional photographer Lawrence F. Abrams, editors with a preference like photographers to use Kodak film. However, the majority did not indicate a preference. Most important was the photo quality.

In the same survey, 95 percent of the editors said they preferred that unmounted (or unmatted) photos be submitted. However, always protect your photos by putting them between two pieces of sturdy cardboard, then wrapping the cardboard with two rubber bands. If sending more than one photograph, separate them with tissue paper or other paper that won't stick to or scratch the print surface. Except in rare instances, *never* send a negative.

Do *not* paper clip a photo (or any artwork) to a sheet of paper or thin sheet of cardboard because the clip will almost always bend or dent the picture. Unless specifically asked, do not send digital photographs either on disk or at an e-mail attachment. Be sure you understand the editor's preferred graphical format.

Insert slides, sometimes called transparencies, in the pockets of a clear plastic slide holder sheet available where most camera and film supplies are sold. Use this method to protect your own slides if they are important to you. However, avoid sheets made with plastic containing polyvinyl chloride (PVC) if the slides will be stored for a long time. Be sure to identify every photo and slide you send.

You can safely write on the cardboard sides of slides, though some photographers type and attach small strips of self-sticking paper with their name and address. Many professionals have an inexpensive rubber stamp made with their name, address and copyright notice, plus blank lines to write other identifying information about the slide.

Unless you are sending just a portrait-type photograph of yourself or someone else (often called a head shot), always provide a photo caption that identifies the people and describes the action. You may have room to place this information directly on the photo back. However, also submit a sheet listing all captions in one place. Number or code each photo or slide in correlation with its caption.

Photos and slides may be submitted directly with a manuscript. There are some markets, however, that only want to receive them at the editor's request.

To ensure at least one good photograph or slide, many photographers bracket their pictures by taking several shots at different settings, a good practice for any photographer. However, don't send a batch of photographs to an editor or contest expecting someone else to select the best ones. That's *your* job. When selecting your photos, look for clear, clean pictures with good contrast and interesting content. An action shot is preferable. Make sure your photo's subject takes up most of the frame. Don't send a photo of someone riding a bicycle with the rider and bike just distant specks. Avoid chopping people's arms, legs, wrists and ankles off at their joints. As with writers and artists, a good photographer improves with practice.

KEEP A COPY FOR YOURSELF

Always make a copy of any manuscript you submit, especially when your work won't be returned, as insurance against a damaged or lost manuscript. Occasionally, an editor will want to discuss your manuscript with you over the phone, a much easier task when you both have a copy.

Make your copies by using carbon paper, retyping a piece, using a photocopying machine or storing a copy on a computer disk.

KEEPING TRACK OF SUBMISSIONS

Once you decide to submit material to an editor or contest, devise a system of keeping track of your manuscripts, especially if you are eager to be published and will be sending several manuscripts simultaneously.

One way to keep track is with 3″ × 5″ index cards kept in a file box. Prepare a new index card for each manuscript you send. Record the title of your manuscript or contest entry, the date you mailed it (not the date you wrote it) and the name of the market or contest to which you sent the manuscript. Under Notes you may want to record the postage needed and how you submitted the work (by e-mail or another method). Also include the cost of the self-addressed, stamped envelope or postcard.

When you receive an answer from the editor or contest, note the date under the Date Returned heading. Under Notes or on

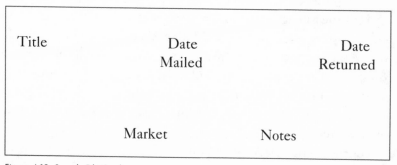

Figure 4-12. Sample File Card

the card back, mark whether the manuscript was accepted or rejected, how much you were (or will be) paid for the piece and the expected date of publication.

If the manuscript was rejected, select another market from the lists. Mark the new information on the same card.

If submitting material as part of a class project, keep an accurate record of all student submissions and editors' remarks in one file box.

Similar records may also be kept in an extra notebook or in a computer disk file.

ADDITIONAL TIPS

Think ahead! If you're really eager to submit material, send for market guidelines, sample copies and detailed contest information before your manuscript is in final draft form. Don't send away for all of them at once, however. Choose a few markets and contests looking for material similar to what you are most interested in writing. Also consider markets and contests directed toward people your age.

Store your market and contest information so that you can consult your files and choose the best place to send your manuscript first. Keep this information in a desk drawer, file cabinet or even a shoe box. Or make your own personal marketing guide, using a large, three-ring binder and a box of top-loading vinyl sheet protectors. Use tab dividers to separate various types of markets and contests or to file information alphabetically.

When a sample copy and guideline sheet arrive, slip them into a sheet protector for safekeeping. Some sample copies may not fit into the sheet protector, so store these elsewhere. Attach a note to the corresponding guideline sheet to remind yourself where the sample copy is. Insert a reference sheet at the front of your binder to record which market and contest information you have. Also include the date you received the information and the date of the sample copy so you'll know when you need to request more current information.

Your personal marketing guide is also an excellent place to keep additional writing notes, new market and contest names and addresses, samples of well-written published material and even your submissions record. If you attend young author conferences or writing workshops, or if published authors speak to your class, store your notes or any handout material in your marketing guide for easy reference.

Author's Tip:

The standard formats and advice featured in this guide will suit the needs of most young writers. For more information about manuscript formats and the marketing process, read *The Writer's Digest Guide to Manuscript Formats*, by Dian Dincin Buchman and Seli Groves. The detailed checklists and submissions logs are particularly helpful for anyone planning to do a lot of writing and marketing.

Chapter Five

Answers to Questions Young Writers Ask Most

QUESTIONS ABOUT GETTING PUBLISHED

Why don't you include more listings for book publishers?

Of all the questions I receive from young writers, this is the most common one. I wish I could say that there are many book publishers who like to receive submissions from young writers, but I'd be lying to you. That's not to say that some young writers haven't been successful in having a book-length manuscript accepted and published by reputable companies or that some editors aren't willing to read a young writer's book-length submission. It's just that most editors don't want to go on record saying so. So, to access book publishing opportunities, young writers must research publishers in more adult-oriented references such as *Writer's Market*.

It is often much harder to understand what a book publisher is looking for, what that certain "something" is that would make them interested in your project. If you persist in trying to market your novel or nonfiction book, be prepared for the possibility of facing many rejection slips. However, persistence could also make you the author of a published novel or nonfiction book someday.

Why should I include an SASE?

All editors and most contests insist that writers include an SASE with their manuscript so that the editor can send you an answer or return your manuscript if it is rejected. To prepare an SASE, write your name and address on the front of an envelope as if you were mailing it to yourself. Put the same amount of postage on your SASE that you put on your mailing envelope.

Example: If it costs you $.55 to mail your manuscript, you must also put $.55 on your SASE. Put your SASE inside the mailing envelope with your manuscript when you mail it.

Special note about the U.S. Postal Service: Always use regular postage stamps on your SASEs. Avoid using metered postage tape or the post office may not return the envelope to you because the metered postage tape will show the date you originally mailed the manuscript or letter rather than the date when the SASE was mailed back to you.

A friend told me she used to always include an SASE with her submissions, but now she only occasionally includes one. Aren't you always supposed to include an SASE?

Before computers, printers, e-mail and the Internet made it easier to edit and reprint documents and send them to others, writers were sternly warned by editors to never break the rule about enclosing an SASE with their submission. Many traditional printed markets and contests still expect to receive an SASE with every submission. Others are not so strict anymore. The only way to know for sure is to read a publisher's guidelines.

Some writers, mostly those with computers, feel it is easier and cheaper to simply print out new copies of manuscripts when needed rather than have editors return them. Under these conditions, writers should *still* include a #10 self-addressed, stamped envelope or a self-addressed, stamped postcard for a reply when submitting to editors or contests that expect SASEs. Explain in a cover letter or a short note what the editor should do with your submission if it's rejected, such as suggesting that the paper be recycled.

Some writers are afraid to suggest to an editor that their manuscript be destroyed rather than returned if not accepted. They worry that it might give an editor the wrong impression about the manuscript's quality or the writer's talent or self-confidence. If this method makes you uncomfortable, then enclose a traditional SASE when appropriate. I personally do not share this fear. Today's editors are too busy to question a writer's preference. In addition, many will appreciate and respect the writer's effort to make the unpleasant process of a possible rejection as quick and inexpensive as possible. More important is that an editor recognize the writer as someone who knows what is expected when submitting a manuscript.

Enclose a regular SASE, however, if you suspect that an editor may offer suggestions and comments on your manuscript even if it is rejected.

An exception to the rule: Do not enclose an SASE when submitting to online markets or contests or traditional ones that *specifically* state in their guidelines or rules that manuscripts are not returned. Sometimes they will return an enclosed self-addressed postcard to acknowledge their receipt of your submission.

I sent a self-addressed, stamped envelope with my manuscript but never received a reply. What should I do?

An editor may take four to eight weeks to respond. If you have waited this long, send a polite letter to the editor asking whether or not your manuscript was received and if a decision has been made. Include an SASE or self-addressed, stamped postcard for a reply. Remember: Some markets receive so much mail that they do not respond at all unless a manuscript is accepted for publication or wins an award. Check the market's listing or guidelines. If a market says, "Does not respond" or "Does not return submissions," don't enclose a self-addressed, stamped envelope. If you want to make sure an editor or contest has received your manuscript, enclose a postage-paid *postcard* addressed to you. (See Figure 4-10 on page 73.)

If you still receive no answer from a market that normally responds and returns manuscripts, write one more time, saying that you are withdrawing your manuscript from consideration and would like it returned to you immediately. Some professionals feel that if an editor hasn't responded within a reasonable time (normally about two or three months), writers may simply submit their manuscript elsewhere without notifying the first editor.

Most editors try to be as prompt as possible.

Can I send a manuscript to a publication not listed in *The Young Writer's Guide to Getting Published?*

For various reasons, not all publications that consider material written by young people are listed in this guide. Some editors have asked not to be listed because they prefer that only their readers submit material. If you have read a notice in a publication asking for submissions, you are considered a reader and may send them your submission whether or not they are listed in this guide. Be careful to follow their guidelines.

Editors who currently receive more submissions than they can handle or use sometimes ask not to be listed in a particular edition. A good example of an excellent writing contest for young writers that is not listed is the *USA Weekend* Teen Short Story Contest. You'll find information about the contest on the newspaper's Web site and in some issues throughout the year.

There may be other publications of which I was not aware or that were too new at the time this edition was printed that may also consider your manuscript. (If you discover a market not listed, please send me its name and address so that I may contact them to see if they would like to be included in future editions.) Send your suggestions to me at the address listed on page 241, in the contest listings.

Check other resources such as *Writer's Market* or *Literary Market Place* or the many writing related Web sites for additional market and contest opportunities. Several writers organizations (such as the National Writers Association) and many trade magazines for writers (such as *ByLine*, *The Writer* and *Writer's Digest*) are also useful sources of current market and contest information. Note, however, that it may be more difficult to locate opportunities for young writers in some of these resources.

Why don't you include the editor's name and phone number with all the listings?

Phone numbers are only listed when the editor includes the information on the survey sheet returned to me *and* indicates that it may be included with the listing. (For examples, see the listings for *Stone Soup* and *Merlyn's Pen*.) Most editors do not want their phone number included because they do not want to answer phone calls from people who should be sending their questions by mail. If you have a legitimate reason to call, you can usually locate the phone number on the guidelines sheet or masthead in your sample copy.

The same criteria applies to including the name of an editor or contest coordinator. If you send for guidelines and/or a sample copy *before* submitting material as advised, you will have access to the names of editors and contest coordinators.

May I send the same manuscript to more than one magazine at the same time?

Sending the same manuscript to more than one market at the same time is called multiple or simultaneous submission. It is not recommended for either adult or young writers. However, you may send different manuscripts to separate publications at the same time. Keep a record of which manuscript you sent to which market.

Most contests want only new material that has not been previously published or submitted to another contest or market. A few contests (for example, see NWA Novel Contest) state in their guidelines that you may also submit entries to a publisher. The only way to know for sure is to read the directions.

Why does a listing say "send holiday or seasonal material six months in advance"?

It takes the entire publication staff several months to collect, edit and print a single issue. Therefore, they must consider material several months in advance of the issue's scheduled appearance. Editors frequently read Christmas stories in July and surfing stories in December. This is called *lead time* (pronounced like "reed"). Different publications have different lead times. Generally, a magazine's lead time is much longer than newspaper's lead time.

What is an International Reply Coupon?

International Reply Coupons (IRCs) are redeemed at post offices for postage, similar to how subway or bus tokens substitute for coins. The *value* has been paid for in advance. Writers should send IRCs instead of putting postage stamps on their self-addressed envelopes (or postcards) when submitting manuscripts to foreign markets. For instance, U.S. postage cannot be used by people in other countries, including Canada, to return a letter or package. You also cannot mail a letter *from* the United States *to* Canada with a Canadian stamp. Sending IRCs instead of stamps allows an editor in one country to purchase the appropriate stamps to respond to a writer in another country. If you wish to submit to a foreign market, ask a postal clerk for the appropriate amount of International Reply Coupons to enclose with your self-addressed envelope instead of a regular stamp.

Many markets and contests outside North America are now easily accessible by e-mail or from their Web sites.

If I submit a manuscript to a Canadian magazine, do I need to spell words like color "colour"? I live in the United States.

It's usually best to spell words the way you normally would, provided that you spell them correctly, of course. If you normally speak and write American English, then spell words like "color" and "favorite" the way you usually do. Do not try to fool an editor into thinking you're Canadian. There are more differences between Canadian English and American English than just the spelling of some words. The same advice applies for Canadians sending manuscripts to the United States. The words you choose to express yourself and even the traditional way you spell them are part of the overall style you bring to your manuscripts. Editors in Canada and the United States will edit such spellings if they think they are necessary. Otherwise, editors will leave the spellings as they are.

Can my friend and I send in a story we wrote together?

Usually, this isn't a problem, especially when submitting manuscripts to markets. Some contests, however, insist that an entry be the original work of one writer. Again, it's important to check the guidelines sheet.

Why doesn't my favorite magazine publish more poems or short stories by young people?

A publication is limited in how much material it can print in each issue or display on its Web site. This is usually determined by the amount of advertising used or, in the case of publications that carry no advertising, a predetermined number of pages or Web site space. Try writing to the editor, explaining that you would like to see more poems (or short stories or whatever) by young people. Also, look for more opportunities to publish your work in your local area. You may even want to consider starting your own newsletter.

My story won first place in a writing contest. Can I send it to a magazine to be published too?

Some contests retain the copyright to entries and some do not. It should state in the rules when and if you may submit your manuscript elsewhere. For instance, NWA contests say that you *may* submit contest entries to a market. However, The Ayn Rand Institute College Scholarship competition guidelines state "all entries become the property of The Ayn Rand Institute." An entry submitted here, whether or not it wins, cannot be submitted anywhere else because the manuscript would no longer be your property. By entering it, you agree to relinquish (give up) your rights to it. Consider this when deciding where to submit your work.

Do I have to subscribe to a magazine before I can send them a manuscript?

It depends. Some magazines want material only from their current subscribers, such as *Poets at Work*. Subscribers can usually find submission guidelines in current issues. Some magazines prefer submissions from readers, though not specifically subscribers. If you don't have this type of magazine delivered to your home but read it in your school, library, church, etc., you are still considered a reader and may submit material. For most magazines, newsletters and newspapers, you do not need to subscribe before you submit material.

I don't own a typewriter or computer. What can I do?

Some editors will accept handwritten manuscripts if they are legible, which means neat and easy to read. Almost all markets for teens and adults, however, require manuscripts to be typed. Try borrowing or renting a typewriter (perhaps at school), or find someone who will type your manuscript for you. Consider saving your money to buy a used typewriter, a no-frills word processor or computer system if you can't afford a new one. The point is, if you are serious about getting published, you will find a way to get your work typed. Don't bother complaining that such policies are unreasonable to writers who don't own typewriters or don't want to find other ways to get their manuscripts typed, as some frustrated beginning adult writers do. Expecting manuscripts to be typed is no more unreasonable than expecting someone who wants to play hockey to get a pair of ice skates.

Remember that "typed" means produced with either a type-writer or computer as long as the final printout is legible.

My story is 1,927 words long, but the magazine I want to send it to only accepts stories 800 words long. Should I send it anyway?

You have three choices: (1) Cut, revise and polish your story until you get it down to the 800-word limit or close to it. A little over, say 50 words, is usually acceptable. This type of editing usually produces an even better manuscript. (Stories may always be under the word limit.) (2) Look for a different publication that accepts longer stories. (3) Send it as is and take your chances. Obviously, the first two suggestions are the best to follow.

Remember, do *not* go over the maximum word limit when entering a contest. Your entry will be disqualified.

When the magazine published my story, they changed some of the words and left some parts out. I liked it better my way. Why did they do that?

There are several reasons an editor may change your story. It may have been too long to fit the available space, or the editor may have felt a different word or phrase would make your mes-sage more understandable. This happens with all types of work. Editors have a responsibility (it's a large part of their job) to edit material when they think it is necessary. Thoughtful editing can make a good manuscript even better. Thankfully, most editors will only make minor editing changes on their own. If they think more changes are needed, they will make suggestions and ask the writer to make them.

Unfortunately, if a piece an editor changes has already been published, there really isn't anything you can do about it except go on to your next project. However, when an editor requests that you make some changes in your manuscript before she will consider publishing it, you must decide whether making them will or will not help your work. If you don't understand what you are being asked to do or if you don't agree with all the suggestions, discuss your feelings with the editor by phone or in a letter. Explain why you think some or all of the suggested changes are unnecessary and/or make new suggestions of your own. This give-and-take between writers and editors happens all the time. Don't be afraid of it. If you and the editor can't agree on what to do, either the editor will not publish it or you can submit the manuscript elsewhere.

All manuscripts are edited, even those by famous authors. It is a necessary part of the publishing process.

Note: If you self-publish your work, it should still be edited. Rewriting, revising and polishing are key steps to producing quality work. You may be able to do all the necessary editing on your own, but it is wiser to enlist the help of someone with editing experience.

A story I sent to a magazine was rejected. But the next issue had a story almost like mine. I think they stole my idea. What can I do?

First, because of a publication's lead time (see page 84) it is very unlikely that someone stole your story. Second, many writers have the same idea for a story, although they do not write the story in the same way. Your story was probably rejected because the editor had already accepted the one you read before your manuscript arrived. Send your story to a different market, and get busy writing new ones. Ideas, by the way, like titles, are not protected by copyright. Many of us have similar ideas, but we write them in different ways.

I'm afraid someone will steal my story and publish it if I

send it to an editor. Is there some way to keep people from stealing it?

It is very unlikely that anyone will steal your story, especially if it is unpublished. When a story is stolen and someone pretends that he wrote it and gets it published or enters it into a contest, this is called *plagiarism*. Plagiarists are usually discovered and can be taken to court.

Plagiarism is a serious offense. It means to use or submit someone else's work as your own original work. Plagiarism often hurts innocent writers in ways that are not always apparent.

For example several years ago I was one of fifty judges who evaluated entries in a large student writing competition sponsored by the *Detroit Free Press*. Many of the entries were so well written that some judges (many were public schoolteachers) were genuinely surprised yet pleased at the level of talent displayed by the young entrants. Then, halfway through the first day of judging, I read an entry that I knew without doubt was plagiarized material. The student had copied two entire chapters out of a juvenile novel by Dorothy Haas. Not even the names of the characters had been changed.

Immediately the judging atmosphere changed. Judges who moments before had been surprised and delighted to discover well-written manuscripts among the hundreds of entries were suddenly wary and suspicious. Whether consciously or unconsciously, we all feared the same thing: Was this another plagiarized entry? Can such a young student really write this well?

If the student who submitted this plagiarized entry thought no one would be hurt by the deception, he or she was wrong. True, no harm was done to Mrs. Haas, the original author. But consider the harm done to all the young writers whose work was judged after the plagiarized entry was discovered. Hurt most were the most talented young writers because their entries drew the most suspicion and they may have been given lower marks than they would have been given the day before.

There is a poem that I really like, but it does not have the poet's name on it. Can I submit it?

No, especially if you hope someone will think that you wrote it. That would be plagiarism. Someone wrote that poem, but it wasn't you.

Are there any exceptions to the plagiarism rule?

Yes, there are situations when you may submit something published in one publication to another. A good example is found in *Reader's Digest*, which publishes many short, usually funny, items published in other magazines and newspapers. The difference is that the person submitting the material, called a *clipping*, does not pretend that he created it himself if he did not. If you submit this type of item, always credit the person who wrote it and/or the publication where it was originally published.

I've never even heard of some of the magazines listed in your book. Where can I find them?

Many of the publications listed are available only by subscription, although some can be found on the Internet, at libraries, bookstores or magazine and newspaper stands. If you are interested in submitting to a magazine you have never read, send for a sample copy and its writer's guidelines. The cost of a sample copy varies among publications. Occasionally, a sample is free upon request or free if you send an appropriately sized self-addressed envelope with your request. However, it is becoming more common to charge the price of a single issue to receive a sample copy. Check the market listing for that information. You can now access stories and articles for some printed magazines directly on their Web sites or by subscribing to their e-mail list services.

My dad says that charging for sample copies is just a way for magazines to make money by selling extra copies. Shouldn't they be willing to send them to writers free so we can see what type of material they publish?

A few do. They are hoping that once you see a copy, you'll want to subscribe to it. Most publications simply can't afford to send a free copy to every writer who wants one. Saving money to send for sample copies is not always easy; however, if you are serious about writing and publishing, it's money well spent. In some ways, it's almost like paying for lessons to learn how to play the piano better.

It's not necessary to send away for every sample copy that's available. Concentrate on the publications to whom you really feel you can sell your work. Also, you can read issues of many magazines for free at the library or online. You may also be able to get samples of old magazines from waiting rooms at some businesses. For instance, since my kids are now too old to want a subscription to *Highlights for Children*, I take home old copies from my chiropractor's office, with permission of course.

Is there any benefit to entering a contest if I don't really think I have a chance of winning?

That depends. If you just write and write and never bother to consider how revising, rewriting and polishing your work might make it better or if you just pick any contest to enter without careful consideration, you might not think you have a real chance of winning. And you'll be right. There won't be any real benefit to your entering.

On the other hand, if you lack self-confidence, you may think you don't have a real chance of winning even if you've taken the time to write and edit until it's the best work you can do and gone to the trouble to find a contest that is appropriate for your manuscript. You might not win, but you'd be wrong to think that you didn't have a chance. If you don't enter, you'll miss the benefit of the experience and a chance at placing.

Do I have to submit to magazines only for kids, or can I send material to the ones my parents read too?

There are a number of magazines for adults that regularly publish material from young people. Some are listed in this guide. Judge for yourself whether a publication not listed would consider publishing a submission by you. Review the section on "Studying and Comparing Opportunities," which begins on page 33. Incidentally, there are *no* circumstances that I can think of where it would be wrong for you to express your opinion on a certain topic and address it to Letter to the Editor.

Why should I bother sending my material to a publication that doesn't pay for it?

As a young writer, you should be more interested in gaining writing and submission experience rather than making a lot of money for having your work published. In fact, very few writers of any age get rich by selling their manuscripts. You will gain valuable experience with every "sale" you make to a publication, whether or not you are paid in cash for your efforts. It is hard for poets, in particular, to find paying markets for their work. Of course, you can choose not to send material to a publication that does not pay young writers. It is entirely up to you. (Beware, however, of markets and contests that want *you* to pay to have your work published!)

If this advice still doesn't make sense to you, pretend for a moment that you want to become a major league baseball player earning a million dollars a year when you grow up. How much do you expect to be paid displaying your baseball skills while playing Little League or on a school team?

Why do some magazines pay a lot for manuscripts, some just a little and some not at all?

How much a publication pays for a manuscript varies greatly with the publication's operating budget and editorial policy. In general, the markets listed in this guide, which normally pay for material, pay the same rates to young people as they do to adults. Publications that include advertisements often, though not always, pay at least a little for accepted manuscripts. People and companies selling products and services pay for adverting space. This money increases a publication's operating budget, making it more likely that it will have money to pay for accepted manuscripts.

On some guidelines I've read "pays on acceptance" and on others "pays on publication." What's the difference?

A publication that pays on acceptance will send your check soon after your manuscript is accepted, without waiting for it to actually be published. Markets that pay on publication wait until they have actually printed your manuscript in the scheduled issue before sending you a check. Waiting for a pays-on-publication market to pay you is sometimes very frustrating. It may take up to a year or longer before your manuscript is published. When deciding between two markets with similar guidelines, submit first to the one that pays on acceptance.

Do I have to cash the check I got from a magazine? I want to frame it.

By all means, cash it. Consider framing your printed piece and/or a photocopy of the check instead to signify your first "for pay" sale.

What does it mean to get a "$500 advance against royalties"?

Normally, when a writer sells a manuscript to a book publisher, she receives a contract which, among other things, tells how much money she will earn for every book that the publisher sells. This is usually based on a percentage of the book's selling price. For example, if the writer's contract says that she will earn 10 percent for each of her books the publisher sells at retail for ten dollars, the writer will receive one dollar for each book sold. (When you purchase an item in a store, you pay the retail cost.) This percentage of sales is known as the *royalties*.

Sometimes, instead of retail cost, royalties are based on the publisher's *net* price, in other words, the price for which the publisher actually sells the book rather than the price listed on the cover. For instance, bookstores buy books from publishers at less than the cover price listed. (Bookstores pay the net price rather than the retail price.) This allows the bookstore to make money (for profit and to cover expenses such as salaries and rent) by selling the books to customers at the retail price. In the example above, if the publisher sells the ten dollar book at net for five dollars, a writer earning a 10 percent royalty based on net would only earn $.50 for each book sold.

Royalties are normally paid out to writers twice a year.

Question: How much money would a writer make on a book earning 10 percent royalties based on the retail price for a book that sells for $6.95 if 1,000 books are sold?

Answer: $6.95 \times 1,000 \times 10\% = \$695$.

Question: What if the 10 percent royalties were based on a percentage of net and the publisher sells each $6.95 book for $3.00?

Answer: $3.00 × 1,000 × 10% = $300.

Since it often takes a year or more between the time a writer sells a manuscript and when the book begins selling, publishers often offer writers an *advance against royalties*. An advance is a certain sum of money that the publisher gives to the writer when the contract terms are agreed upon but before the book is actually published. This is not free or extra money that the writer gets. When the book is finally published and copies are sold, the publisher will deduct the amount of the advance from the total royalties due to the author.

Therefore, a five hundred dollar advance against royalties means that a writer will not receive any money earned from royalties *until* her royalties exceed five hundred dollars. That's the downside of advances. However, writers always try to get as big an advance from their publishers as they can against royalties (preferably based on retail) because the writer can keep all of the advance money even if the book doesn't sell enough to earn royalties.

An article I submitted was rejected because they had printed a similar piece a few months before. How can I know what subjects have been covered without reading every back issue of every magazine to which I'd like to submit?

This happens most with information, how-to articles or stories with a common or seasonal theme (Christmas, springtime, love, death, etc.). For magazines to which you, your friends or neighborhood library subscribes, scan at least the table of contents of several back issues. For other publications, have your school or public librarian show you how to use two reference collections called *Reader's Guide to Periodic Literature* and the *Children's Magazine Guide*. Both list by subject, title and author articles published in many publications. These same or similar resources are often available on the library's computer system, through an online information source such as CompuServe or via the Internet. Finding information is much easier and quicker by computer. However, check with an adult before using an online information source because access fees may be charged to the user's account.

Don't worry too much if your subject has been covered recently if you've written an essay or opinion piece. Editors often repeat certain subjects if the writer presents a different or interesting viewpoint.

What is a "theme list"?

Some magazines and contests plan issues around a certain topic or theme, such as medicine, sports, dating, Colonial America, holidays, etc. Most listings will specify if a publication or contest follows a theme list. The deadline dates for submitting material will be included to help you meet their lead time.

I'm confused. Do I send my original manuscript and keep the copy, or do I send the copy and keep my original?

Generally, you would send your original manuscript and keep a copy. Note that "original" here means both something new you created on your own *and* the actual final draft you made of it. Markets and contests that accept handwritten work by young people, like *Stone Soup*, are more likely to want the actual work you created and not a photocopy or a copy retyped in standard format. Markets and contests that only accept work in standard typewritten format don't really care if they receive the original or a copy as long as what they receive is clear and easy to read.

The most important point to remember is to *never* send the only manuscript you have. *Always* keep a carbon copy, photocopy, disk copy, extra handmade or typed copy, computer printout or the original just in case something happens.

Some contests specifically request originals; others request a copy.

What should I do with rejected material?

First of all, don't take it personally. There are many reasons a manuscript may be rejected, and some have nothing to do with how well, or poorly, it is written. Reread your work and see if you can improve it. If you like it the way it is, look for another market. Be sure to follow all guidelines and any theme or deadline requirements. Remember that even famous writers have material rejected. Some manuscripts are not bought until the fifth or even thirtieth different submission. The key is to keep trying and to keep writing new material.

What does "copyright" mean?

For writers, "copy" means their written work. (Don't confuse this with making a copy of something.) "Right" refers to the person who has the authority to sell or offer a certain piece of written, drawn, photographed or computer-created work for possible publication. When you write something, you automatically become the copyright owner by law. If an editor agrees to publish your manuscript, he will buy the rights to it. Sometimes, magazines buy *one-time rights* or *first North American rights*, which gives them permission to print your manuscript one time. The rights are then returned to you, and you may offer the same manuscript to another editor for *second* or *reprint* rights. A number of publications and some contests buy *all rights*, which means that once you agree the publication can print your manuscript (or you submit to that particular contest), the work becomes *their* property (they hold the copyright) and it is no longer yours. You may not send it to another market or contest. Even though you no longer own the copyright to it, if it is published, your name as author will be included.

The copyright of a message or library file on an online information service such as CompuServe is held by its author and, in certain cases, jointly with the service. You must obtain the author's permission to make further distribution of any portion of a message or file. Material available on the Internet is also covered by copyright laws. Just because online material is easy to access and copy does not make it legally or morally right to do so.

Copyrights can be very confusing. See page 43 for more information.

What is a model or material release form?

Occasionally a publication will ask the writer to provide a statement signed by the person granting an interview or appearing in a photograph to prove that he or she agreed to being interviewed or photographed. Some editors can supply you with a model or material release form. You can make your own release form using a clean sheet of paper containing your name, address and phone number and the name, address and phone number of the person being interviewed or photographed or whose work you will be quoting. Have that person write a sentence or two that shows he or she understands that the information or photograph may be published, and then have the person sign his or her name and the date. Most people don't mind providing this information. If you are writing something about or taking a photo of someone eighteen or younger, have a parent or guardian also sign the release form. You do not need to provide this form unless the publication's guidelines specifically request it or if there is any doubt that you received permission to use information or photographs in a manuscript you intend to submit to a market or contest.

Should I include a letter with my manuscript when I mail it?

If there is special information that you wish to share with the editor and it is not included in your manuscript, you may send a short, one-page cover letter. Often this is not necessary. When receiving a manuscript prepared in standard typewritten format, the editor assumes that you are hoping it will be accepted for publication. Note that some markets and contests want you to include a cover letter particularly if you are under eighteen years of age. For more information see page 67.

Is a cover sheet the same thing as a cover letter?

Not exactly. While a cover letter may also serve as a cover sheet, many contests use the term *cover letter* to mean the form that should accompany an entry.

What is a query letter?

Writers send a query letter to editors when they want to know in advance whether the editor would be interested in receiving a manuscript about a certain topic. Most editors prefer that young writers send a complete manuscript, though older teens attempting to publish in adult publications may send query letters outlining their proposed article. Many book publishers and literary agents also prefer to see a query letter first rather than the full manuscript or proposal for book-length projects.

Someday, if you've sold several manuscripts to the same editor, you may be surprised to receive a query letter from that editor asking you to write on a certain subject. The editor will feel confident doing this because she is already familiar with your previous work and knows that you are dependable. Of course, it will be up to you whether or not you accept the assignment. Most of the editors, contest sponsors and young writers profiled in the guide received queries from me asking them if they would be interested in contributing.

What does "solicit" mean?

To solicit means to ask for something. A publication that solicits poetry is indicating that it wants to receive poetry submissions to consider for publication.

A solicited submission means that an editor has either specifically asked a writer to submit a particular manuscript or agreed in advance to consider a manuscript when it is submitted. For example: If you query an editor if she would be interested in seeing your manuscript about "What Kids Can Do to Protect the Environment," your manuscript becomes a solicited submission.

An unsolicited submission refers to a manuscript mailed to an editor without her prior knowledge and approval; in other words, the editor hasn't asked to see it. Unsolicited submissions waiting to be read and answered are often referred to as the *slush pile*.

What does "in-house" publication mean?

When a company or organization publishes something such as a newsletter intended primarily for its employees or members, it is often referred to as an in-house publication. In other words, it is not meant for the general public. A student school newsletter is a good example of an in-house publication.

Some people also use the term *in-house* to mean that all the work done creating a publication is done without assistance from outside sources. You may hear, for example, "We did it all in-house."

What's a press pass, and how do I get one?

A press pass is a type of identification card or badge. Writers, especially journalists, TV or radio reporters, use press passes to gain entry into special events especially when gathering behind-the-scenes information or interviewing someone special. Staff members and writers on assignment (someone an editor has told to pursue a specific topic because of an interest in publishing the proposed article) can request a press pass from their editors. For example, members of your school yearbook staff get a type of press pass that allows them to attend sports and other activities free to get information and photographs.

Read about Michael LaFontaine in chapter seven in the fifth edition of the guide. He used a press pass to attend a political rally for President George Bush during the 1992 presidential campaign.

An article I read in a writer's magazine gave tips on being polite and treating editors right. One tip was to compliment the editor who will read your manuscript. On what should I compliment her?

First of all, the article you mentioned referred to compliment-ing an editor *after* she has contacted you and, unfortunately, re-jected the manuscript or idea you submitted. Many rejection notes and letters will contain the editor's name. The author of this article was suggesting that writers send the editor who re-jected their material a short note that basically says: Thank you for taking the time to read my manuscript and consider it for publication.

Sometimes writers who get rejection notices write very nasty letters to the editor no matter how kind the editor tried to be. So I'm sure many editors would prefer receiving a nice thank-you note instead. However, I don't think this is necessary unless an editor has sent you a very personal letter that perhaps offers some words of encouragement or advice for improving your manuscript.

What is the genre's trade journal?

The word *genre* means a specific type or kind of writing. Science fiction is one type of genre, as are picture books, cookbooks, romances, biographies, even comic books. Every different type of writing can be considered a different genre.

Many professions have magazines (also called journals) devoted specifically to that profession. For instance, doctors have magazines about medicine. Mechanics have magazines about fixing cars. Teachers have publications about teaching. Writers and editors have special magazines for their professions too. You're a writer and you read *Writer's Digest*. The "Markets" section of *Writer's Digest* often lists the names of editors. Editors and publishers also have special magazines, such as *Publishers Weekly*. So, one example of a writer's genre trade journal would be *Writer's Digest*.

How do I find a publisher to whom I can send my novel? There are only a couple markets and contests listed that want book-length manuscripts.

Unfortunately, there just aren't many publishers who want book-length manuscripts specifically from young writers. However, there are hundreds of markets that publish novels and nonfiction books. It won't be easy, because the competition is tough. Your manuscript will be competing for attention with thousands of other manuscripts written by older and often more experienced writers. Make it the best it can be in content and presentation.

Make sure you've really written a novel and not just drawn out the events of what should have been a short story. Understand that novels aren't novels just because they are longer than what you are used to writing. Read some of the many good how-to-write-a-novel books if you aren't sure of the differences, or see if a novel-writing course is offered in your area.

When you're sure you've got a marketable book-length manuscript, check out one of the many other market reference books available such as *Writer's Market* or *Novel & Short Story Writer's Market*, both published by Writer's Digest Books.

Be market savvy. Beware of fad topics. Book publishers often plan their lists as much as two years in advance. "So," as one Atheneum editor says, "if a topic is 'hot' right now, it may be 'old' hat by the time we could bring it out."

Author's Tip:

A good book on novel writing is *Get That Novel Started! And Keep It Going 'Til You Finish* by Donna Levin. Published by Writer's Digest Books, it helps you write a novel with step-by-step directions.

Do your homework! Everything you've learned here about preparing your manuscript and studying the markets still applies. Once you find a few potential markets, read some of the recent books they've published. You may want to market test your manuscript by entering it first in a novel contest such as the one sponsored by the National Writer's Association.

As a young writer, your chances of getting a novel published are slim, but it can and does happen. Gordon Korman did it (and his weren't even long books). So has Jessica Carroll, whose *Billy the Punk* was published by Random House in Australia in 1993. She was seventeen at the time.

I wish you the best of luck! Let me know how you do.

I'm afraid I won't know what to do if my book manuscript gets accepted and the publisher sends me a contract. What should I do? Will the publisher decide not to publish it when they find out I'm just a kid?

Publishers are interested in publishing good books. They really don't care what age the author is as long as they feel the author will act in a responsible, professional manner (reread the beginning of chapter three). Contracts can be confusing, but don't be afraid of them. If there is something you don't understand (and there probably will be), talk it over with your editor. Also get some outside help from a trusted adult. The main things to look for in a contract are: What rights does the publisher want to buy? How much will you be paid and when? What is the deadline for you to turn in a final, polished manuscript? What other responsibilities does the publisher expect from you? (For instance, if your book will have photographs or illustrations, who pays for them, you or the publisher?) What happens if the editor does not like your final manuscript? How will the copyright be registered? Must you give this editor first choice for accepting your next book?

I write on a school computer that has a special software program that helps me make up stories. Can I send my story to a market or contest?

There are many computer software programs that help students learn how stories are put together by showing part of a story on-screen and asking the student to fill in missing parts. They encourage creativity and help students learn new words but really do not help students create original stories. These types of stories are not suitable for submitting to regular markets and contests because the work is not entirely your own.

Occasionally, someone will sponsor a special writing contest based on one of these programs. In 1988, for instance, The Learning Company and Tandy (the company that makes the computers sold by Radio Shack) sponsored a "Silly-Story" writing contest. Every student used the same story "shell" that came with one of The Learning Company's software programs. They filled in the story blanks with as many creative nouns, verbs, adjectives and adverbs as they could.

QUESTIONS ABOUT WRITERS AND WRITING

What's the difference between a writer and an author?

If you write, that is, creatively arrange words in some fixed form (usually on paper) to create a poem, story, article, etc., then you are a writer. But you are also the author of the piece you have written. The term *author* is most often used when referring to the writer of a particular piece of published work. Example: Kathy Henderson, author of *The Young Writer's Guide to Getting Published*, will be our featured speaker.

How can I tell a good idea from a bad one?

Often you can't. William Saroyan once said, "You write a hit play the same way you write a flop." You've got to have faith in yourself and follow your instincts. Sometimes, it's not the idea that's bad, but the way the writer used it. For some tips about getting and recognizing good ideas, refer to chapters two and three.

I love your book but still have lots of questions. Can I write to you?

Yes, you may write to me. I always look forward to hearing from readers. Send your letters to me or visit my Web site at the addresses listed on page 241. You can also e-mail me directly at kathy@youngwriternetwork.com.

Could you help me choose the best place to send my work? I'm afraid of picking the wrong place.

As much as I'd like to help, I prefer not to choose the places where young writers send their work. For one thing, I'd never have time to write and market my own work! Second, I can't because most times I've never seen the letter writer's manuscripts, so I have no way of evaluating them to know which markets or contests might be most appropriate. Third, marketing your own manuscripts is kind of like homework; if you're going to learn anything, you've got to do it yourself.

Some writers, myself included, find marketing much easier than writing. I like researching the possibilities, analyzing and comparing the differences, weighing the benefits of submitting first to one market instead of another—all essential elements of choosing where to send a manuscript. For me, the process is inspiring. New ideas for articles, stories and books pop into my mind as I read what editors are looking for. Turning those ideas into finished manuscripts, though, is a constant struggle. I have a hard time letting go of a project until I feel it's the best I can make it. (And I'm a tough judge of my own work!) Sometimes, I've got so many ideas I don't know which one to work on first. It's too easy to stop working on one thing when the writing gets tough and start another. (If you have this problem, too, read *Becoming a Writer* by Dorothea Brande.)

Most writers, however, are more comfortable with the writing process. They really don't like worrying about how to market their work. They balk at learning which editors want the kind of manuscripts they have to offer. In fact, they would prefer to skip the marketing process all together if they could.[1] But, like me, they want to be a published writer. So, whether we enjoy the process or not, we do each step because it has to be done. If you accept the challenge and learn to enjoy the process, you'll have a much better chance of getting published.

Of course, studying and comparing opportunities doesn't do any good if you're afraid of picking one because your manuscript might not get accepted. This is a fear with which all writers struggle. It's no different than a baseball player worrying that he might strike out at the plate. If you simply cannot decide, put the names of your best choices (see "Studying and Comparing Opportunities" beginning on page 33) into a hat and draw one out after another, keeping a list as you go along; then start submitting.

This all seems too much like work. I thought writing was about inspiration and being creative. Isn't that more important?

For many people, that is what writing is all about. They enjoy being creative and, whenever inspired, they write. If that's how you want writing to be for you, that's fine. But serious writers can't rely on inspiration alone. They need to approach their craft like anyone serious about improving, using and promoting their talent and skills. Writing when inspired might get you a nice seat on the players' bench, but it won't put you in the starting lineup. How many top athletes do you know who only practice or show up for games when inspired?

If I sent you my manuscript, would you tell me if it is good or not?

Well . . . this is a really hard one for me to answer. I love to read the work of young writers, and I don't want to discourage anyone from writing to me. When I have time, I do read manuscripts and make a few comments if asked to do so. Occasionally, I'll work with one or two young writers on a more detailed level

---

[1] Some writers, after achieving some success, do skip the marketing process by paying a literary agent to do it for them. Unfortunately, that's an arrangement out of reach for many writers, especially young ones.

each year. These are usually students I've met during workshop presentations. Unfortunately, it's simply not possible to give a detailed critique to everyone who writes. Bear in mind that I am primarily a nonfiction writer, although I do write and have published some fiction. Like a maid who doesn't do windows, I'm a writer who doesn't do poetry. So, while I love to read poetry, I am not a good person to ask for help writing or publishing it.

Here are some guidelines for those who would like to write to me:

1. To receive a quicker response, and as a courtesy, please include a self-addressed, stamped envelope (SASE) with your letter when you write.

Note: I receive many letters each year from students and teachers that I cannot respond to because there is no SASE and no return address on either their letter or envelope. So, even though I want to respond, I can't because I don't know where the writer lives.

2. Tell me a little about yourself such as your age, school and the kind of writing you like to do.

3. Feel free to ask me specific questions. Here, for example, are what three students at Warrensburg Elementary in Warrensburg, Illinois, recently wrote to ask me:

From where do you get your ideas?

What made you become an author?

What is your favorite animal?

Did you write any books about your childhood?

What is your favorite book you wrote?

(By the way, my favorite animal is my newest calico cat, Jiffy. My favorite book that I wrote is this one.)

4. Please ask me questions that you, personally, are interested in knowing. Don't, for example, ask the same thing everyone else in your class is asking. If everyone wants to know something, send one letter like the Warrensburg students above did.

5. Please do not ask me to give you answers to things you can easily find in my book. That's why I wrote *The Young Writer's Guide to Getting Published* in the first place . . . so you would have

the basic answers. It is very bothersome to receive six letters (especially all from the same class) that say:

> Dear Ms. Henderson: *(or: To Whom It May Concern)*
> I am in the fifth grade and am planning to send some things for publication. I need to know the requirements— handwriting, paper size, etc. Who should I send this to?
> Thank you.
> Sincerely,
> So-and-so young writer

Unfortunately, I receive several packets of such letters every school semester.

6. If you include a sample of your work, please limit it to five pages. I especially enjoy receiving photocopies of things young writers have had published. *However, I do not publish writers' work myself, except profile essays associated with this guide and a few things on my youngwriter.com Web site.*

7. Please be patient while you wait for me to respond. I try to answer within two weeks, but sometimes it's longer. In addition to writing, I also have a full-time job and sometimes travel to speak at schools and conferences. Don't forget that it may take a few extra days for your letter to be forwarded to me from Writer's Digest Books.

8. Occasionally things get lost in the mail, so if you don't hear from me after a while, feel free to write me again. Include your address on both your letter and envelope in case they get separated. (You would be shocked at the many letters I get that have no return address on them.) Please include an SASE if at all possible. Send letters to me or visit my Web site at the addresses on page 241. Or e-mail me at kathy@youngwriternetwork.com.

May I write to other writers?

I can't speak directly for other writers, but generally, yes, you may write to other writers. It's always a pleasure hearing from readers who have enjoyed our work. If you don't know where a writer lives, send your letter to the company that published the book or to the magazine where you read the work. Your letter will be forwarded if possible. It may take several weeks for a writer to receive a letter forwarded from the publisher. I once received mail two years after it was sent to a publisher with whom I used to work. So, please be patient. Many writers now also have Web sites that can be found by using a search engine.

Does it make you happy to get published?

I don't believe having things makes one happy. Once you get it, you always think having more or getting something else will make you happier. Having my work published makes me feel good and excited and proud. But I get happiness from being me and pursuing my goals. I think Margaret Lee Runbeck said it best: "Happiness is not a state to arrive at, but a manner of traveling."

I wish you all good luck and much happiness as you travel the path to getting published.

PART TWO

Chapter Six

Young Writers in Print

You've come to my favorite part of this guide, where I get to introduce a new group of young writers who have found from a little to a lot of publishing success.

Even before I finish working on one edition of *The Young Writer's Guide to Getting Published*, I've already begun to collect information and references for the next. I never grow tired of meeting young writers or of reading and hearing about their experiences. Many people have asked how I learn about young writers in so many different parts of the country, around the world and from such different backgrounds. (Each new edition features a different group of young writers, a total of forty-nine so far, not counting celebrity guest young writers.)

Finding young writers is the easy part. Many write to me each year from the United States. and around the world. I have received letters and e-mail from Canada, England, Australia, New Zealand, France, Belgium, the Netherlands, Germany, Puerto Rico and the U.S. Virgin Islands, Malaysia, Japan, China, Spain, Ireland, Scotland, Korea and India. Some send samples of their work, share good and bad experiences they had marketing and entering contests, want to know more about me personally or ask for more information about writing and marketing. Some I chat with online. Many of their questions and experiences find their way into new editions.

I also learn about talented young writers by asking for recommendations from the editors and contest sponsors I'm interested in featuring. It's not always possible, but I prefer to feature both an editor or contest sponsor and a young writer with ties to the same market or contest. This gives you, the reader, a unique two-sided look behind the scenes.

Each young writer essay must include three things: (1) something of value to share; (2) some words of inspiration or encouragement, such as advice about becoming a better writer or marketing tips; and (3) a way of expressing themselves or experience with a different type of market or contest. I always ask them to share at least one good and one not-so-good experience. Of course, I have to get their submissions in time to meet my book deadline. But if you asked, they would tell you that I give them very few guidelines about how to write their personal experience essays. What I give them is a skeleton. They must construct a strong body.

The most fun, however, is when I receive everyone's photo, because I rarely know what anyone looks like in advance! It's also fun right now, when I get to introduce them to you. I know you'll enjoy meeting and learning from them as much as I have.

In the last two editions, two celebrity guest "young writers" were featured. The first was Stephen King. The other celebrity guest young writer was Gordon Korman, whose first novel, *This Can't Be Happening at Macdonald Hall*, started as an English assignment and was published by Scholastic's Canadian division when he was a seventh grader. He published four more novels before graduating high school and has made writing his career.

You might be amazed at the number of successful people who enjoyed writing and publishing success in their youth. Some, like actress Elizabeth Taylor, who had a small storybook published as a child, did not pursue a writing career; others did, such as C.S. Lewis, author of *Chronicles of Narnia*, started writing his first book when he was only eight or nine years old. Did you know that U.S. naval officer and Antarctic explorer Admiral Richard Byrd, as a twelve-year-old, had letters he wrote home when he traveled alone to visit his godfather in Europe published in the local paper? Here are some highlights about other well-known writers:

- Edgar Allan Poe (1809–1849) published his first book, *Tamerlane and Other Poems*, in 1827 when he was eighteen.

- Walt Whitman (1819–1892), most famous for his book of poetry, *Leaves of Grass*, started writing seriously and had many poems published in his youth. By the time he was nineteen, he was working as a newspaper editor.
- Louisa May Alcott (1832–1888) spent many hours writing stories and poems as a teen just like Jo in *Little Women*. She was first published at age eighteen, when a poem appeared in *Peterson's Magazine* in 1851.
- Ernest Hemingway (1899–1961) wrote poems and stories as a high school student in Illinois. His first published story, "The Judgement of Manitou," appeared in his school literary magazine when he was sixteen.
- Langston Hughes (1902–1967) wrote his first poem for his eighth-grade graduation and had many poems published in his school magazine. By age nineteen, he had two poems published in *The Brownie's Book*, a magazine for African-American children, as well as collecting his first professional adult publishing credit for his poem, "The Negro Speaks of Rivers," in a magazine called *The Crisis*.
- Sylvia Plath (1932–1963), known for such works as her novel, *The Bell Jar*, and published poems in many major magazines, had a short story published in *Seventeen* magazine before she was eighteen.
- Nadine Gordimer, winner of the 1991 Nobel Prize in literature, published her first short story at the age of fifteen.
- Richard Branson, now chairman of the Virgin Group of Companies, which owns Virgin Atlantic Airways, Virgin Entertainment and Virgin Cola, started a magazine when he was fifteen. That magazine eventually developed into a national magazine called *Student* for young people in the United Kingdom.
- Richard Lowry, who became editor in chief of the *National Review* at age twenty-nine, was originally invited to join the staff in 1992, after finishing second in its young writers contest.

Even Jewel (Kilcher), best known now for her singing and songwriting, started writing poems while growing up underprivi-

---

Author's Tip:

....

Very few markets and contests react positively to poems and stories full of grief and woe. Yes, it's a universal feeling. But, oh so many adolescents and teens submit so many manuscripts heavily laden with it that it's hard to sell heartbreak to a publisher. To see how well and touchingly the issue of grief can be handled, check out *Word Painting* by Rebecca McClanahan. Study pages 55–56 in particular.

---

leged in her native Alaska. Her debut album, *Pieces of You*, featuring a collection of songs written when she was eighteen, finally helped her talent and patience pay off. Selling ten million copies and remaining on the U.S. charts for three years, it has become one of the Top 10 debut albums of all time. That's a stupendous payoff for a creative and talented young person living in a world where it's hard for even established and well-published adult poets to earn much for their work.

A SPECIAL CELEBRITY GUEST YOUNG WRITER

Getting published is often an exhilarating experience. But life is filled with joys and sorrows, ups and downs, successes and rejections. It is the combination of these opposites that makes life, as well as the pursuits of writing and publishing, so fascinating and challenging. Stories that focus only on all good or all bad are boring, no matter how eloquent the actual writing might be. The story and writings of a very special celebrity guest young writer are being featured in this edition. Her name is Celia Pinson Iskandar.

CELIA PINSON ISKANDAR
1974–1998

It's quite likely that you've never heard of Celia or read any of her published work. But her prolific publishing history started before she turned ten and continues to this day, even though Celia died in 1998 at the age of twenty-three. I never had an opportunity to meet Celia in person, but we became writing pals when she was just eleven. I've asked her mother, Maxine Pinson, an editor and publisher herself, to share Celia's story with you.

> *Writing has helped me in numerous ways and provided rewarding experiences since I was five years old. In the year 2000, I hope to be more concerned with how my writing can help others than with how it can help me. My goal is to write stories providing cheer and hope to those in need, to provoke thinking, to make reading fun. Through writing, immortality becomes possible.*
> —Celia Pinson, age 13

When I see these words, penned by my young daughter, on the front page of a newsletter for writers, I beam with pride. I am delighted with my daughter Celia's writing credits, but I am even more pleased with her stated values and goals. I think about a fable, written by Celia, recently published in a Christian children's publication, *Clubhouse.*

> . . . Oliver the Worm was a kind creature who crawled about doing good deeds for others. Clara the Robin was frivolous and conceited and never helped others in any way. As Oliver was slithering home one day, after visiting an ill friend, Clara the Robin swooped down and clutched Oliver in her big beak. Before Oliver died in Clara's silly gossipy

mouth, he said: "It is better to live a short life doing good than to live a long life doing evil."

An entry into an essay contest brought Celia her first formal recognition as a writer when she was ten years old. She was awarded a plaque, which still hangs above her little oak writing desk. Fourteen years later, October 1998, a journal of creative writings was dedicated to her. Opening the booklet, a special collection of writings by cancer patients, one reads:

> "I Have Marks to Make" Journal is dedicated in memory of Celia Pinson Iskandar—a courageous 23-year-old Georgia woman whose deep faith and rich sense of humor sustained her and inspired others during a difficult two-year struggle with cancer.

The first poem in the anthology is entitled "Baldheaded Babe." It was written by Celia while undergoing treatment for a rare form of cancer, mycosis fungoides. Drawing from her wit and relying upon her faith, she concludes her poem with the following lines:

> Well, woke to hair all on my pillow, in my eyes,
> my ears, my nose.
> Hair fallin' in the shower past my neck and knees and toes.

> Said, "How 'bout some Rogaine? Just a little
> Vitamin?
> Bald's beautiful on Grandpa, yeah, but not, no
> way, on me."

> So I stuck on this wig for the very first time,
> the blonde one I call "Sue,"
> Wonderin', well, can everybody tell? an' wishin'
> for Super-glue.

> Oh, ya know, Clark Kent, he's got nothin' on me,
> High Flyin' Superman.
> Slippin' on tights in telephone booths, shootin'
> off as fast as he can.

> He's a-leapin' tall buildins' in a single bound,
> got muscles made of steel.

I'm a-tacklin' stone walls day by day, got prayer
and an iron will.

Melissa, Celia's best friend and eighteen-year-old sister, was
asked to read the poem to a gathering at Savannah, Georgia's
Telfair Academy of Arts and Sciences. Wearing a "best friends"
necklace of interlocked hearts, given to her by Celia, Melissa
read the poem with expression and flair. I could sense Celia's
smile and approval. Following the reading, my husband and I
were presented a framed version of Celia's poem. It hangs outside
her old bedroom next to a piece Celia wrote for Melissa her last
Christmas, a piece published in an Advent booklet. "Better than
Barbie" expresses Celia's deep devotion and love for her sister.

A sister, I decide at age three, would be more fun to play
with than Barbie. A sister is what I want more than anything
in the world. When I am five-years-old, I get one. She has
red hair and a loud mouth. And she is more fun to play with
than Barbie and Ken combined.

Her name is "Melissa." . . . The most precious gift I ever
received, came not from Santa, but from God. She is a gift
who makes Christmases extra special and other times, too.
She is a gift better than Barbie any day. She's my sister,
Melissa.

Always a free spirit, Celia requested that she be cremated and
that her husband, Antoine, scatter her cremains. Celia and Antoine were married just a little over a year before Celia developed
her terminal illness. But, in spite of the suffering she endured
after the cancer began progressing, she said that the three years
she was married to Antoine were three of the happiest years of
her life. When we went to the funeral home to select an urn,
Antoine was asked what Celia's occupation was. With pride, Antoine answered, "She was a writer. She was working on a novel
when she died." Antoine supported Celia's passion for writing,
and she loved him for it.

James Byron Spencer, the minister who baptized Celia and
provided ongoing encouragement for the development of her

writing talent, offered the closing prayer at Celia's Memorial Service:

Our Creator God and Loving Father, we have gathered in this sacred place to worship and to express appreciation for your sharing with us this special life: so delicate, yet creative in her expression; so determined in her objectives; so anxious to express kindness in her relationships; so unique in her faith and affections. She accomplished so much and taught us more in her one score than most given four.

Dr. Spencer quotes Celia: "I can't wait to write my novel!" And she didn't wait. She wrote it with her life.

Yes, through writing, immortality becomes possible. One of my most cherished possessions is a collection of stories and newspaper articles written by Celia over a period of eighteen years. I will never be able to spend time again with Celia in this life, but her stories enhance my memories and enable me to relive special times we shared as she, unknowingly, trained me as a writer and introduced me to the publishing world. Melissa and I are now coauthoring a book. It will be dedicated, with love and gratitude, for Celia and the lasting contribution she made to our lives.

Celia concluded her original profile essay in the second edition of *Market Guide for Young Writers* with, "This experience shows what I believe: God never closes a window without opening a door." In my e-mail to Mrs. Pinson asking for two photos of Celia I said, "I expect Celia's smiling down from Heaven seeing how much her writing and life are still reaching out and touching others."

God chose to close the window on Celia's life on Earth, but in doing so a door was created that Maxine Pinson has opened in the form of an online publishing opportunity focusing on grief and heartbreak. Details are on page 179.

STEPHEN KING
Former Young Writer
Bangor, Maine

Stephen King (one of today's most famous and prolific writers) started writing in his youth. The following is a reprint of a story that was self-published in the magazine written and published (photocopied and stapled!) by Mr. King and a boyhood friend. They produced several, but to his knowledge, only one copy of each still exists. When they sold them for $.10 to $.25 to the kids in school, Mr. King realized for the first time that one could write something and get paid for it. School officials eventually made them stop.

In a 1986 letter to Carol Fenner, managing editor of Flip, *a student literary magazine no longer published, he had this to say about his story:*

This has been very painful for me, but I have managed to dig up the rotting body of one of my stories written as a teen of thirteen. I think your readers will see what a really dreadful story it is, but I think they will also see maybe the first delicate sprouts of what has become the world's best-selling Venus flytrap. If you don't want to use the story, I'd be delighted. But for what it's worth, you have my permission.

Unfortunately, the issue of Flip *that was to have featured Mr. King's story was never published due to lack of funding. I'm grateful to Ms. Fenner for her cooperation in helping me access this story and to Mr. King for allowing me to reprint it here.*

THE HOTEL AT THE END OF THE ROAD

"Faster!" Tommy Riviera said. "Faster!"

"I'm hitting 85 now,' Kelso Black said.

"The cops are right behind us," Riviera said. "Put it up to 90." He leaned out the window. Behind the fleeing car was a police car, with siren wailing and red light flashing.

"I'm hitting the side road ahead," Black grunted. He turned

the wheel and the car turned into the winding road spraying gravel.

The uniformed policeman scratched his head. "Where did they go?"

His partner frowned. "I don't know. They just–disappeared."

"Look," Black said. "Lights ahead."

"It's a hotel," Riviera said wonderingly. "Out on this wagon track, a hotel! If that don't beat all! The police'll never look for us there."

Black, unheeding of the car's tires, stamped on the brake. Riviera reached into the back seat and got a black bag. They walked in.

The hotel looked just like a scene out of the early 1900s. Riviera rang the bell impatiently. An old man shuffled out. "We want a room," Black said.

The man stared at them silently.

"A room," Black repeated.

The man turned around to go back into his office.

"Look, old man," Tommy Riviera said. "I don't take that from anybody." He pulled out his thirty-eight. "Now you give us a room."

The man looked ready to keep on going, but at last he said: "Room five. End of the hall."

He gave them no register to sign, so they went up. The room was barren except for an iron double bed, a cracked mirror, and soiled wallpaper.

"Aah, what a crummy joint," Black said in disgust. "I'll bet there's enough cockroaches here to fill a five-gallon can."

The next morning when Riviera woke up, he couldn't get out of bed. He couldn't move a muscle. He was paralyzed. Just then the old man came into view. He had a needle which he put into Black's arms.

"So you're awake," he said. "My, my, you two are the first additions to my museum in twenty-five years. But you'll be well preserved. And you won't die.

"You'll go with the rest of my collection of living mummies. Nice specimens."

Tommy Riviera couldn't even express his horror.

FIONA CULL
Barnsley, England

By the time you read this, Fiona's story will have been published in the January/February 2001 issue of Stone Soup *magazine. She's eleven years old and attends her local Secondary School Foulstone. Her favorite (or "favourite," as Fiona spells it) subjects are art, English and geography. She enjoys taking horse-riding lessons every fortnight (two weeks) and recently started cross country running. Fiona's home includes her three pet rats, three snails belonging to her brother, lots of gold fish and six stick insects.*

I have no idea where my passion for writing stories comes from, but my mother says it's all the books that I read. I confess, I'm a bookworm! My bedroom is full to burst with fiction books, not including a selection of *Animal Ark* books and *Harry Potter* novels! My younger years account for some of it though: At the age of three I could recite a story from memory and make up one just as interesting from my imagination. My junior school teacher was always telling me I thought of excellent descriptive words and would try to make up something just as good—but failed.

I think for any young writer to write a story well they need to have a baseline first. I always write a story about either horses or big cats, as these are my 'favourite things.' Both my parents say I know more about horses than they could ever learn; it's the same with big cats.

I started a publishing 'streak' when the annual school magazine was being made. (This was at my junior school.) I first made four pages of information on dogs, birds of prey, horses and big cats (one page each). Then I went on to win the vote for the front cover and wrote two more stories to go in the magazine! After my dad had read all of this he said, "You know Fiona, you should get a story published!"

In the meantime I had been very busy writing up a horse magazine on the computer. (Every young writer should be able to use and get access to one.) ALL BY MYSELF! When this was finished and everyone had bought one, I settled down to write a story about cheetahs. I then set about the task of finding a publisher that might take my story; at last I did. *Stone Soup!* The editor, Gerry Mandel, let me illustrate my story named, 'The Chase,' and is going to publish it in the January/February issue in 2001. So far this is the only story I have had taken in [published], but there are loads more in the pipeline. We have just been on holiday [vacation] in our camper van and this inspired me to start a volume of stories—the 'Carly Greene' adventures. I'm still in the process of finishing the third one of five total. That's just about it up to the present time. By the way, if you are a young writer and willing to take on the challenges, then take my advice, go for it!

JESSICA RENEE LEVING
Highland Park, Illinois

Twelve-year-old Jessica introduced herself to me by e-mail one day. She said, "I have a lot of different interests, including practicing karate, playing tennis, dancing, talking with friends, baby-sitting, woodworking and traveling to cool places like London, Paris, Rome and Hawaii. But my favorite thing to do is write. I write stories and poetry."

She lives with her mom, stepdad and a younger half-brother, but sees her dad frequently. If you count a much older stepsister, Jessica is a "middle" child but says she thinks of herself as the oldest.

Writing ever since she knew how, Jessica displayed her creativity even before then while playing Barbie dolls with her mom, who let her be bossier than any of her friends would let her be. In her essay, Jessica mentions several excellent writing contests that declined listing in this edition. If you are interested in entering them, you should be able to find information on them with a little bit of Internet research.

Teachers and family friends often ask me how long I have been writing. My answer is forever. Before I could put my ideas into words, I translated them into creative play. I was what my mom called her "Little Make-Believer," constantly fussing about the lives of my Barbie dolls.

Once my Barbies found a new home in a box in my closet, my imagination found $.99 notebooks. I began writing constantly. Many of those stories were similar, about orphaned girls who traveled to many different foster homes. Most were never finished because a new idea would pop into my head and old ones would be abandoned.

In third grade, my teacher introduced me to the world of poetry. I now prefer writing poetry to writing stories because with poetry, there are no rules. I can do whatever I want. It doesn't have to rhyme; but when it does, I can read it aloud and it puts me in a better mood when I hear the music and realize that it is solely my creation. However, it can be frustrating when I have composed a beautiful poem in my head, and then I write it down, but no matter how much I play with the words, it just doesn't sound right.

When I was younger, that aggravation caused me to throw my work in the garbage and give up. Now that I am older, I realize that without perseverance, there is no production. Often, to inspire myself, I read. I have found that reading plays a huge role in influencing what you write. Now, I read whenever possible if I'm not "creating," as my grandpa calls it. I'm proud to say that my love for poetry and a few wonderful teachers to help me along the way got me published three times in the *Young American Poetry Digest's* annual book of poetry. I was thrilled. For some people, having your work published for no pay is just a hassle and very boring, but not to me. The moment I saw my name printed inside of a book, I knew that writing was what I wanted to do for the rest of my life. In fact, I sat down and wrote a poem about the exhilaration of being published. That poem went on to be included in *Eclipse*, my school's literary magazine. In addition, I have submitted poetry to many magazines such as *Stone Soup*, *Highlights for Kids* and *Boodle*.

That leads me to rejection letters. I have received many of them. If you submit your work continually, chances are you will too. Don't let them discourage you. Most of the time it isn't that they don't like what you wrote, it's just that it won't enhance the quality of their production. Ever since my first rejection, I have lived by my mom's advice: "At least you were dedicated enough to finish something and send it off. Keep trying, and eventually you'll get somewhere."

As for my short stories, around fourth grade I became interested in publishing. Wanting the glory but not the sweat, I began reading over all of my old stories, and, finding nothing but errors in them, I put them back on a shelf and did what all writers need to do: work. My computer became my new storage room. Yet, like most things, because of the effort I put in, stories I can honestly say I liked were what came out.

One of my favorite stories, "Circle of Smiles," was written for a contest related to a fun program I'd been doing after school called Future Problem Solving. My teacher for that year notified me later of a National Problem Solving Bowl Scenario Writing Contest for Illinois. While the contest rules restricted me to a certain story line, it also helped me structure the story and keep "writer's block" from interfering. I won fourth place in that contest.

I think writing is great because you can do so much with it and all you need is paper, a writing utensil and an experience. Every single day, even if it is spent in front of the TV, is an experience. And not only can anyone write, but writing has helped me through many tough times; I use it often as a form of therapy. Writing is a great way to express your feelings, and this way, you can still keep all your secrets to yourself.

My advice to other writers is to always write everything down. Even if you think it probably won't turn into anything, you can never be sure; and in the long run it's better to have the idea handy. Also, when you are writing, just let it flow. Don't worry about grammar or spelling, and lock your door so no one will bother you. I have found interruptions such as those to be very distracting. I forget what I wanted to write. Remember, too, there's always editing. Edit, edit, edit. And don't rush to finish something. A good piece takes a lot of time.

COREY S. DWECK
Allentown, Pennsylvania

As a thirteen-year-old, Corey has already accumulated so many publishing credits—and from an impressively high quality of publishers—that it makes my head spin just thinking about it. He's not shy about using his achievements to help him get his foot in the door with other publishing, reporting and editing opportunities.
He's considering self-publishing a collection of his poems and stories, but he's been wise enough to gather the facts and understand the trade-offs.

More than his published credits, I'm impressed by Corey's eagerness to learn as much about the craft and business of writing and his willingness to risk rejection. He consistently aims high with his submissions, while more timid writers set their sights lower, hoping to minimize the chance of rejection.

Shortly before completing this introduction, Corey e-mailed me again with more good news. You could feel the breathlessness in his words. "I got a phone call last night from the editor of Chicken Soup for the Teenage Soul. *She'd like to use a story I contributed for a book she's editing for Spring 2001. I almost imploded when I found out. You wait, and wait for an answer, and then, when you least expect it—the phone rings!"*

His mom says that when he grows up, he'd like to be either a children's poet or the next Bill Gates. I think Corey could probably manage both careers someday.

From a young age, my mom was constantly reading to me. My favorite author was Dr. Seuss. By age two, I had memorized most of his works. I'd hold his books in front of my nose and recite them to stunned strangers, who thought I could read. Even then, I loved the sounds of words and their ability to make people laugh.

The thing that most influenced my writing career was our computer. I have "fine motor skill difficulty." This means, my hands aren't wired to move the pencil as quickly as my brain. Before the word processor, I'd give up in frustration. My teacher told my mother that I had ADD, attention deficit disorder. She felt that I lacked the concentration needed to complete a poem or story. My mom did not agree. She rarely does!

She taught me to touch-type, using a kid's software program. I caught on pretty quick. It reminded me of the video games I loved to play. I practiced my typing like you'd practice a piano—every day. Soon, I was typing over forty words per minute. This new talent enabled my fingers to fly as swiftly as my mind. I don't believe in handicaps. Robert Frost, a famous poet, once said, "I took the road less traveled, and that has made all the difference." Sometimes you have to find your own "road," which might be off the beaten track. You have to advocate for yourself. My mom did it in this case. But, there have been times since, when I've had to tell a big adult teacher that there is more than one way to get from point A to point B.

The Internet afforded me my first publishing experience. I was the Grand Prize Winner of the Chevron "Car of the Future Essay Contest." I won a $2,000 computer system for my school and some pretty cool prizes for myself. I was psyched. Later that same year, I placed second in the Real Kids, Real Adventure(tm) Essay Contest. I won a check for $50. But, even cooler than that, the author, Deborah Morris, asked permission to publish my poem in her next book. Since then, we've established an e-mail relationship. She's a great human being, writer and mentor for all us aspiring young writers.

This brings me to my next piece of advice . . . keep on moving. Explore all options and exploit all opportunities. Being a little hyper can sometimes be a *good* thing. I never stop. If I'm not writing, I'm reading books, newspapers, magazines or surfing the net. You never know where you might find your big break. After coming in second in Ms. Morris's contest, I volunteered my services as her junior PR man. I have traveled to different bookstores, plugging her books. My mom is always in tow, acting as chauffeur/bodyguard. *Always have a responsible adult watching out for you!!*

Anyway, I digress. Keep your eyes and ears open. You never know where one brief communication might lead you. It was Deborah Morris, who suggested I buy *The Market Guide for Young*

Writers. Taking her advice has led me to my next publishing experience, which you are reading right now.

My writing niche is humorous kid's poetry, along the lines of Jack Perlutsky. I'm working on compiling enough poems for a book. I don't mean to suggest you should limit yourself to only one genre. I've entered a lot of different kinds of writing contests, everything from science fiction to romance. Through experimentation, you'll develop your own style. Don't be afraid to dip your word brush in all different kinds of paint.

In writing poetry I've developed a writing process that works for me. You'll find yours. I start out with a funny concept in mind. I actually begin with the last line first. I think to myself, what line will leave my reader laughing—and thinking? It's easy to put myself in my reader's shoes. After all, I'm a kid. Then I read the poem out loud to myself. Does it make me chuckle? Next I walk away for a while and come back later to read it again. Sometimes you need to clear your head. Finally, I read my poems to other kids, like my ten-year-old brother, Michael. Unfortunately, most of the poems he laughs at end with the word "cootie." But don't discount your audience's opinion. I'm *always* listening to other kid's conversations. You might think I'm nosy, but I get my best ideas listening to what they're laughing at in the cafeteria.

When I'm stuck for a word, I reach for my bag of tricks. I work on a computer connected to the Internet, with a thesaurus, a dictionary and a rhyming dictionary. My favorite rhyming site is poetry.com. It's not cheating to use aides. They inspire you to go in directions you may never have considered. Just make sure that your wording isn't just for the sake of rhyme. It helps to make sense. I love silly poetry, but I also want it to tell a story.

My best advice is to be different. *Warning!* There are teachers out there who will order you to always color your grass green. Don't let conventionality mow down your creativity. Sure, everybody goes to the cinema to watch the movies. But what if the movies were watching *us*? Being able to think beyond conformity makes interesting reading. And don't fill the page with worn-out analogies like "That man is strong as a bull." That's the easy way out, and it's destined to put your reader to sleep. That same man gains dimension when described as "having muscles with such massive girth, they popped the seams of his tightly worn T-shirt," or something like that!

The best time to write, for me, is in the morning. That's because my mind is freshly pliable from dreamland. In this post-sleep state, I'm freer to let my mind wander, and that's "key" to expressing yourself. On weekends I lie in bed extra long. My dad thinks I'm being lazy. But, I'm really letting the creative juices ooze. I keep a notebook beside my bed to jot down ideas, which can disappear as quickly as my dreams.

And now, a brief word about rejection. Last week I asked a girl out to the movies. She gave me some lame excuse about having to give her dog a pedicure. And I was cool with that. In fact, it even made great material for a new poem. Keep things in perspective! *Rejection is part of life!* I just keep sending things out every day . . . to magazines, contests, whatever. If you keep your brain occupied with new challenges, you won't have time to gloom and doom over some publisher's thumbs down or lack of response. You just got to keep on moving! Remember, bob and weave, and your opponent won't ever get the chance to knock you down.

I think it's appropriate to close with my poem about that backwards movie house I mentioned earlier. I hope it makes you smile.

> If I went to the cinaplex, this is what I'd see;
> the actors on the screen, would all be staring back at me!
> It is a backwards movie house, so they are watching you.
> The actors pay five dollars each, for this disturbing view.
> "You'd better entertain us!!" One surly actor said.
> Then he scooped inside his box, and threw some popcorn at my head!
> This kind of shook me up, and made me kind of shutter.
> I had popcorn in my hair, and my nose was dripping butter.
> And, when the lights went on again, it was as I had feared.
> The actors all walked off the screen, and I just *disappeared*!

KAMEEL STANLEY
Port Huron, Michigan

On Saturday, October 14, 2000, I partici-
pated as one of the workshop presenters for the
"World's Largest Writing Workshop" jointly
sponsored by Barnes & Noble Bookstores and
Writer's Digest Books at hundreds of locations
around the United States. In the audience at
the Port Huron Barnes & Noble store where I was scheduled sat a young
teen, her bright brown eyes twinkling with eager anticipation and a dog-
eared copy of the fifth edition of my Market Guide for Young Writers
propped atop her notebook. She didn't seem to mind that all the other
attendees were far older than she. We had an opportunity to chat during
a break, and I was delighted to learn about Kameel's writing interests
and publishing background. Since I like to feature at least one young
writer from Michigan in each edition and hadn't yet invited one to submit
a profile for this edition, I asked her if she'd be interested but warned
her that I needed her essay within the next few days or it would be
impossible to add it in time to meet the book's production schedule. To
my delight, Kameel said yes and started drafting her essay that day.

Kameel is thirteen and attends Chippewa Middle School. I think most
of you will appreciate and relate to both the highlights and low points
she shares in her essay.

Once upon a time . . .

That's how all my stories started out when I first began writing.
I don't know why, maybe it was because I was three or because
that was the only phrase I could spell without mistakes. Anyway,
that's what all my paragraph-length stories started with. My
grandma was the person who inspired me to start writing. She's
a writer also, and I loved to watch her sit at the kitchen table and
write. So one day I got some yellow paper, flung myself on the
gray living room carpet and wrote my first stories: "The Mop"
and "The Funny Fruit Tree." I love writing, and to this day I'm
never bored with it.

I wrote all the time. I'd write down everything. I remember
how proud I felt whenever I finished a story. I was about six

years old when I finally wrote my first three-page story. I ran throughout the house with a grin on my face. I found my stepfather and thrust the papers into his face saying, "Here, edit," not really knowing what the meaning of editing was. My stepfather later gave me the story back. I looked at it and burst into tears. He had marked and "edited" all over my story with blue ink. I screamed at him. "You ruined it. You ruined it!" It took both my mother and my grandmother to calm me down.

I kept writing though. I wrote continuously. Getting that one piece "ruined and edited" had made me more determined to be a better writer. By the time I was in third grade I'd had two works published. It felt so good to see my name in print. It seemed like everything was perfect.

Then I started middle school. Everyone around me was either an athlete or was "cool." I knew no other young writers. This depressed me and I eventually stopped writing. I figured people wouldn't like me if they knew I loved to read and write, so I didn't tell anyone, not even teachers.

My family knew that I had stopped, and they would always ask when would I start writing again. I ignored them for a year and a half. In fact, it took a mandatory English assignment in seventh grade to get me writing again. That assignment turned out so good that I'm now in the process of getting that story published.

That brings us up to present day. I am now in eighth grade and I haven't stopped writing since that assignment. Now, I guess I'll give you some helpful tips, but I'm not going to tell you a mile-long list of laws and dos and don'ts. I hate when grown-ups do that to me, so I'm not going to do it to you.

1. Don't be afraid to let someone edit your work.
2. *READ*. The more you read, the better you write. Trust me.
3. Don't let adults dictate how you write or what you write. Every person has his or her own style, remember that.
4. Keep trying and try not to get depressed. All writers will eventually get a rejection or returned manuscripts.

Finally, I want to say one more thing. Writing is not always fun, but you make the choice whether you want to produce good fruit or bad fruit. Stick with it.

JONATHAN COFSKY
Briarwood, New York

Jonathan Cofsky is sixteen years old and recently graduated from Townsend Harris High School in New York City. He started writing at age twelve for Anton Community Newspapers in Long Island before going on to regularly write and publish articles for Newsday. *Additionally, he has been published in* Sports Illustrated for Kids *and the* Times Herald Record Jr. *(an upstate New York newspaper). While writing for these publications, he has had the opportunity to interview many sports figures, such as Bobby Valentine, Jim Fassel, Ron Artest, Jesse Armstead, Michael Strahan, Jason Sehorn and Amani Toomer. Recently he finished with honorable mention in the 2000 Salomon Smith Barney Quality of Life Research Competition and second place in the 2000 Eldred WWII Museum Essay Contest.*

My Writer's Digest Book editor, Michelle Howry, brought Jonathan to my attention after he submitted a book proposal to Jack Heffron, another WDB editor with whom I had worked. Although the editors eventually turned down Jonathan's book idea, Kids Can Get Published Too, A Kid's Guide to Writing and Getting Published, *they were impressed enough with his work to suggest him as a young writer profile prospect here. Perhaps no one can empathize more with Jonathan's experience with WDB than I. After all, they were the first publisher to turn down my first book proposal in 1986. It was for the very first edition of* Market Guide for Young Writers. *And look who publishes it now (grin).*

I started writing when I was twelve. I don't know whether it was by accident or by fate; either way I just seemed to trip over it. I never really liked writing, nor did I ever consider myself a "writer." I preferred math, science, business, sports, video games, anything other than writing.

My mom wrote a freelance article for Anton Community Newspapers and noticed that it had a kids' page. Being a normal, nagging mom, she told me to write something for the kids' page. I had no clue what to write about, and I wasn't too happy about the extra work. I would rather be with my friends playing football or baseball or video games until my eyes saw colors that didn't exist. I decided to write an article about investing in the stock market on a kid's budget. The editor liked it and ran the article, and barely any revisions were made. I started sending more articles in—about sports, video games or anything else I felt like. The editor published about 75 percent of my submissions. He was so impressed with my work that he would publish almost anything I wrote. I've been extremely lucky because I have received very few rejection letters and have worked with editors who have given me free range and have had open minds.

Eventually I decided writing articles was fun, but it would be more fun to interview athletes on the teams I rooted for. I proposed to my editor that I would send a letter to some local teams to try to obtain an interview with their coaches. Well, the scheme worked, as the New York Giants and New York Mets both complied with my request.

Shortly after completing those interviews (I was about thirteen), Anton Community Newspapers decided to discontinue their kids page. So I sent a query letter and an article to an editor of the Kidsday section of *Newsday*, a large New York newspaper. Most people I know thought that the effort would be futile. As it turned out, it was anything but. The editor published the article. As I had done with the Anton newspaper editor, I started sending this editor articles on topics ranging from sports to dragging my dad to a Nine Inch Nails concert. Most of my articles were published, and the editor even gave several assignments to me. One article he assigned to me was an interview of former St. John's star, Ron Artest. I was paid twenty-five dollars for expenses. This marked the first time I was paid for my work.

When I was fifteen, I decided it was time to start making money, or at least trying. After calling and proposing several ideas to editors at *Sports Illustrated for Kids*, they finally liked one and sent me up to the New York Giants training camp to interview Michael Strahan, Jason Sehorn, Jesse Armstead and Amani Toomer. They even paid me four hundred dollars (enough to cover the memorabilia I bought to get autographed).

For the most part, I've only had one really negative experience in the several years that I have been writing. I proposed an article to a newspaper and received approval to write the article. The article involved interviewing a doctor at a local hospital. I called the hospital and received permission to conduct an interview, until they realized my age. Once they realized I was only fifteen, they complained to the newspaper and I wasn't able to write the article.

Writing has been great for me. I enjoy writing articles, conducting interviews and writing fiction. Writing has been a release. Whenever I'm tired or frustrated, I just write. I am lucky enough to have found something I enjoy doing and something that gives me an opportunity to be heard. I have been places and met people I never would have if I didn't write. I'm sure it helped my SAT score. I received a 770 verbal, and I don't exactly enjoy reading the dictionary.

Honestly, I don't have any tips on writing technique or style, other than be yourself. Write what you want, however you want it. It doesn't matter if you are published or if no one ever knows that you write. No one writes your stories but you. Stories aren't always unique for their ideas, but the voice they're told in is yours. Generally, my English teachers haven't praised my writing, but that never stopped me. Rather it made me more driven to prove them wrong. Keep an open mind, but don't let anyone destroy or distort your vision.

MEGAN R. MATTINGLY
Pine Mountain Club, California

Megan, seventeen, home-schooled since sixth grade and the oldest of four children, is part of a family where everyone is actively involved or interested in some aspect of the entertainment industry. Both of her parents are writer/ producers. When she wrote me, they were producing a movie and a series for television that they had written together. Both brothers, Matthew and Jacob, are aspiring animators, and sister Jayne wants to be an actress as well as an architect. Under the director of doctors at the Shriner's Hospital for Crippled Children in Los Angeles, Megan handles a lot of the home-based physical therapy for Jayne, who was born with spina bifida and is paralyzed from the knees down.

In addition to writing, Megan's major interests are acting, reading and dance, including ballet, tap, jazz and even Balkan folk dancing. Megan hopes that through her writing she can bring attention to a number of important issues. Drawing upon her knowledge and experience as an insulin-dependent diabetic, she's working on a cookbook for diabetic teens. She's also started a teen awareness campaign to help bring attention to problems associated with devil worship cults and ritual sacrifices. Says Megan, "I'd like to mention my friend, Ryan. His sister, Elyse Marie Pahler, was murdered five years ago in San Luis Obispo, California, after being kidnapped, tortured and raped in a ritual sacrifice to the devil. I've started a teen awareness campaign and hope that, through writing, Elyse's memory will not be lost."

Sitting at the miniature desk in my nursery, I folded the single sheet of drawing paper in half. My creation was no longer a picture with poorly spelled captions. No, it had become the two-page saga, "MaryAnne's Surprise." It was the touching, if somewhat shocking, story of a little girl who goes out to play one sunny summer afternoon and unsuspectedly steps on a firecracker, blowing herself to smithereens. Crayons still in hand and with an ear-to-ear grin on my face, I went to give the story to my mom. But I wasn't taking it to her as Megan Mattingly. I was "Megan

Margaret," a "writing name" I had created for myself years earlier at age three.

I handed her my story and waited anxiously for her to finish, holding my breath the entire two seconds it took her to read it. She stared at me with her mouth open for a long time before finally asking what could have possessed me to write such a story. "You don't like it?" I asked, my eyes starting to fill with tears. "Well," she said as she sat me down, "I like that you put so much effort into it." Then she gently explained that people wouldn't understand the reasoning behind that kind of senseless violence. I nodded. I understood. As I hopped out of the room, I promised to remember what she said and, peeking around the doorframe, said, "But Mom, I can *guarantee* that MaryAnne was surprised." I was six. So began my humble career as a young writer.

Because my parents are writers and fostered a creative academic environment, it was almost inevitable that I became a writer. Looking back, I see that I probably couldn't have escaped it even had I wanted. We were always reading, writing, talking and *always* telling each other stories. They taught me the importance of expressing my thoughts and opinions. Writing continually fascinates me because anyone, no matter who he is, can write down what he thinks or how he feels and others will read it. That makes writing one of the most powerful activities one can do.

During my years in elementary school, I participated in many short story and essay contests. I did very well, usually placing at least an honorable mention. But by calling yourself a "writer," you accept a great deal of responsibility, inviting tremendous pressure to flourish to "write well." It wasn't until my freshman year of high school, when my talent started to flourish, that I really began to consider myself a "true writer." I'd written an environmental commentary on frog mutations that I felt was both intelligent and witty. (If you can make frog mutations a fun topic, then you know you've got something!)

The time for dabbling was behind me; I was finally ready to devote real time and effort to my work. No longer just a fashion accessory, my oversized totebag carried the tools of my trade; notebooks, ink pens and Liquid Paper pens go with me everywhere. After all, I never know when I'll have an amazing idea in the food court at the mall.

The saying goes, "Write what you know." But I look at it like this: *Write what you know, and what you don't know—research.* When I used to get an idea for a short story I would mistakenly tell myself that there would be absolutely no research involved. Then my brain would go to work and turn my simple idea for a ten-page story into a two-hundred-page Hollywood-worthy epic. So that, of course, meant spending endless hours pouring over every scrap of information on my topic. It's hard work, but in the end it all pays off.

For me, it wasn't enough to write for myself. I still entertained the dream that my work would be read by people I'd never meet or even see. So after firmly dismissing the millions of "what ifs" that cluttered my mind, I gathered my courage and made my first submission. I sent a characteristically humor-filled essay to the teen zine, *Readers Speak Out!* To my absolute relief, it was accepted and I was able to cultivate a positive relationship with the publication and its editor, Ron Richardson. I now serve as an adviser for *RSO!*, and in turn, Ron has done an excellent job advising me on how to make smart submissions. Under his direction, my work has appeared in magazines such as *Teen Voices* and *Positive Teens*, and I have even earned some spending cash.

Working with editors isn't the easiest thing in the world, and I'm glad my parents conveyed the importance of tact and assertiveness. I've found these qualities very useful. If I believe in something I've written, I will stand my ground. That's being assertive. However, if an editor doesn't share my vision, then I make sure to go elsewhere without slamming any doors behind me. That's where I use a lot of my tact.

Since childhood, my life has reflected a love affair with words. A lot has changed since I wrote "MaryAnne's Surprise." I've grown as both a writer and a person. And, by age eight, I replaced "Megan Margaret" as my writing name with Megan R. Mattingly. Through it all, my love and appreciation for writers and their work have never faltered. I look forward to a career in writing and hope someday to be counted among the great authors I have cherished.

JESSICA & DANIELLE DUNN
Sugarland, Texas

Twins Jessica (top) and Danielle Dunn first contacted me via CompuServe on June 1, 1997. They were sixteen at the time, going into eleventh grade at Dulles High School, and had been writing and publishing (on their own as well as together) for five years. They were writing to share some of their experiences, including writing a how-to book together that Prufrock Press had published a year earlier. The eighty-four-page book, A Teen's Guide to Getting Published, *puts a special teen focus on submitting work for publication. The teens' contract with Prufrock earned them 10 percent royalties on sales. They were diligently at work on a new nonfiction book proposal full of tips on how a good student can become a great student in school.*

"We've learned a lot through our experiences," they said. "A lot of young writers seem to think that being young makes it difficult to have work published, but we see it as an advantage. Who better than a teen to write a book on coping with life as a teen?" Unfortunately, they dropped the project after it was rejected by Free Spirit Press and they became busy with other things.

Now attending Rice University, the girls maintain a strong interest in writing, still tackling some things individually and some things in tandem. For this edition, I've asked the twins, now twenty-years-old, to share individually their publishing experiences. They may be frequent writing partners, but each has a mind of her own. Jessica gets to go first because she got her essay to me first.

JESSICA DUNN
I first attempted to publish my writing at age twelve by submitting a lot of poems and a few short stories to children's magazines like *Creative Kids* and *Merlyn's Pen*. I had some success with the poems, but it didn't take me long to realize that fiction was not my forte. I couldn't write a suspenseful plot to save my life!

Under the circumstances, I enjoyed the publishing far more than the writing itself, so I turned to other creative pursuits. By age thirteen or fourteen, I discovered puzzles. Children's magazines often publish puzzles and word games because children love to solve them, but relatively few young people realize how much fun it is to create them. Puzzles can also help writers break into any number of magazines.

In addition to puzzles, I began to focus on writing nonfiction. Many kids love storytelling, but they think that nonfiction is limited to book reports or research papers for school. How about discussing a unique interest, sharing a creative solution to a common problem or teaching a skill that you feel others may find useful? For instance, my sister Danielle and I wrote an article for *Creative Kids* on some unusual summer activities for kids. We also wrote an article for *Skipping Stones* on Russian nesting dolls, the wooden ones that each open up to reveal another one inside. We both love to collect such unusual items and thought other teens might enjoy reading about them. Just remember: Nonfiction isn't limited to topics like "Characteristics of Helium" or "How to Make a Peanut Butter and Jelly Sandwich"! However, by far my most amazing experience was the publication of *A Teen's Guide to Getting Published*, the book I co-wrote with my twin sister. Five years later I still shake my head in wonder that it was accepted at all—and that was just the first step. Stephanie Stout, an editor at Prufrock Press, went through several drafts of the manuscript with Danielle and me for over a year. She marked minor changes, recommended topics for whole chapters to be added and then sent it back to us so we could make the changes on our computer. It was a daunting task and at times very frustrating. I felt a bit hurt when Ms. Stout asked us to cut out a whole chapter that she felt was not very useful. Also, Danielle and I disagreed with one or two of her suggestions and convinced her to leave the manuscript as written in those cases. Most of the time, however, I agreed with and wholeheartedly appreciated Ms. Stout's revisions. When she suggested that we add a chapter on how to "present a professional image," I thought, "Of course! Why didn't I think of that before?" To Danielle's delight as well as mine, the book doubled in length and greatly improved in content as a result of her help.

Most of all, I was glad Prufrock encouraged our involvement throughout the editing process. For years I had sent my work to editors whom I never had a chance to meet or talk to personally. It was like submitting my thoughts to a deity and anxiously awaiting judgment from on high. Finally, here was my opportunity to offer my input in the postacceptance editing process! I spent half an hour on the phone with Ms. Stout discussing last-minute changes to be made to the final author's proofs, which show all the pages in their actual layout, just as they will look in the book itself. Especially for a person of my age, it was a really cool experience.

After waiting anxiously for several months, I was elated when I received the first printed copies of the book in the mail. Danielle and I continue to receive royalties for it to this day. Given that it is sold only through catalogs and has a relatively small audience, we have been very pleased with the sales.

About a year later, Bonnie Drew, the editor of *Young Entrepreneur Newsmagazine*, happened to see an article that Danielle and I wrote for the *Houston Chronicle*. She wrote a letter asking us to write an advice column for her magazine's readers on how to publish their own work. I loved being able to submit articles by e-mail, and I also liked having "steady work." Rather than receiving acceptances sporadically, I had my writing published every four to six weeks for about a year and a half. Ms. Drew even offered us a raise to $.35 per word.

Not everything about publishing has gone perfectly for me, though. I attribute quite a bit of my success to good luck, but it wasn't always with me. A case in point: my next attempt at publishing a book. Danielle and I again collaborated to write *A Teen's Guide to Achieving Academic Success*. We studied the catalog of Free Spirit Publishing, which carries books on "self-help for kids," and it seemed like a perfect match for our manuscript. We sent them a book proposal, including a query letter, outline and sample pages from the book; but the editors felt that they had too many other books in their catalog with topics similar to ours, and they declined to look at the full manuscript. Danielle and I continued to work on it off and on for three years and sent out several more book proposals but never found a publisher. It still disappoints me when I consider the incredible amount of work that I put into that manuscript. Perhaps someday we will return to it, include some advice about college and try again to get it published.

In the meantime, my life has shifted into the amazing alternate universe they call college! I am now twenty years old and a sophomore at Rice University, a private school in Houston, Texas, studying chemical engineering and bioengineering. Many people have expressed surprise that I do not plan to be a freelance writer for a living, but I have always had a great interest in math and science as well. However, writing will remain one of my hobbies. I keep a journal, and I would like to write articles for trade magazines someday after I become a practicing engineer. At the very least, I think that publishing has enhanced my life and has also improved my communication skills. Many of the best memories of my life thus far have come from my experiences in publishing. I don't think I could have asked for a more exciting hobby.

DANIELLE DUNN

I was twelve years old when I first learned that young writers like me could get their work published. It sounded like fun, so I read a couple of guide books on publishing, including an earlier edition of *Market Guide for Young Writers*, and eagerly submitted my stories and poems to several youth magazines. The majority were rejected; in fact, I tried repeatedly to get something printed in *Stone Soup*, one of the better-known magazines written by and for children, but I never succeeded in breaking into that market before exceeding its age limit. Happily, by eighth grade I had had several poems and puzzles accepted for publication elsewhere.

I was hooked by the excitement of seeing my work and my name in print. It was like I had been initiated into a secret club. Apparently, most of my peers knew very little about opportunities in writing and publishing and had never even heard of the magazines to which I frequently submitted my work. I wanted to share what I had learned and let them know how enjoyable and gratifying it really was.

My twin sister Jessica, whose own publishing efforts had also begun in the sixth grade, agreed with me. Suddenly we found ourselves enthusiastically composing a how-to guide for young writers, containing all that we had learned along the way about the writing and publishing process. We spent many hours brainstorming subtopics to include, individually writing different sections and then editing our own and each other's contributions. As our excitement grew along with the manuscript, we considered submitting it to a book publisher.

The young writer's magazine *Creative Kids*, in which Jessica and I had each been published, provided the link we needed. Prufrock Press, the publisher of the magazine, also printed educational books for students and teachers. Thinking that maybe our involvement in the magazine would give us a foot in the door regarding our book, we sent in a query letter and later the full manuscript, upon the editor's request. I was truly ecstatic when I received a letter in the mail several months later saying that Prufrock would publish the book, called *A Teen's Guide to Getting Published*—and pay us both royalties for it!

Hooked on the idea of writing more nonfiction, I got a summer job writing news and feature articles for a local weekly newspaper, the *Fort Bend/Southwest Sun*. About once a week, the editor, Trinh Le, would give me a lead for a story assignment, usually about a local organization or an individual resident who had done something exciting or unique. I would take it from there, reading whatever background information Ms. Le gave me and gathering further details if possible, usually on the Internet. The rest of my material came from interviewing people—on the phone, by e-mail or in person. I even took photos to accompany a few of my articles. Being a reporter, writer and photographer all at once was a really neat experience.

However, one of my feature articles about a local resident turned out to be quite a hassle because the husband of my interviewee was extremely overbearing. He had very specific ideas of what he wanted me to say about his wife and her achievements, and he called me several times to check on my progress. I laugh about it now, but at the time it was very irritating. Never let anyone dictate what you should write!

Anyway, my hard work paid off almost immediately after I

e-mailed each finished article to Ms. Le; the paper only had a one-week lead time! Ms. Le almost always edited my work, frequently changing my headlines and lead paragraphs. I really did not mind, however, because her improvements, as I saw them, helped me to learn and to hone my own skills.

Having had such a wonderful variety of experiences in writing and publishing, I have come to recognize that the publishing world is like a giant buffet. Don't be afraid to sample your options and try out new directions; you may discover something even better suited to your talents, and even more fun, than what you've already tried. Experiment with writing poems and short stories, fiction and nonfiction, even puzzles and word games. Look for new markets for your work, magazines as well as newspapers. Write about a variety of subjects. The solid advice to "write what you know" served me well when I was working on *A Teen's Guide to Getting Published*. By contrast, for the *Sun* I really enjoyed writing not what I knew, but what I could find out. By interviewing people and researching for my articles, I learned about everything from the art of quilting to suicide prevention to the history of Mickey Mouse, and then I shared this information with the *Sun's* readers.

I am now twenty years old and a sophomore at Rice University, studying to be an engineer. I may never be a full-time writer, but I know that my communication skills will help me in any career path I might choose. Meanwhile, writing makes a fantastic hobby!

Chapter Seven

Editors Are Real People Too

I n this chapter, you'll have the opportunity to meet five adults who work as editors or contest sponsors, plus Rachel Hubbard, the teen founder, publisher and editor of a zine named *Splash!* Two of them were highlighted in earlier editions: Christine Clark, when she was editor of *Humpty Dumpty* magazine published by the Children's Better Health Institute, and Gerry Mandel, in William Ruebel's behind-the-scenes look at *Stone Soup* who cofounded and edited the magazine with her.

Shirley Jo Moritz, Young Writers editor at *Skylark*, the literary arts annual magazine of Purdue University Calumet, was delighted to comply with my request to share about *Skylark*. When she suddenly faced a serious medical problem, *Skylark*'s editor in chief, Pam Hunter, stepped in to help her draft and submit her profile to me just in time.

Many of you may recognize the name of Deborah Morris, creator and author of the very popular book and television series *Real Kids, Real Adventures*. If you're looking for a special manuscript critique group just for young writers, you'll want to visit her Web site and sign up.

Ronald A. Richardson (an adult) and Rachel Hubbard (a teen) both have ties to Mr. Richardson's small teen-focused and traditionally published zine, *Reader's Speak Out!* Rachel also publishes and edits her own zine called *Splash!*

I hope that putting faces to names, learning a bit about their backgrounds and letting them share what they do behind the scenes will help you see these professionals as real, everyday people. Use what they have so graciously shared to better write and market your work.

RICH WALLACE
Senior Editor, *Highlights for Children*
Honesdale, Pennsylvania

Rich Wallace, a senior editor for the past five years, began his career at Highlights for Children *as a copywriter thirteen years ago. In addition to his editorial work, Mr. Wallace is also a noted author of young adult novels. His latest book,* Playing Without the Ball, *was published by Knopf in September 2000. It, like his first two books (also by Knopf), has a sports-related focus. His first book,* Wrestling Sturbridge, *was a top-ten pick by the American Library Association.* Shots on Goal *was his second book.*

Interest in book writing apparently runs in the family. Both of Mr. Wallace's two teenage sons are avid writers. "They have both been writing novels since about the third grade," he says. Although Mr. Wallace also wrote as a child, success did not come early or easily.

When I was a kid, my favorite part of any magazine I read was always the jokes and riddles. That's the first section I'd turn to in *Highlights for Children* or *Humpty Dumpty* in my annual visits to the dentist's office. And, as a subscriber to *Boys' Life*, it's also the section I often submitted work to, hoping to find myself published.

It never happened. Even when I was sure I'd discovered the funniest joke, told it with perfect timing and sent it off in the mail, I'd invariably see that same joke published (and told better than I had done) a month or two later, attributed to some other kid.

Many years later, after I'd become an editor at *Highlights*, I realized just how enormous was the competition for space on the pages of those magazines. At *Highlights*, we receive more than a thousand pieces of mail from our readers each week, and nearly all of those envelopes include work being submitted for publication: stories, poems, drawings, jokes, riddles, tongue twisters and other items. And even though we devote a fair amount of space to kids' work each month—about five or six pages, on average—

it is still only a tiny fraction of that volume that ever gets into print.

Ask any editor at *Highlights* and they'll tell you that the single hardest job we have is choosing which pieces of kids' work to publish. With stacks and stacks of creative writing and drawings to look through each month, how do we determine which pieces should get in? It's not an easy job.

Let me tell you about the process. First I should say that we don't expect jokes, riddles or tongue twisters to be original. Of course, as editors, we've read most of the more common jokes and such a thousand times, so we probably won't be as tickled by "Why did the chicken cross the road?" as by a joke we've never heard before. But items like these feel somehow like community property, so we're happy to share a joke that a kid has heard in school or elsewhere.

But when it comes to stories and poems, we seek originality without fail. Some kids do submit poems that they've read or heard elsewhere. Published work is protected by copyright laws, of course, and we wouldn't want to give someone credit for work that is not their own. We are very careful to have all poems we are considering checked by an expert, but occasionally a poem that's been copied will slip by us all and get into print. It's not only embarrassing, but it's aggravating to know that the poem took space that could have been devoted to another child's original work.

So be original. And be creative.

I love poems and stories that only could have been written by one specific kid. That is, if you've had a funny experience with your cat or a deep thought while watching the moon come up, find a way to tell about it that makes it yours alone. The poems or stories that seem to jump out at us as we work our way through a stack are the ones that convey a child's very own senses and emotions. The writer's words help us share that experience. And that makes us want to publish the work.

Editors select things for publication that move them in some way. This is true of the stories, poems and articles we purchase from adult writers as well as the work we select from our readers. Any piece that causes me to react—to smile or be entertained or even to feel sad—will definitely get a second look. If it has made me feel some emotion, then it will do the same for other readers as well.

Here are my top tips for any kid hoping to submit stories or poems to *Highlights*. (I've already given two of them, but I'll repeat them because they're so important.)

1. Be original. We can nearly always detect copied work.

2. Be creative. We read lots of poems about falling leaves. Either find another subject or find a new way to tell us.

3. Be careful. It does make a difference if words are misspelled or writing is not neat. Always check your work and recopy it if necessary. Carefully prepared pages let us know that the writer takes pride in his or her work.

4. Be patient. You will receive a letter or postcard letting you know that we've received your work, but it will be at least six months before your work might be published. And the chances are great that it won't be. We always encourage kids to keep writing and drawing and to be proud of their creative work, whether it is published or not.

5. Be aware. It will be obvious from looking through a few issues of *Highlights* that we don't publish lengthy poems and stories by children. Pay attention to the type of work that your magazine is publishing. Most kids' magazines list some sort of guidelines in their pages. (Check the box on "Our Own Pages" in *Highlights*, for example.)

6. Keep trying. The more you write or draw, the better you will become at it. Successful writers and artists keep at it for a long time, and that is true of children as well as adults.

GERRY MANDEL

Editor, *Stone Soup*
Santa Cruz, California

*My how time flies! It's sometimes hard for me
to believe that* Stone Soup *has been publishing
high-quality writing and art by children for
almost thirty years. Gerry Mandel, along with
William Rubel, is both cofounder and editor.
Mr. Rubel, profiled in the* Market Guide for Young Writers *third
edition, published in 1990, is working mostly on a consulting basis these
days.*

*"We love what we do," said Ms. Mandel back then. And while the
faces and names of the young writers and artists featured in its pages
continually change, Ms. Mandel hasn't lost any of her love for her work.
"It's very satisfying to be able to encourage young writers and artists by
presenting the best of their work in* Stone Soup.*" Here Ms. Mandel
illustrates the truly global appeal and reach of its readers and
contributors.*

When I checked my e-mail this morning, it included poetry
submissions from young people in England, Finland and the
West Indies—what a thrill! *Stone Soup* has always been an international forum for young writers and artists, but the Internet has
made it easier than ever for young people the world over to share
their work with one another. Envelopes and postage, which may
be difficult for some children to obtain, are no longer a problem,
and writers are not at the mercy of postal systems that may be
unreliable.

This year in *Stone Soup* we published "Meet Soon Soon," a
story by eleven-year-old Sarah Heng Blackburn of Beijing, China.
Sarah's story recounts the experiences of a little girl whose family
is torn apart by the Cultural Revolution. It's both a moving story
and a fascinating history lesson, showing us an important period
in world history through the eyes of a young person who knows
about it firsthand. This year also saw the publication of "Winter
Light," an exquisite poem by twelve-year-old Miyo Kurosaki of
Kyoto, Japan. The poem appeared in *Stone Soup* in both English

and Japanese, and our readers got to admire the beautiful Japanese characters submitted by the author. Our January/February 2001 issue will include "The Chase" by eleven-year-old Fiona Cull of South Yorkshire, England. Like many children all over the world, Fiona is an animal lover, and her story about a family of cheetahs trying to survive on the plains of Africa has universal appeal.

This may sound corny, but "universal appeal" is what I like best about publishing work from other countries in *Stone Soup*. When children read the work of their peers from other countries and realize that young people share the same concerns and interests regardless of where they live, it brings us all closer together.

The Internet is a great way for young writers around the world to reach *Stone Soup*; it's also a great way for everyone everywhere to have access to vast quantities of work by children. For over twenty-five years, *Stone Soup*'s covers have featured international children's art. Just in the last year we have published art on our covers from Indonesia, Russia, Greece, China, South Africa and Cyprus. Go to our Web site at www.stonesoup.com and see all twenty-five years' worth of covers in one place, reproduced in sparkling color! In addition, our Web site includes a growing sample of international children's art from our own collection of over one thousand works. Before long we plan to offer links to the Web sites of children's museums around the world, including the Museum of Greek Children's Art in Athens and the International Museum of Children's Art in Oslo. Children who speak English can share their writing across country lines—all children can share their experiences and feelings through the common language of art.

These are exciting times. When magazines like *Stone Soup* can build on their foundations with expansive Internet offerings, a whole world of opportunities opens up for young people everywhere. We're proud to play our part in the Internet revolution and overjoyed that we can provide new outlets for talented young writers and artists around the world.

SHIRLEY JO MORITZ
Editor, *Skylark*
Hammond, Indiana

The copyright page of Skylark *magazine includes this statement: "This magazine publishes work by children and by adults on the
acknowledged premise that children and more
mature literary artists should be published side
by side." True to its claim, the pages of* Skylark *are filled with wonder-
fully inspiring and thought-provoking writings and artwork by children,
teens and adults.*

*In this profile, Shirley Jo Moritz focuses most on sharing how she
chooses artwork by students, keen to include color and black-and-white
art that serves to truly complement the text nearby. If you are a young
artist, you'll want to pay particular attention to the advice Ms. Moritz
gives for what she looks for and how she discovers the young artists and
writers whose work she publishes in the pages of* Skylark. *You'll be able
to apply what you learn here to improve your chances for success submitting to other markets and contests. Included at the end of this essay is
some special advice aimed just at teachers.*

As editor for the "Young Writers" section of *Skylark*, I experience
stimulating, inventive powers that allow me to grow more creative
with each new issue. In fact, each year, as I work to blend text and
artwork into my section of the magazine, my own creativity is called
upon constantly and is expressed in various ways.

I enjoy working with my readers in order to select the poems,
essays and short stories that are submitted to the magazine by
young writers all across the nation and around the world. When
I discover a young person who writes with a sense of humor
or who can express a sad situation in a moving, yet not overly
sentimental way, I become very excited. What really gives me a
thrill, however, is taking these well-written pieces of writing and
matching them to a complementary or contrasting piece of art
that also has been created by a young person. I feel that an excellent poem paired with a beautiful line drawing or full-color illustration offers the reader a double treat.

There are two ways that I solicit artwork. I make a general request for sketches, color drawings or photographs to the local community. And to reach a wider pool of artists, I list *Skylark*'s needs in several market guides, such as *The Young Writer's Guide to Getting Published*. But now that our magazine is becoming better known for publishing national and international young writers and artists, I have built a network with artists whose work has appeared in past issues. I encourage these individuals to submit new work they have subsequently finished. In addition, I provide them with a list of specific subjects I would like illustrated. Then, it is up to them to take up the challenge.

To me, many of the submissions are so awesome that I have a hard time choosing what to publish. In the end, I select the best examples of as many different artists as I can. If someone is especially willing to draw, I may send a copy of a poem or short story that I have accepted for him or her to illustrate. The end results are often surprising because what impresses them so often is the contrast to what impresses me as an editor. I find this to be a valuable learning experience.

If an artist submits freelance work and gives me the flexibility to use any or all of his or her work in any way I choose, I take advantage of all of the possibilities that are open to me. This is how I work with the students of Dr. Martyna Bellessis of University Elementary in Bloomington, Indiana. For several years now, she has sent a variety of artwork to *Skylark* that has been created by students in the gifted and talented program of the Monroe County Community School Corporation. It is a joy to encounter the work of young people who compose pictures with such originality of color, form and texture. And I am given permission to use any part or all of any illustration in order to most enhance the text.

In 1999, Dr. Bellessis submitted collages done by sixth-grade students who used construction paper and markers to express interpretations of their favorite artists. I received examples that emulated Monet and Klee. Along with these was a piece entitled "Pink Flamingo" by Isaiah Stroup, which I published in color to open my section. Isaiah's bird reflected the work of John James Audubon. But this young artist employed a bold color scheme, and the stance of the flamingo reveals Isaiah's own personality too. Perhaps that is why Cindy Duesing, production editor for *Children's Writer's and Illustrator's Market*, chose it to accompany *Skylark*'s listing in its 2001 edition. Because of this, Isaiah gets a free copy of the guide and will also receive a fifty dollar reprint fee. To say that this selection surprised and pleased just this young artist is only partially true. Equally thrilled were Dr. Bellessis, the students and educators in Bloomington and all of the staff at *Skylark*. Here, indeed, is an example of student, teacher and literary publication working together to express and communicate both verbally and visually.

Now that *Skylark*'s budget allows more inside pages in color, I am even more eager to work with young artists. Reader and sponsor response to our last issue, including the "Young Writers" section, was highly enthusiastic for its format. So, choosing artwork, both in color and in black and white, which will integrate with the rest of the magazine, is a challenge for me and for all of the young artists who will be submitting in the future.

SPECIAL WARNINGS, TIPS AND ADVICE

To have a greater chance at being accepted for publication at *Skylark*, artists should submit work that is drawn on clean paper with no creases. Artwork will be returned carefully packaged so it does not sustain damage in transit.

Both art and text that are submitted with complete information about the artist or author in a cover letter have a better chance of being published. Follow the current *Skylark* guidelines.

Finally, the *Skylark* staff does not jury English composition assignments. To judge writing as good or bad, in order for a student to receive a certain grade at school, is not the function of a literary magazine. Poetry and prose submitted to *Skylark* may be rejected for a variety of reasons. Factors such as timing, content or availability of space have forced its editors to return many well-crafted poems and short stories. However, staff does encourage teachers to submit their students' work in order for students, as writers, to learn the mechanisms of getting work published. In addition, *Skylark* editors may offer suggestions. Then it is up to the teachers to work with their students in ways that will benefit the students' writing abilities most.

DEBORAH MORRIS
Sponsor, Write Your Own
    Adventure Contests
Author, *Real Kids, Real Adventures* books
Garland, Texas

When people ask Deborah Morris, who has wanted to be a writer since the sixth grade, why she chooses to write terrifying true stories about kids who've been attacked by sharks, caught in forest fires or faced other mortal dangers, they're often shocked by her enthusiastic—some would say ghoulish—response.

"I love it!" says the forty-year-old Garland, Texas, resident. "I guess I need the excitement. Looking back, my whole life has been a series of real-life dramas." Her background includes a stint as a commercial fisherman in Florida, a partnership in an Arizona gold-mining venture, a year on the road with her husband and children in a Mayflower moving truck, even several years as an Avon lady. Then in 1987, Morris added a death-defying experience to her resume.

"My family was on vacation in Florida when a tractor-trailer ran us off the highway," she recalls. "It sent us spinning down end over end into a ravine. It should have killed us, but we all walked away from it. I wrote the story for Guideposts *. . . and that's how I found out dramatic storytelling was a lot of fun. It wasn't long before I was writing dramas for* Reader's Digest *and* Good Housekeeping, *which eventually led to the* Real Kids, Real Adventures *series.*

She's quick to admit, though, that not all her adventures involve high drama. "I'll never forget the time I conducted an interview in broken Spanish, only to realize later that I had repeatedly called the family dog a—there's really no nice way to say this—a "fart" because I couldn't roll my r's correctly," she laughs. "Now I always bring a translator."

In addition to writing about the real life adventures of real kids, Ms. Morris also has a companion Young Writer's Clubhouse Web site where writing contests with exciting themes are regularly sponsored and where young writers can find tons of how-to information, as well as participate in a kid-focused manuscript critique group. Below is an excerpt from some of the "Keys to Writing Success" advice she shares on her Web site.

Plus each writing contest assignment features special writing tips to help you write a dynamite entry.

> Kid: "Mom, I want to grow up and be a writer!"
> Mom: "Sorry, honey. You can't do both!"

That's an old joke, but in a lot of ways it's true. Writers need "childish" traits like curiosity, stubbornness and an imagination to succeed. Since you happen to be a kid, you're already miles ahead of all the adults who've outgrown their imaginations. All you need are a few pointers to get you off to a good start.

HOW WRITING WORKS

First, how do you turn your ideas into articles, poems or books that people will want to read—and publishers will want to print? There are six basic steps (although they don't always occur in this order):

1. You get an idea for a story/article/book/whatever.
2. You write to publishers till you find one interested in your idea.
3. You write your story (or article or whatever).
4. You submit it (send it in) to the publisher.
5. You revise it if the publisher asks you to.
6. You get paid!

Sounds easy, right? The problem is, where do you find your ideas? How do you know which publishers to write to? What if none of them are interested? What if you send something in and they don't like it? You'll find answers to all those questions if you do your . . . homework!

No, no, I'm not talking about school homework! (Although, come to think of it, that's not an entirely bad idea.) I'm talking about learning the basics of how to send for writer's guidelines from different publishers, how to write good query letters and how to type your manuscript.

Work hard on your query letter. A "query" is a question, so a "query letter" is simply a letter asking an editor if he's interested in a certain idea or story. Think of it as a sales letter. It should be fun, friendly, but not foolish! Let your writing do the "talking" for you. For more details, buy or check out *How to Write Irresistible Query Letters* by Lisa Collier Cool, or browse *Inkspot*'s "Resources for Young Writers." (There's a link to *Inkspot* on the Clubhouse "Links" page.)

Make sure your manuscript is typed correctly. A "manuscript" is what you actually send in to the publisher. It needs to be typewritten (double-spaced) on clean white paper, with nice, wide margins at the top, bottom, left and right edges of each page. Only type on one side of each page, and don't use funny-looking fonts. It might look boring to you, but that's the way editors want it. It's your writing that should be exciting, not the paper! This is a good book for learning more details about manuscripts, or read the Beginning Writer's FAQ available at *Inkspot*. For questions about grammar, where to put commas, sentence structure and things like that, browse through *The Elements of Style*, an excellent online reference book. For a step-by-step guide to preparing a fantastic book proposal, buy or check out Jeff Herman's *Write the Perfect Book Proposal: 10 Proposals That Sold and Why*.

When I was a kid, I wanted to be a writer. But I didn't think that was an attainable goal. Why not? Mainly because when I was a kid, all the adults told me it wasn't an attainable goal. You know the routine—if you're a kid and you say, "I want to be a writer (or artist or soccer star or whatever)," parents and teachers mostly just smile. If you persist, they start giving you all the depressing statistics to show how hard it is and how few people make it. I think we talk a lot of kids out of their dreams that way, and that's a crime. Anyway, I didn't even try writing until I was an adult myself with three kids. When I finally did, I soon found out I could make it. I'm just sorry I wasted so much time.

RONALD A. RICHARDSON
Editor, *Readers Speak Out!*
Seattle, Washington

I've never come across a publication like Readers Speak Out! *before or a publisher/editor like Ron Richardson, who is so dedicated to mentoring young writers and helping them learn to improve their skills and publishing successes.* RSO!, *a single, two-sided sheet, nonfiction-only publication, uses a question and answer format where teens express their stances on controversial and pertinent issues in mini-essays of 50 to 150 words. Teens themselves, working as volunteer interns, think up most of the thought-provoking questions. Questions encompass virtually any topic, including all aspects of the arts (music, architecture, visual and performing arts), ethics and religion, and philosophies of life.*

And the teens who speak out in the pages of RSO! *don't hold back any punches. They may express opposing points of view, but both the questions and essay answers are well expressed, with the authors displaying a knowledge of history and societal concerns, as well as a sensitivity and respect for others.*

When I graduated from a Seattle high school in 1964, I aspired to become something that I would not have been happy at: a high school teacher. For me, *Readers Speak Out!* is a way to hang with some of the most intriguing teens in America. Many of my writers and advisers are unschoolers (such as home-schooled), but *RSO!* welcomes submissions from any teen: high school students, preppies (a prep school student served for several months as an assistant editor), dropouts, and I've also published responses by two college students.

I'm disabled by a severe eye disease. My modest income and ample time on my hands allow me to do *Readers Speak Out!*, mentor teens, correspond with adolescent pen pals (many are autodidacts, someone who is self-taught) and critique writing, especially poetry, short stories and personal essays by teenagers. I am a published poet myself.

Readers Speak Out! gives selected teens a chance to actually help run a zine. Internships are offered via correspondence. Interested teens can learn publishing procedures by volunteering to help in the behind-the-scenes workings of a small press zine. We have an ongoing need for mailbox interns in these areas:

- Associate editor—These *RSO!* partners write questions for the zine, work with manuscripts and have full autonomy and creative freedom.
- Acquisitions editor—Recruits people to write for *RSO!*
- Advisers—These interns suggest ways to improve our zine.
- Copyediting—Learn proofreading, grammar, spelling and meticulous light editing that respects an individual writer's unique voice.
- First reader—Assays and ranks submissions, recommending for or against acceptance.

I also have an informal teen advisory board. Plus I have a healthy slush pile, competent teen advisers and the will and financial stability to continue *Readers Speak Out!* for the duration of *The Young Writer's Guide to Getting Published* and probably well beyond.

RACHEL HUBBARD
Editor & Publisher, *Splash!*
Glen Ellyn, Illinois

Rachel Hubbard, sixteen, a sophomore at Glenbard West High School, really enjoys writing and publishing. To her, having a zine is a fun and easy way to express her feelings about things going on today. She believes it may even help her get into a good college or obtain a writing job someday. Rachel also enjoys being a teen correspondent for the magazine, Positive Teens, *as well as a staff writer for her school newspaper. Other publishing credits include* Skipping Stones *and the* Chicago Tribune.

For Rachel, her "voice" has been heard through her writing, and she has seen a dramatic improvement in her life because of it. She has been enriched by what she has learned from researching topics, from people she has corresponded with, and just from the writing process itself. "I now have a higher self-esteem and have found something I'm good at. To me, that's the best gift of all!" She also says she encourages people to get involved with writing because, as she puts it, "It's a truly remarkable experience. And, what do you know, you just may be good at it."

Ronald A. Richardson, editor and publisher of Readers Speak Out!, *recommended Rachel as a young writer, editor and publisher profile prospect. I'm glad he did. Look for details about her magazine,* Splash!, *in chapter eight.*

Ever since I was young, I dreamed of creating my own magazine. I remember talking with my best friend about the magazine we would create someday. We spent hours brainstorming the perfect name for it and talking about how big of a hit it would be. That never happened though, and soon I began to lose interest in writing. I didn't have any teachers to motivate me to write, and therefore that spark that had once been inside me was slowly disappearing.

However, after my first experience in the writing world, in eighth grade, that spark soon came alive again. It all happened one day when I found an address for a free zine in a teen magazine. I didn't even know what a zine was, but I was curious. So

I wrote to this man, Ron Richardson, and he began writing back to me. He told me about the "underground press"—the world of zines and writing. He also told me that I, too, could start my own zine. I, too, could be a part of the underground press.

I wanted to be a part of that world, so I began the task of creating my own zine, which I called *Splash!* I wrote articles about things that were going on in the world today and things that interested me. With the help of my parents, I designed the layout of my zine and thought about an appropriate title. I decided on the price, how often *Splash!* would be published and what *Splash!* would consist of. Then I mailed free copies of my zine to family, friends, teens, other zines and whomever else I thought might be interested in it.

I worked hard to publicize *Splash!* I put ads in zines and magazines and was fortunate enough that my zine was reviewed by other publications. Teens, adults, parents, grandparents, magazines and schools started helping me out by submitting articles, poems and stories. Through these people around the country, I learned about their hopes and dreams and thoughts and ideas.

I soon discovered that I *was* a good writer, and I did have a talent. I was able to write my thoughts about different topics and get them published. Through writing, I could "speak" my thoughts and people would listen. To me, this is wonderful. To have a zine, be a teen correspondent and be published in many magazines was beyond belief. Yet, here I am, telling you my story. I do consider myself lucky to have accomplished all this in just two years and to see my writing get better and my self-esteem rising in the process. To have accomplished all of this and not speak out is a shame, though. As a result, I now go to elementary schools and speak to children about zines and publishing. I tell them that they, too, can create their own zine or get their work published . . . that they can also accomplish their dreams.

To feel that spark that every day is growing inside me starting to spark inside these children is wonderful. So, I repeat what I tell these children to you: You can do it! You can do whatever you put your mind to, and you can accomplish it because dreams do come true. I should know; it's happening to me!

PART THREE

Chapter Eight

The Market List

On the following pages you will find the special market listings for young writers. However, as mentioned in chapter three, many of the best and most easily accessible markets are not listed here. They are the publications with which you are already familiar, such as your hometown newspaper, the regional magazine insert that comes with the daily paper, your own school or church publication and the special publications sponsored by clubs and organizations to which you may belong. For those of you who have Internet access, don't forget to check what might be available in your special interest areas. They are all potential markets for your work. You may submit material to them using the same formats and advice you have learned about here.

Include a short cover letter when you first submit to a local or regional market, especially ones not listed here. Tell the editor where you are from and include a brief personal history, including such things as your school's name and your grade. Add a line or two about your writing and publishing desires. However, as previously noted, don't waste time telling the editor what a great (or miserable) writer you are or that you have enclosed (or want to send) a great story, poem or article you wrote.

Never mention how great (or yucky) your family, friends or teachers find your writing.

Local editors, like editors elsewhere, are usually very opinionated people when it comes to submissions. If you are a good writer and have submitted a really good manuscript, the editor will know. If the editor doesn't agree with your ability assessment, boasting won't convince him otherwise. In general, editors are very skeptical about working with people who think too highly of themselves or their work. If your writing needs an explanation from you to be understood and appreciated, then it isn't ready for submission. Let your writing speak for itself.

The biggest benefit of submitting work to the types of markets mentioned above is that if a local editor likes your work and finds that you are willing to listen to his comments and ideas, plus can accept editing of your work without much fuss, you may find yourself being hired to do special writing assignments or asked to write a regular column.

UNDERSTANDING A MARKET LISTING

Markets, which include secular and religious magazines, newspapers, newsletters, theater groups, book publishers and other opportunities, are listed alphabetically, including those accessed through online computer services.

Each listing contains three individual sections of information that will help you understand (1) the type of publication it is, (2) what material it will consider from young people, and (3) the preferred formats for submitting your work. There are two optional sections. "Editor's Remarks" are quotes directly from editors or their guidelines sheets. They provide additional information to help you understand and evaluate whether the market would be an appropriate place for you to send your work. "Subscription Rates" has been included as an extra service since so many of the publications listed are available by subscription only.

New additions to this edition's market listings are preceded by a checkmark (✔). Markets that are of special interest to young people are preceded by an asterisk (*). Markets that require an entry fee are marked with a dollar sign ($). Canadian markets are identified with a maple leaf (✿). Listings based outside the United States and Canada or that are especially global in nature are preceded by a globe icon (▦). Look for an envelope icon (✉) for online-only publishing opportunities, as well as those that accept e-mailed submissions.

A few listings are also marked with a double cross (‡). This indicates that this market should be considered only by serious teen writers. Competition for acceptance is likely to be tough because you will be competing against adults, the market receives many more submissions than it can use or has an unusual focus that may not be understood or appreciated by young writers. To help you remember how to interpret the codes and listing information, author's notes have been placed at the bottom of some listings.

The following chart and sample market listing will help explain the information contained within each section. You may want to review the sections "What's New in This Edition" and "More About the Listings" in chapter one, plus the advice in chapter three, "Studying and Comparing Opportunities," before reviewing these listings.

MARKET LISTING CHART

SEC.	YOU WILL FIND	PAY SPECIAL ATTENTION TO
1	Name of Publication. Mailing address for manuscripts, guidelines and sample copies. Brief description including how often it is published, the age range, and interests of its readers.	Who reads this publication and the general theme followed in each issue.
2	Types of written material, art and photography, that are considered for publication. Specific material that is not accepted.	Any special columns or departments written exclusively by young writers. Any specific types of material that are never used.
3	More detailed information to help you write and prepare your manuscripts. Payments offered; rights purchased. Word limits; line limits for poetry. Availability of guidelines and samples.	Any special instructions for submitting manuscripts. Whether you need to include a signed statement from your parents, teacher or guardian.
4	Advice and helpful tips especially for young writers, quote directly from the editor.	What the editors say they do and do not want from young writers.
5	Subscription rates Subscription mailing address when it differs from the editorial office.	Included as an extra service for young people, parents and teachers.

SAMPLE MARKET LISTING

1 _____ **THE ACORN**, 1530 7th St., Rock Island, IL 61201. For young people in grades K–12. Published four times a year, this 10-page publication offers a showcase for young authors.

2 _____ **Publishes:** Fiction on any subject of interest to young people, except killing of humans or animals or "love" material. Uses 4″×5″ black ink drawings on any subject. Uses material only from young authors. Uses *no* nonfiction articles.

3 _____ **Submission Info:** Handwritten material OK if readable. Photocopies of original work are permissible. Prefers standard format. Maximum length for fiction is 500 words; poetry up to 35 lines. *Always* put author's name, address, age or grade on manuscript. Submissions will *not* be returned without SASE. Reports in 1 week. Guidelines available for SASE. Sample copy $3. Material not accompanied by SASE will be destroyed. More than one manuscript may be submitted; send together with either one or individual SASE for each.

4 _____ **Editor's Remarks:** "Just be yourself. Write your feelings; dare to be different. You never know when what you have to say might be of help and encouragement to other young authors. No pay, but it isn't necessary to purchase a copy to be published. We like to give young authors who have never been published before a place in *Acorn*."

5 _____ **Subscription Rates:** One year (4 issues: Feb., May, Aug., Nov.) $10.

* THE ACORN, 1530 7th St., Rock Island, IL 61201. For young people in grades K–12. Published four times a year, this 10-page publication offers a showcase for young authors.

Publishes: Fiction on any subject of interest to young people, except killing of humans or animals or "love" material. Uses 4″ × 5″ black ink drawings on any subject. Uses material only from young authors. Uses *no* nonfiction articles.

Submission Info: Handwritten material OK if readable. Photocopies of original work are permissible. Prefers standard format. Maximum length for fiction is 500 words; poetry up to 35 lines. *Always* put author's name, address, age or grade on manuscript. Submissions will *not* be returned without SASE. Reports in 1 week. Guidelines available for SASE. Sample copy $3. Material not accompanied by SASE will be destroyed. More than one manuscript may be submitted; send together with either one or individual SASEs for each.

Editor's Remarks: "Just be yourself. Write your feelings; dare to be different. You never know when what you have to say might be of help and encouragement to other young authors. No pay, but it isn't necessary to purchase a copy to be published. We like to give young authors who have never been published before a place in *Acorn*."

Subscription Rates: One year (4 issues: Feb., May, Aug., Nov.) $10.

* AMERICAN GIRL MAGAZINE, 8400 Fairway Pl., Middleton, WI 53562. Web site: www.americangirl.com. Bimonthly magazine for girls ages 8 and up. Mission is to celebrate girls, yesterday and today. *American Girl* recognizes girls' achievements, inspires their creativity and nurtures their hopes and dreams.

Publishes: See details in magazine for written, art and photography submissions sought (usually in connection with contests).

Submission Info: Accepts handwritten, typed or e-mailed submissions. Carefully read guidelines in magazine to determine accepted lengths or limits. Provide an SASE only if you want your work returned. *Please—No stories about the American Girl Collection* *characters (Felicity, Josefina, Kirsten, Addy, Samantha or Molly) or about America.*

Editor's Remarks: "Each issue of *American Girl* contains information on our current contests. Our contests include various art or photography contests as well as writing contests, including at least one short story contest each year. Generally, this is the best way to get your work published in *American Girl*.

Subscription Rates: One year (6 issues) $19.95; single issue $3.95.

* $ AUTHORSHIP, National Writer's Association, 3140 S. Peoria #295, Aurora, CO 80014. Web site: www.nationalwriters .com. Accepts submissions, students welcomed as members. Published bimonthly.

Publishes: Articles on writing only. No fiction or poetry.

Submission Info: Use standard typed format. Maximum length is 800 words. Payment $10 plus two copies and credit given for professional membership in the National Writer's Association. Submissions will not be returned without SASE. Reporting time one month for unsuitable materials. If it's held longer, we are considering it for publication.

Editor's Remarks: "We have an excellent article by a 14-year-old in our Summer 2000 issue."

Subscription Rates: Individual membership includes subscription. For schools or institution, one-year membership costs $18. Student membership is $35 with copy of student I.D. We also give $10 credit toward membership in lieu of *Authorship* payment.

[**Author's Note:** See profile of Executive Director Sandy Whelchel in the 5th edition of *Market Guide for Young Writers* or on my Web site: www.youngwriternetwork.com.]

BREAD FOR GOD'S CHILDREN, P.O. Box 1017, Arcadia, FL 34265. Monthly magazine for Christian families; designed to be a teaching tool to enhance the knowledge of the Word of God. Published six times a year.

Publishes: Two freelance stories and two columns for children and teens. Stories should teach walking in faith and overcoming through Jesus. Articles for The Team Page and Let's Chat columns should relate to some aspect of daily living through biblical principles. Also considers short fillers.

Submission Info: Use standard format; include SASE. Limit articles to 800 words or less. Limit stories for older children and teens to 1,500 words maximum. Limit stories for younger children to 800 words. Pay some publication: $50 for stories for teens; $40 for stories for children; $25 for articles; $10 for short fillers. Send SASE for guidelines. If you have not asked for them before, they will send you two or three sample copies upon request. Include SASE (9″ × 12″ envelope with five first-class stamps).

Editor's Remarks: "If writers will study copies of *Bread for God's Children* to get an idea of our thrust, it will be appreciated by us and save them from having a manuscript held up in our office when it really fits another publication."

CAMPUS LIFE, 465 Gundersen Dr., Carol Stream, IL 60188. *Campus Life*'s purpose is to help Christian teens navigate adolescence with their faith intact. Target audience: Teens in high school and early college.

Publishes: Personal experience stories from and about teens. Uses very little poetry and fiction.

Submission Info: Query only; no unsolicited manuscripts. Pays 15¢-20¢ per word. Reports 3–5 weeks. Send SASE for guidelines. Sample copy $3. Use standard format; include SASE.

Editor's Remarks: "The first-person or as-told-to first-person story is the best way for new writers to break into *Campus Life*."

✔ * ▦ ✿ ✉ **CBC4KIDS WRITERS CORNER**, Room 2A400, P.O. Box 500 Station A, Toronto, Ontario M5W 1E6 Canada. Web site: www.cbc4kids.ca. Canadian Broadcasting Corporation's Web site devoted to kids 8 to 14.

Publishes: Original poems, short stories, essay reports and book reviews online that are written by 8- to 14-year-olds who visit the Web site on a weekly basis.

Submission Info: Submit directly online or by regular mail. See guidelines, examples and related information. Click on the

Words section to find the Writers Corner. There are also sections to submit book reviews, and another called Never Ending Story, where you can add to a story started by a famous Canadian author.

Editor's Remarks: "CBC4Kids wants to know about the books in your life. What are your favourite books? Was there one you particularly didn't like? Have you read one of the books profiled in our book lists or Book Looks? This is your opportunity to share your views with us and with other CBC4Kids users across Canada and around the world."

✔ * ❁ **THE CLAREMONT REVIEW,** 4980 Wesley Rd., Victoria, British Columbia V8Y 1Y9 Canada. E-mail: aurora@ home.com. Web site: www.members.home.net/review. Publishes fiction and poetry by young adult writers in North America (in English language only).

Publishes: Poetry, fiction (including short plays), art and photography by young writers ages 13–19 or in grades 8–12. All work received is edited.

Submission Info: Use standard format. All work should be neatly typed and carefully edited. Put name of author at top of each page. Double-space fiction. One poem to a page. Include SASE and brief biography with all submissions. Replies in 2–6 weeks, not including the months of July and August. Published authors receive one copy of magazine. Cash payment is possible depending on availability of grant monies. Check Web site for more information.

Editor's Remarks: "We publish anything from traditional to postmodern, but with a preference for works that reveal something of the human condition. We strongly urge contributors to read back issues. That is the best way for you to learn what we are looking for."

Subscription Rates: One year (2 issues) $12; two years $20; back issues $5.

✔ * ▣ ✉ **CLUB GIRL TECH,** www.girltech.com. E-mail: girltech@girltech.com. Features special Girls Views section on the Girl Tech Web site.

Publishes: Book reviews and opinions by girls around the world.

Submission Info: See Web site for details and links to submit book reviews and other material. Selected submissions are available to read on the Web site.

[**Author's Note:** It's hard to describe the eclectic nature of this Web site. But I found it fun and interesting to read the opinions that were submitted.]

✓ * ▨ **THE CONCORD REVIEW,** Will Fitzhugh, Editor, P.O. Box 661, Concord, MA 01742. E-mail: fitzhugh@tcr.org. Web site: www.tcr.org. The first and only journal in the world that publishes the academic work of secondary students, so reprints usually make a distinctive contribution to an author's college application materials.

Publishes: Essays by secondary students of history from around the world. Submissions accepted on a "rolling admissions" basis.

Submission Info: Essays should be in the 4,000- to 6,000-word range, with endnotes. (But has published essays fewer than 4,000 words and more than 14,000 words.) Must be typed or sent on Macintosh disk. Papers should be unformatted (no page numbers, etc., and with notes and bibliography placed at the end. Visit Web site for complete submission guidelines, form to accompany essays, sample essays, history of the *TCR*, subscription information, review plus additional advice such as feedback, questions and comments options. Authors receive a copy of the issue in which their essay is published and at least twelve reprints of their published essay. If school library or history department does not yet subscribe, write *TCR* or call (800) 331-5007 for a free copy.

Editor's Remarks: "The best way to judge the quality of the history essays we have published is to read one or more of the issues of the journal. We offer young people a unique incentive to think and write carefully and well. We advise that the author should prepare with considerable reading on the topic and that the essay go through at least one draft before it is polished and proofread for submissions. Essays are not rejected, nor are they returned unless requested and accompanied by an SASE. A good rule is: When in doubt, send it in. We have not yet received essays from history students at all of the perhaps 30,000 eligible secondary schools around the world, but there is already a high level of international competition."

Subscription Rates: One year (4 issues: Sept., Dec., March, June) $35; mail to TCR Subscriptions, P.O. Box 476, Canton, MA 02021. Orders for class sets (26 or more) receive 33 percent discount.

[**Author's Note:** Excellent opportunity for serious teen writers. Beware you will face a lot of tough competition.]

* CREATIVE KIDS, Prufrock Press, P.O. Box 8813, Waco, TX 76714-8813. Web site: www.prufrock.com. Kids from all over the nation contribute to the largest magazine written by and for kids.

Publishes: Stories, games, puzzles, poetry, artwork, opinion and photography by and for kids 8–14. Work must be original and submitted by the author. Work submitted to *Creative Kids* should not be under consideration by any other publisher.

Submission Info: Each submission must be labeled with child's name, birthday, grade, school and home address and must include a cover letter. All submissions must include SASE for reply. Send SASE for detailed guidelines. Sample copy $3.

Editor's Remarks: *"Creative Kids, The National Voice for Kids* bursts with new ideas and activities to entertain, excite and encourage the creativity of kids ages 8–14. The magazine includes exciting examples of the most creative student work to be found in any publication for kids."

Subscription Rates: One year (4 issues), published quarterly, $19.95.

* ▣ CREATIVE WITH WORDS, P.O. Box 223226, Carmel, CA 93922. Publishes anthologies, many of which are by children.

Publishes: *CWW* is devoted to furthering (1) folk/artistic tales and such; (2) creative writing by children (poetry, prose and language arts work); (3) creative writing in special interest groups (senior citizens, handicapped, general family). Particularly interested in prose language arts work, fillers, puzzles and poems from young people. Publishes according to set themes.

Submission Info: Submissions from young writers must be their own work and not edited, corrected or written by an adult. Will work with individual young writers if editing and corrections are necessary. Do not send personal photo unless requested. Use standard format for preparing manuscripts. Poetry must be 20 lines or less. Prose should not exceed 1,000 words. Shorter poems and articles are always welcome. Do not send previously published material. Copyright reverts back to author after publication. No payment is made to contributors, but they do receive a 20 percent cost reduction on publication in which their work appears. No free copies in payment. Send SASE for return of manuscript and/or correspondence. Send SASE for current guidelines and theme list. Address submissions to B. Geltrich.

Editor's Remarks: "*CWW* is an educational publication, which means that it serves both the academic and nonacademic communities of the world. The editors publish themes relating to human studies and critically analyze manuscripts for minimal charge. Writers of each publication compete for 'Best of the Month' entry with one free copy of the issue."

Subscription Rates: One year (12 issues, each 50–100 pages) $60.

‡ **CRUSADER MAGAZINE**, P.O. Box 7259, Grand Rapids, MI 49510. Christian magazine for boys aged 9–14; official publication of the Cadet Corp. Web site: www.gospelcom.net/cadets/.

Publishes: Sports articles up to 1,500 words, accompanying photos appreciated; crafts and hobby articles, articles about camping in nature (how-to or "God in nature" themes); fast-moving fiction stories of 1,000–1,300 words that appeal to a boy's sense of adventure or sense of humor. Avoid "preachiness" and simplistic answers to complicated problems. Avoid long dialogue and little action. Also boy-oriented cartoons. All submissions must relate to upcoming theme.

Submission Info: Use standard format, include name and address in upper left corner along with number of words and statement regarding terms of sale (all rights, first rights or second rights). Enclose SASE for return of submission. Payment for manuscripts 3¢ per word and up (first rights with no major editing). Cartoons $5 and up for single gags; $15 and up for full-page panels. Puzzle rates vary. Photos $5 for each one used with an article. Send SASE for guidelines and theme sheet.

Editor's Remarks: "A writer desiring to sell to *Crusader* should request a list of themes."

[**Author's note:** This is the same information supplied to adult writers as found on guidelines.]

✔ * ▦✉ **CYBERTEENS**, Cyberkids/Cyberteens, c/o Able Minds, Inc., 1750–1 30th St., #170, Boulder, CO 80301. E-mail: editor@cyberteens.com. Web site: www.cyberteens.com. Publishes creative work from teens 13–17 on Web site.

Publishes: Always interested in articles of any type, art, poetry and fiction, particularly humorous stories. Work may be on any subject appropriate to teens. Illustrated articles and stories get special attention (can be illustrated by someone other than the author, but clip art is not acceptable).

Submission Info: Submissions may be e-mailed or sent by regular mail. Include name, age and country. Poetry, articles and stories should be pasted directly into the e-mail message. Art should be sent as an attachment to the e-mail containing your name, age and country. Prefers jpeg and tiff formats for art, but can open a wide variety of graphic formats. See Web site for samples and additional information.

Editor's Remarks: "We get a lot of angst-ridden poetry; thus poems in the lighter vein are more likely to get noticed by our editors."

✔ * ▦ ✉ **CYBERKIDS**, Cyberkids/Cyberteens, c/o Able Minds, Inc., 1750–1 30th St., #170, Boulder, CO 80301. E-mail: editor@cyberkids.com. Web site: www.cyberkids.com. Publishes creative work from kids 7–12 on Web site.

Publishes: Always interested in articles of any type, art, poetry and fiction, particularly humorous stories. Work may be on any subject appropriate to teens. Illustrated articles and stories get special attention (can be illustrated by someone other than the author, but clip art is not acceptable).

Submission Info: Submissions may be e-mailed or sent by regular mail. Include name, age and country. Poetry, articles and stories should be pasted directly into the e-mail message. Art should be sent as an attachment to the e-mail containing your name, age and country. Prefers jpeg and tiff formats for art, but can open a wide variety of graphic formats. See Web site for samples and additional information.

Editor's Remarks: "We get a lot of angst-ridden poetry; thus poems in the lighter vein are more likely to get noticed by our editors."

✔ * **ENCOUNTER—MEETING GOD FACE-TO-FACE**, Standard Publishing, 8121 Hamilton Ave., Cincinnati, OH 45231. Eight-page, full-color, weekly magazine for Christian teens; distributed through churches in United States and other English-speaking countries.

Publishes: Nonfiction (400–1,100 words) on current issues and topics of interest to teens, from a Christian viewpoint, including school, family life, recreation, friends, part-time jobs, dating and music. Also uses type of nonfiction such as profiles, quizzes. Fiction (up to 1,100 words) must appeal to teens. Also needs professional quality photos; see details on guidelines. Poetry is accepted from teens only. Devotions and artwork are done by assignment only. Pays on acceptance; see guidelines for payment rates and terms. Allow 8–12 weeks for reply.

Submission Info: Use standard format, include your social security number and approximate word count on first page. Send SASE for detailed writers guidelines. Author's date of birth *must* accompany all poetry submitted. Include SASE with submission or it will not be returned.

Editor's Remarks: "Submissions must present a Christian point of view. The main characters in fiction should be contemporary teens who cope with modern-day problems using Christian principles. Stories should be uplifting, positive and character building, but not preachy. Conflicts must be resolved realistically, with thought-provoking and honest endings. Please write to us if you'd like to be considered for a devotions or artwork assignment."

‡ * **FACES: People, Places and Cultures**, Cobblestone Publishing, 30 Grove St., Suite C, Peterborough, NH 03458. A world cultures magazine aimed at students in grades 4–9. Each month *Faces* introduces readers to a specific world culture or region. Published nine times a year—September through May.

Publishes: Variety of feature articles and in-depth, personal accounts relating to themes. Word length: about 800. Also uses supplemental nonfiction, 300–600 words. It includes subjects directly or indirectly related to themes. Some fiction, activities, photos, poetry, puzzles and games with a connection to an upcoming theme. Young writers have best chance when submitting letters, drawings, poems, short essays relating to theme.

Submission Info: Manuscripts from young writers should be typed or printed. Use standard format. Operates on a by-assignment basis but welcomes ideas and suggestions in outlined form. Ideas should be submitted at least six months prior to the publication date of related theme's issue. Pays on individual basis. Guidelines with theme list available for SASE. Sample copy $4.95 plus 7½″ × 10½″ (or larger) self-addressed envelope with $2 postage. Students receive two complementary copies of the issue in which their work appears.

Editor's Remarks: "Unfortunately, we do not have enough space to regularly publish students' work other than the letters, drawings and short poems sent to *Faces* for Letters Page. We occasionally have contests that involve creative writing. Keep an eye out for these contests. All submissions for feature material, from students and adults alike, are evaluated equally."

Subscription Rates: One year (9 issues) $29.95; two years (18 issues) $48.95. Customer service: (800) 821-0115.

✔ * ▣ ✉ **GIRL ZONE**, www.girlzone.com. E-mail: publisher@girlzone.com. Online magazine and community for girls ages 12–16 where every girl is cool.

Publishes: Opinions, book reviews, poetry. Features six different community bulletin boards, each focusing on different topic: True Love & Crushes, Friends & Family, Who You Are, Animals & Nature, The Whole Wide World, and Whatever. Expresso section is showcase for girl's creativity via poetry. Also always looking for girls to write book reviews for the Words books section.

Submission Info: See details on Web site or e-mail the magazine for more information. Be sure to tell them the specific information you are interested in receiving. Best to check the Web site first.

Editor's Remarks: "Girls can come share what's on their mind in our bulletin boards. Our fiction book reviews are written by real girls. (And you get to keep the new book we send you to review!) Simply click on one of the categories to share *your* thoughts, feelings and poems with girls all over the world. Your poems don't have to be perfect or any certain style; they only have to express what's inside of *you*."

[**Author's Note:** A very active and interesting Web site for young writers who also happen to be female.]

✤ **GREEN'S MAGAZINE**, P.O. Box 3236, Regina, Saskatchewan S4P 2H1 Canada. Quarterly literary magazine for general audience, including libraries and many writers.

Publishes: See writer's guidelines for specifics. Material targeted to a general audience. Study sample copy.

Submission Info: Send complete manuscript with SASE or self-addressed envelope (SAE) with adequate IRCs. Send cover letter and biographical information with manuscript. Buys first rights that can be reassigned to authors on written request with SASE or SAE with IRC. Do not send multiple submissions. Generally reports in 8 weeks. Payment two copies. Send SASE or SAE with IRC to receive writer's guidelines. Sample copy $5.

Editor's Remarks: "We do not go out of our way to publish young writers but report happily that we have published many, including preteens."

Subscription Rates: One year (4 issues) $15. Single issue $5 each.

‡ **GUIDE MAGAZINE**, 55 W. Oak Ridge Dr., Hagerstown,

MD 21740. Weekly Christian publication for young people ages 10–14; emphasizing positive aspects of Christian living.

Publishes: Devotional, adventure, personal growth and Christian humor stories. Present stories from a young person's viewpoint, written in the active voice, concisely and with clarity. Avoid stories with violence, hunting, etc. Prefers true or based on true stories. Must have a spiritual emphasis.

Submission Info: Use standard format; be sure to include name, address, phone and social security number in upper left-hand corner of first page. Include SASE with submissions and requests for guidelines and sample copy. Pays upon acceptance; complimentary copies sent when published. Reports in 3–4 weeks. Considers first rights, reprints and simultaneous submissions.

Editor's Remarks: "When writing for *Guide*, please strive to set forth a clearly evident Christian principle, without being preachy. (This doesn't mean kids don't have important issues to address. It just means there are effective and ineffective ways to deal with their problems.) In general, *Guide* is interested in creative approaches to topics that will provide young people with ideas and tools to help enrich their lives in Christ."

Subscription Rates: One year (52 issues) $39.97. Higher outside U.S. Send check or money order to above address or call (800) 765–6955.

[**Author's Note:** These are the same guidelines given to adult writers.]

✔ * ▦ ✉ **GUIDEPOSTS FOR KIDS**, P.O. Box 638, Chesterton, IN 46304. Web site: www.gp4k.com. Annual contest for kids ages 7–12.

Publishes: True stories for God's Mysterious Ways section; first person accounts of how God has worked some wonder in your life. Specific incidents only.

Submission Info: Accepts handwritten, typed, MS Word, or e-mailed submissions. SASE required for God's Mysterious Ways. Reports in 6 weeks. Guidelines available upon request.

Editor's Remarks: "Articles should present specific incidents only, please. For example, one recent God's Mysterious

Ways piece was about a girl who put on her bike helmet after hearing a voice tell her to do so. She was later involved in a bike accident and would have sustained head injuries if she had not been wearing her helmet."

[Author's Note: *Guideposts for Kids* is an excellent market and contest publication for young writers with strong Christian values and interests to consider.]

* HIGHLIGHTS FOR CHILDREN, 803 Church St., Honesdale, PA 18431. Published monthly for youngsters ages 2–12.

Publishes: Poems, drawings and stories from readers. Also runs many reader-response features a year to which readers submit their creative responses. For writers 16 or older, also reviews submissions of short stories, factual features, puzzles, party plans, crafts, finger plays and action plays. Seldom buys verse.

Submission Info: For writers up to age 15, drawings may be in color or black and white. Prose may be no more than two double-spaced typed pages or three double-spaced handwritten pages. Acknowledges all material submitted. However, material is not returned; *do not enclose SASE.* No payment made for contributions from writers 15 or under. For writers 16 or older, consult regular freelance guidelines available free. Fiction should not be more than 800 words; pays 8¢ and up per word. Science and factual stories within 800 words bring $75 and up. Other material brings $25 and up. Those 16 and older should send complete manuscript with SASE. All submissions need to include name, age and complete home address. Personal photo is unnecessary.

Subscription Rates: One year $26; three years $70. Write *Highlights for Children*, 2300 W. Fifth Ave., P.O. Box 269, Columbus, OH 43216.

[Author's note: Be sure to read the foreword to this book, written by Kent Brown, editor of *Highlights*.]

✔ * ▥ ✉ INKSPOT FOR YOUNG WRITERS, www.inkspot.com/young. Online writer's Web site with special section, Young Writers Room, for writers 18 and under.

Publishes: Variety of opportunities to share your thoughts and written work in various departments of the Young Writers section. Also has an area for manuscript critiques.

Submission Info: Click links on Web site to areas of interest and follow the instructions for submitting or participating.

Editor's Remarks: "At the present time, we don't purchase stories, poems or articles from young writers for display on the section. We also have The Hopper, where young writers can send in writing advice, which is posted for other young writers to read. Once again, although I credit the author, there's no compensation . . . it's more of a tool than anything else."

Subscription Rates: Free opt-in e-newsletter. See Web site to sign up.

[**Author's Note:** Inkspot is one of the oldest and most respected Web sites devoted specifically to writers and writing. You'll find updated market and contest information here, as well as tons of other useful information about writing and getting published.]

✔ * 🖥 ✉ **KIDS' HIGHWAY**, P.O. Box 6275, Bryan, TX 77805-6275. E-mail: kidshighway@att.net. Web site: http://home .att.net/~kidshighway. Printed magazine published five times yearly, targeted especially to young and new writers; family-oriented; started and edited by 18-year-old, Miranda Garza. Also features some submissions on Web site.

Publishes: Anyone may submit, especially writers under the age of 17. Accepts fiction, poetry, jokes, fillers and nonfiction that's "fun to do, see, hear, feel, read, eat, make or try." Material should be entertaining and leave our readers with a smile. Accepts most genres, however, does *not* want submissions on the following topics: politics, occult (ghosts, magic or horror), seasonal or holiday material. Also open to column proposals.

Submission Info: Put your name, address and word count on everything you submit. Students should include their age. Maximum preferred lengths: stories for adults under 2,000 words; stories for kids under 1,500 words; nonfiction between 250–500 words; poetry 20 lines. Will consider other word lengths for fiction and poetry only. For Career Watch series, articles should be between 200–250 words (including title and name) and discuss in detail one career only. Article should inform youths between the ages of 11–16 what is required in that profession and how they can start preparing now for this career. Include an exciting experience or two, as well as a list of sources for additional research. May submit by e-mail or regular mail. See Web site for detailed guidelines and submission tips. Include SASE with mailed submissions. Be sure you include your e-mail address in the body of your message for e-mailed submissions. Buys one-time rights and selective, nonexclusive, one-time electronic rights. Will consider previously published material, but be sure to include details. Payment is $5 per story or nonfiction over 400 words, $2 per poem, and a complimentary copy of issue in which work appears. For pieces 400 words and under, pays in copies.

Editor's Remarks: "*Kids' Highway* editors would like to challenge writers to submit more material for our adult audience. We haven't received enough in any of the special sections for adults. We would also like to assure our readers that *nothing* in our pages is meant to offend or single out any person/group in a derogatory manner. Our sole purpose in publishing *Kids' Highway* is for the enjoyment of our readers and to encourage writers in the publishing process. Please check out our Mission Statement."

Subscription Rates: See Web site.

✔ * ▣ ✉ **LIKEWISE MAGAZINE**, based in United Kingdom. Editor: Gavin Leigh. E-mail: editorial@likewisemagazine.co.uk. Web site: www.likewisemagazine.co.uk. General consumer magazine with a U.K. circulation (although available anywhere else by subscription).

Publishes: Open to writers of all ages. Features and articles, including a "creative section" with pieces that normally span 4–6 pages. All creative writing must be self-contained pieces—no excerpts. Open to unsolicited submissions; reads all submissions.

Submission Info: No restrictions on the length of articles. Pays a "highly competitive rate" per word. See "Guide for Writing for Us" on the Web site. Prefers e-mailed submissions.

Editor's Remarks: "Although we are a general consumer magazine, it differs from other magazines in that it doesn't tell the reader what they should buy or wear or what lifestyle they are assumed to follow. Instead it offers a solid read that is intelligent, sometimes irreverent and often funny. Anyone can write for the magazine. It's the content of the writing that gets it published, not the writer's background or CV [curriculum vitae], and all are paid the same."

Subscription Rates: Check Web site or e-mail request for rates.

* MAJESTIC BOOKS, P.O. Box 19097M, Johnston, RI 02919. Publishes anthologies of stories by writers under age 18. Founded to give young writers an opportunity to be published in a quality format.

Publishes: Short story anthologies two to three times a year. All submissions must be written by writers 18 or younger. Readers range in age, so submissions should be for a general audience. Length limit for stories and poems is 2,000 words. Does not use illustrations of any kind.

Submission Info: Use standard format; include SASE with all submissions and requests; be sure to indicate age of author. Payment is in royalties. Sample copy $5.

Editor's Remarks: "Use *your* imagination and be original. We prefer stories that leave a reader thinking long after the last word is read. Manuscripts are judged against others of the same age group, and we use anything that is considered good for that age group. Make sure to include your age. We comment on manuscript if requested. To get an idea of what we like, send for a sample copy of one of our books at our drastically reduced cost of just $5, which includes shipping."

✔ * ▦ ⊠ MEMORIES, www.the-innside-scoop.com/celia.htm. Web site link is to the Celia Pinson Iskandar's Memorial Site.

Publishes: Provides an online publishing opportunity for writers ages 8–15 to express, through a poem, grief experienced by them resulting from the loss of a special someone or a beloved pet. Black-and-white sketches or colored illustrations may be included.

Submission Info: E-mailed submissions only! Must be in

MSWord format. Poems limited to 2 typewritten pages (based on standard typed format). Illustrations must not be larger than 8″ × 10″. No submission fee is charged; no payment is offered. A certificate of recognition will be sent for each poem selected for display on the Web page. One poem will be selected bimonthly. Authors of selected poems will be notified within 6 weeks.

Editor's Remarks: "The poems are selected and the site maintained by Melissa Pinson. It was established in loving memory of her sister, Celia (1974–1998). Both Celia and Melissa were published as young writers."

Subscription Rates: Individuals wishing to receive notification of new poetry additions may request being added to the mailing list for *Memories* by e-mailing: rememberingcelia@aol.com.

[**Author's Note:** This is one of those rare publishing opportunities that is open to poems that focus on the topics of personal grief, dying and heartbreak.]

* **MERLYN'S PEN: Fiction, Poetry, and Essays by America's Teens,** P.O. Box 910, East Greenwich, RI 02818. (401) 885–5175, (800) 247–2027. E-mail: merlynspen@aol.com. Web site: www.merlynspen.com. Magazine written by students in grades 6–12. For middle school and high school students. One 100-page issue per year.

Publishes: Short stories, short-shorts, poems, personal essays, plays. We do not consider works longer than 30 manuscript pages. *Merlyn's Pen* does not publish artwork, book reviews, news articles or research papers.

Submission Info: All submissions must include the *Merlyn's Pen* official cover sheet, which is available in the magazine, on the Web site or can be requested by calling or writing *Merlyn's Pen*. Please do *not* send SASE. The $1 submission fee includes postage for our response. Response time: approximately 8 weeks for an acceptance/rejection response, 10 weeks for a comprehensive critique. Upon acceptance, a statement of originality must be signed. For each published piece, authors receive three copies of *Merlyn's Pen* plus payment ($20-$200, based on length).

Standard format manuscripts preferred: double-spaced in a

plain, clear font of at least 10 points. Send hard copy only: no disks or e-mail submissions. Manuscripts cannot be considered without the cover sheet. Reads year-round. Publishes teen writers only, grades 6–12. We will consider work sent during the summer before 6th grade and the summer after 12th grade.

Editor's Remarks: *"Merlyn's Pen* is dedicated to publishing the best writing by teens, and we are highly selective. We publish only about 1 percent of the submissions we receive. Don't let an initial rejection discourage you—we have gone on to publish writers who were rejected on their first (and second and third) try. We sometimes ask an author to revise an exceptionally promising work. To get an idea of the caliber of work *Merlyn's Pen* publishes, authors can read selected works on our Web site, including the winners of our annual short story contest."

Subscription Rates: Published annually. Current issue $19.95. Back issues $17.95. Discounts available for classroom sets (15 or more copies). Issues available through www.merlynspen .com and online booksellers.

[**Author's Note:** See profile of Editor Jim Stahl in the 4th edition or on my Web site: www.youngwriternetwork.com. *Merlyn's Pen* is one of the premier opportunities for young writers. This listing has changed dramatically from previous listings and for the first time includes the nominal $1 submission fee. Because this fee replaces enclosing a standard SASE with a submission, I have decided not to include the $ (dollar sign) code in its listing.]

 ✔ * ▦ ✉ **MIDLINK MAGAZINE, THE DIGITAL MAGAZINE FOR KIDS BY KIDS,** http://longwood.cs.ucf .edu/~Midlink/. E-mail: midlink@sas.com. Award-winning on-line magazine, established in 1994, is a nonprofit educational project sponsored by SAS inSchool, NCSU and UCF. Open to kids ages 8–18.

Publishes: Regularly posts Call for Participation. Solicits submission of student work from teachers; advocates getting student and parental permission to publish student work.

Submission Info: Work may be submitted in any software program format. Examples: Claris Works, HyperStudio, KidPix, MSWord, MSWorks, etc. Teachers must edit all student work before submitting. Visit Web site for complete details and separate directions for schools with a Web page and those without a Web page.

Editor's Remarks: "We welcome new ideas. Our goal is to share creative work taking place in classrooms around the world. Make a suggestion or send us the URL of your [school] Web page. You may be our next article!"

[**Author's Note:** Excellent Web site for teachers interested in helping their students reach a global audience of readers for their creative work. Site also full of resources. It needs to be visited to be appreciated. Especially good site for work by adolescents and younger teens.]

✔ * ▦ ✉ **MY LITTLE MAGAZINE**, P.O. Box 2120, Channelview, TX 77530. E-mail: MyLittleMagazine@cs.com. Web site: http://mylittlemagazine.homestead.com. Online and printed versions. Quarterly magazine dedicated to helping young writers ages 8–18 improve their skills and have fun doing so.

Publishes: Stories and poems by students ages 8–18. Also promotes fiction, essays, poems, book reviews, how-to's and more. Has regular columns featuring work by young writers.

Submission Info: My Favorite Book reviews limited to 60 words; include the title, author's name and what you liked about it. Pays with contributor's copy. Poems up to 16 lines, on any subject suitable for family reading. Pays $2 plus a contributor's copy. Length for short stories is between 300–900 words. Pays $2-$10 plus copy. See details for other featured sections, detailed guidelines and submission information on Web site. Submissions may be mailed or e-mailed.

Editor's Remarks: "Our mission is dedicated to helping young writers ages 8–18 improve their skills and have fun doing so. Our goals are to provide the tools young writers need to bring their work to its best form, stimulate creativity, give information on where and how to get published and to foster determination."

Subscription Rates: One year $16.95 (Canada and foreign higher). Single issue $3.95. Sample copy $2.50 and will count toward purchase of subscription.

[**Author's Note:** Excellent opportunities especially for beginning young writers.]

* ▩ NEW MOON: THE MAGAZINE FOR GIRLS AND THEIR DREAMS, P.O. Box 3620, Duluth, MN 55803-3620. E-mail: girl@newmoon.org. Web site: www.newmoon.org. Bimonthly international magazine for every girl who wants her voice and her dreams taken seriously. Edited entirely by girls ages 8–14.

Publishes: Nonfiction profile articles of girls and women from the present and past; narratives of personal experience (difficult and pleasant); opinion pieces, poetry and some short fiction; cartoons, artwork and photography by and about girls. Especially seeks submissions from girls ages 8–14.

Submission Info: Include name, age, address and phone number. Articles run 600 words; poetry 25 lines or less. Black-and-white photos preferred, but crisp color acceptable. Artwork in black ink/pencil on plain white paper preferred. Don't fold artwork; send flat or in mailing tube. Send SASE for cover art or writer's guidelines and upcoming themes. Pays with copies and 6¢–12¢ per word for articles; $10 for poems and artwork; and percentage of reprint revenue. Sample issue $6.50.

Editor's Remarks: *"New Moon*'s girl editors seek well-written, original work that covers the depth, range and variety of girls' experiences, feelings, opinions, concerns and dreams. Let the girl's voice and soul come through. Make it real. *New Moon* celebrates girls, explores the passage from girl to woman and builds healthy resistance to gender inequities."

Subscription Rates: One year (6 issues) $29. Add $6 for postage to Canada; $12 to all other countries. U.S. funds only. Send check or money order to *New Moon*, P.O. Box 3587, Duluth, MN 55803-3587. Free library sample available.

‡ * ❀ OUR FAMILY, P.O. Box 249, Battleford, Saskatchewan, S0M 0E0 Canada. E-mail: editor@ourfamilymagazine.com. Web site: www.ourfamilymagazine.com. Monthly magazine published for Catholic families, most of whom have children in grade school, high school or college.

Publishes: Nonfiction related to the following areas: people at home, people in relation to God, people at recreation, people at work, people in the world, biography (profiles about Christians whose living of Christian values has had a positive effect on their contemporaries) and inspirational articles. Also spiritual reflection, humorous anecdotes, poetry on human/spiritual themes, cartoons (family type), photos. *No fiction.*

Submission Info: Articles must be between 700–2,400 words. Queries welcome, but articles are only accepted upon final review of full manuscript once it is received. Allow 8–10 weeks for review and response. E-mail submissions are accepted in the following ways: attached as a plain text file, as a WordPerfect 6 file or copied and pasted into the e-mail message. Send for theme list and detailed guidelines for nonfiction and photos by enclosing SAE and 95¢ (Canadian currency) or IRC. (Average cost to return manuscripts is $2 in Canadian currency.) Sample copy $3.50 U.S. Payment: 7¢–10¢ Canadian per word on acceptance. Authors receive 2 complimentary copies of the issue containing their articles.

Editor's Remarks: "The majority of our readers are adults. If young people write for us, they must understand that they are writing and competing in an adult market. Because our publication stresses the personal experience approach, young people could find a slot in our publication by writing as teenagers focusing on teenage concerns. We make no age distinctions. If a particular article/poem/filler effectively reaches a certain segment of the family, we're pleased to purchase it for publication in our magazine. Each month three articles are selected to go on our Web site—we consider the right to online publishing including the first rights or reprint rights purchased from authors, unless otherwise requested."

Subscription Rates: Online subscription form. Published eleven times a year. Regular one year $20.28 Canadian funds ($18.95 + 7 percent GST), U.S. and overseas add $6 per year for postage.

✔ * ✉ **POTLUCK CHILDREN'S LITERARY MAGAZINE**, Box 546, Deerfield, IL 60015-0546. E-mail: NAPPIC@

aol.com. Web site: www.potluckmagazine.com. *The* magazine for the serious young writer. Open to writers ages 8–16.

Publishes: Short stories, poetry, book reviews and artwork by writers/artists ages 8–16. Open to individual and group submissions.

Submission Info: Submit work by mail or as part of the e-mail message, not as an e-mail attachment. New length limit on stories is 500 words maximum; poetry up to 30 lines; book reviews up to 150 words. Be sure to include title, author and any awards received for book reviews. Use standard typed format. Author's name, age, address, e-mail address and word or line count in an upper corner. SASE (#10 size) or an e-mail address must be included for a reply. Do *not* send your only copy; it will not be returned. Will return original artwork provided guidelines are followed. See Web site for detailed guidelines. Deadlines for Spring issue—Dec. 1; Summer issue—Mar. 1; Fall issue—June 1; Winter issue—Sept. 15. Pays with one contributor's copy. Responds six weeks after deadline.

Editor's Remarks: "Writers from across the country fill each issue with imagination, hopes and dreams. Young artists amaze us with their insight and originality. Ninety-nine percent of *Potluck* is written by young writers, one of the highest percentages available in the young writers market today. Perhaps this is why so many young writers have turned to the world of *Potluck*—learning, connecting, achieving."

Subscription Rates: Special prepublication prices available to all accepted writers. See Web site or e-mail for rates.

[**Author's Note:** This magazine has received a lot of recognition by the media, teachers and parents.]

✔ * READERS SPEAK OUT!, c/o Editor Ron Richardson, 4003 50th Ave. SW, Seattle, WA 98116. Small newsletter featuring teen questions and answers on controversial and pertinent issues.

Publishes: Nonfiction, mini-essays from teens who express their opinions on previously posed questions on controversial and pertinent issues of interest to teens. Uses strictly question and answer format. Teens also serve in volunteer editorial internships in a variety of positions, working closely with the publisher and editor. Questions encompass virtually any topic, including all aspects of the arts (music, architecture, visual and performing arts), ethics and religion, and philosophies of life. Example: If someone commits a serious crime as a minor, but isn't charged until years later, should the person be charged as an adult or a juvenile?

Submission Info: Handwritten material OK if readable, but prefers typed manuscripts in standard format. Submissions must be in printed form and mailed (no e-mail or floppy disks). Length for mini-essays is 50–150 words. Request guidelines and a free sample copy from the editor. Any teen who requests a sample copy also receives a list of upcoming questions that they may respond to if interested. Pays in two contributor's copies for published mini-essays or a submitted question that generates a response by another reader.

Editor's Remarks: "Your submissions, including questions you might cook up, receive very meticulous personal attention from me and my teenage advisers. As editor, I also provide manuscript criticism to any interested teen. (There is no charge for this service.) I will critique poems, short stories, personal essays and other forms of writing—but you need to ask before sending writing you want critiqued. After giving you suggestions about how to be a better writer, I will name specific publications that I estimate to be most likely to actually print a given piece of your writing. Teens I mentor regularly appear in *Growing Without Schooling, Positive Teens* and *Teen Voices*. In addition, I critique fine art photography (4″×6″ prints only).

Subscription Rates: Free upon request. Published quarterly.

[**Author's Note:** There is never any charge of any kind to participate in any aspect of the educational mission of this zine or to receive mentoring in writing from editor Richardson.]

* ▣ SKIPPING STONES: A MULTICULTURAL MAGAZINE, P.O. Box 3939, Eugene, OR 97403. E-mail: skip ping@efn.org. Web site: www.efn.org/~skipping. International nonprofit magazine featuring writing and art by children 7–18. Writing may be submitted in any language and from any country. Awarded 1995 Golden Shoestring Award by Educational Press

Association of America; 1997 NAME Award from the National Association for Multicultural Education.

Publishes: Original artwork, photos, poems, stories, pen pal letters, recipes, cultural celebrations, songs, games, book reviews; writings about your background, culture, religion, interests and experiences, etc. May send questions to other readers to answer or ask your pen pal to send a letter. Submissions welcomed in all languages. (Work published in the language submitted, with English translation.)

Submission Info: Prefers original work (keep your own copy). Short pieces (under 750 words) preferred. Include your age and a description of your background. Can be computer printout, typed or handwritten. Free copy of the issue in which your work appears. Material not copyrighted for exclusive use. Reproduction for educational use encouraged. Guidelines available; please enclose SASE or SAE with IRC if possible for guidelines. Sample copy $5. Enclose SASE with submissions. Address submissions to Arun Toké, editor.

Editor's Remarks: *"Skipping Stones* is a place for young people of diverse backgrounds to share their experiences and expressions. Our goal is to reach children around the world, and economically disadvantaged as well as privileged families, including underrepresented and special populations within North America. Please tell us about yourself in a cover letter. For instance: What is your cultural background? What languages do you speak or write? what is important to you? What are your dreams for the future? What inspired you to write or create your submission?"

Subscription Rates: In the U.S.: one year $25; institutions $35; foreign $35 in U.S. funds; airmail $10 extra. Third World libraries and schools or low-income may purchase one-year subscriptions for $15. Free subscriptions available when situation warrants. Contact editorial office by e-mail for information.

[**Author's Note:** See profile of Arun Toké in the 4th edition or on my Web site: www.youngwriternetwork.com.]

* SKYLARK, Purdue University Calumet, 2200 169th St., Hammond, IN 46323. (219) 989–2273. Published annually, *Skylark* magazine annually reserves 15 to 20 pages out of 100 for the work of young writers usually 8–18 years old. Editor Young Writers Section: Shirley Jo Moritz.

Publishes: Prose, poetry and graphics from young writers that show an original bent and have a positive impact. Material illustrated by author welcome. Material must be original and not previously published. Does *not* use trademarked figures in artwork (e.g., Walt Disney characters).

Submission Info: Manuscripts must be typed, double-spaced and mailed with SASE. Poetry 18 lines or less. Prose 800 words or less. Graphics should be suitable for 8½″ × 11″ page; may include black-and-white photos or ink sketches on white paper. Now publishes some art in color. No light pencil or lined paper. No simultaneous submissions. A note from teacher or parent, verifying that the work is original and unpublished, must accompany manuscripts. Please state age or school grade with submission. Manuscripts not proofread for correct grammar and punctuation will be returned on read. Enclose SAE or a response replied only. An SASE must accompany manuscripts if submitted by an individual or groups submitted by a school. We will *not* acknowledge receipt, acceptance or rejection of any work without an SASE. Payment is one free copy of publication per poem; two to three copies for prose or artwork. Entries from schools earn the teacher one free copy too. Schools are credited in issue where student's work is published. Teachers encouraged to submit portfolios of their students. Reporting time three months. Guidelines available for SASE. Sample copy $7 postpaid.

Editor's Remarks: "Our best advice to a young writer: Go with your own feelings and state them as clearly as you can. We look for the spontaneous and creative. Manuscripts should be edited and grammar should be correct. [We are] looking for short stories with interesting plots, including those that provide historical backgrounds or involved, detailed information about certain subjects (e.g., collecting baseball cards or creating graphics on the computer). In other words, the young writer should learn to use specific and accurate details when writing a story. What *Skylark* sees too much of: love stories in which the hero or heroine is beautiful and perfect."

Additional Editor's Remarks to Parents/Teachers: "In

the Young Writer's Section, we publish work by young writers only. If their work is applicable in other sections (e.g., special theme), it will be placed there. However, *Skylark* is a magazine for adults, so much of its content will include adult themes and perhaps some adult language. Parents and teachers who may not like controversial or mature material in the same book with work by young writers should keep this in mind.

"*Skylark* does not appreciate 'homework assignments' being submitted. This demonstrates that some teachers are not defining 'fine arts' correctly."

✔ * ▦ **SPLASH!**, Editor Rachel Hubbard, 635 Hill Ave., Glen Ellyn, IL 60137. Thought-provoking zine recommended for anyone who wants to be heard and to read about topics that are important to the editor and other people from all over the world. All ages welcome.

Publishes: Poems, short stories, articles, commentary, reviews, artwork and anything else on such issues as women's rights, hate crimes, environmental issues, religion, politics and government, gay rights and violence in the schools.

Submission Info: Accepts typed or handwritten manuscripts. Black-and-white artwork only. No word length limits, but prefers pieces not be "very long because *Splash!* issues are only 6–7 pages long each." SASE required if you wish manuscript returned, or want to know when and if work is to be published. Send SASE for guidelines; sample copies of back issues available for $1 each. Published authors receive one free contributor's copy.

Editor's Remarks: "*Splash!* has been raved about in many magazines and by people from all over, including positive reviews in *Skipping Stones* magazine, *A Reader's Guide to the Underground Press* by Doug Holland and by Violet Jones in *SPUNK.*"

Subscription Rates: One year (12 issues) $8. Single copies $1.

[**Author's Note:** Published and edited by a teen.]

* **SPRING TIDES**, Savannah Country Day Lower School, 824 Stillwood Dr., Savannah, GA 31419. Literary magazine written and illustrated by children ages 5–12.

Publishes: Stories and poems with or without illustrations. Illustrations may be black and white or in color.

Submission Info: Any child, ages 5–12, may submit material. Limit stories to 1,200 words and poems to 20 lines. Material submitted should not be under consideration by any other publisher. All work must be accompanied by SASE. Label each work with child's name, birth date, grade, school, home and school address. Also include a statement signed by the child's parent or teacher attesting to the originality of the work submitted. All material should be carefully proofread and typed. All material must be original and created by the person submitting it. Students who have material accepted will receive a copy of the issue in which the work appears. Send SASE for guidelines. Sample copy $5.

Subscription Rates: Per copy price $5, plus $1.25 postage/handling. Georgia residents add 6 percent sales tax. Order from above address.

* ▤ STONE SOUP, THE MAGAZINE BY YOUNG WRITERS AND ARTISTS Children's Art Foundation, P.O. Box 83, Santa Cruz, CA 95063, (800) 447–4569. E-mail: editor@st onesoup.com. Web site: www.stonesoup.com. Editor: Ms. Gerry Mandel. Founded in 1973. Published six times a year for ages 8–13. Mission: It is our belief that, presenting rich, heartfelt work by young people the world over, we can stir the imaginations of our readers and inspire young writers and artists to create.

Publishes: Stories, poems, personal experience, book reviews and art by children through age 13.

Submission Info: *All submissions must be accompanied by SASE and include contributor's home address and phone number.* (Foreign contributors need not include return postage.) Standard format. No length limit for submissions, although seldom publishes anything over 2,500 words. Writing in languages other than English considered; include translation if possible. No simultaneous submissions. Children interested in reviewing books should write the editor, Ms. Gerry Mandel, stating name, age, address, interests and the kinds of books they like to read. Children interested in illustrating stories should send two samples of their artwork, along with their name, age, address and a description of the kinds of stories they want to illustrate. Reporting time 4 weeks if SASE enclosed. CAF reserves all rights. Authors of stories and poems whose work is published receive $25, book reviewers receive $25 and illustrators receive $15 per illustration. All published contributors receive a certificate, two copies and discounts on other purchases. Guidelines available with SASE or from Web site. Sample copies available for $3.

Editor's Remarks: "We can't emphasize enough our interest in your experiences. If something that happened to you or something you observed made a strong impression on you, try to turn that experience or observation into a good story or poem. Whether your work is about imaginary situations or real ones, use your own experiences and observations to give your work depth and a sense of reality."

Subscription Rates: *Stone Soup* is mailed to members of the Children's Art Foundation. Rates are: One year (6 issues) $33; two years $54; three years $74. Canada and Mexico add $6 per year. Other countries add $12 per year. All checks must be in U.S. funds or equivalent amount in foreign currency.

[**Author's Note:** It's believed that *Stone Soup* is the longest surviving literary magazine by and for creative young writers and artists. A profile of the editors first appeared in the 3rd edition of *Market Guide for Young Writers*.]

✔ * ▦ ✉ **STUDENTSWRITE.COM,** P.O. Box 90046, San Antonio, TX, 78209-9046. E-mail: editor@studentswrite.com. Formerly Texas Young Writers' Newsletter; only online version now exists. New editions posted monthly, with an archive of previous months' contributions. Primarily a market for young writers ages 11–20, although age range is not rigidly enforced.

Publishes: Poetry, short stories, essays, humor and personal experience pieces. Maximum length is 5,000 words or 55 lines of poetry. Open to short nonfiction articles related to writing and publishing from experienced writers; include cover letter describing your publishing experience and qualifications.

Submission Info: Use standard typed format, or send word processing files on disk or via e-mail attachment. Include SASE with all U.S. mail submissions. Responds in 2 weeks. Young writers whose submissions are accepted will be asked to provide a disk or e-mail attachment for their manuscript. Guidelines available automatically by sending e-mail to guidelines@studentswrit e.com. Send SASE for paper copy of guidelines. No sample copies available. Check Web site for examples of accepted work.

Editor's Remarks: "I'm very excited about the evolution of TYWN into *StudentsWrite.com*. Please tell readers that if their work is not published the first time they submit, don't be discouraged. There are many reasons why the work might not have been chosen: we may have too many submissions right now, or the work might be too long or we might just like them to develop the work a little further. However, they are encouraged to e-mail or mail their work now! We wish them the best of luck."

[**Author's Note:** Editor Susan Currie, who founded TYWN as a teen, is now in college. She was profiled in the 5th edition.]

✔ ❀ ✉ **SURFACE & SYMBOL**, Scarborough Arts Council, E-mail: scarborough@on.aibn.com. Web site: www.scarborou gharts.com. Monthly online edition of Toronto's only arts newspaper.

Publishes: Welcomes submissions in the following categories: news, features, book reviews, opinions, photography and illustrations. Refer also to the Artery section of the newspaper for two pages of arts opportunities that include calls for entry, auditions, workshops, classes, calls for manuscripts and any other opportunities that allow artists to learn, perform and create.

Submission Info: See printed copy of newspaper or Web site for submission information.

Editor's Remarks: "Our mission is to provide leadership and opportunities for artists to pursue excellence in the visual, literary and performing arts, thereby enhancing the quality of life for all."

Subscription Rates: See Web site or current edition of newspaper published ten times a year.

✔ * ▦ ✉ **TEEN VOICES**, P.O. Box 120-027, Boston, MA 02112-0027. The premier magazine written by, for and about teenage and young adult women ages 13–19.

Publishes: Fiction, poetry, editorials, artwork on any subject welcome.

Submission Info: Accepts handwritten, typed or e-mailed submissions. Please label submissions: Attention: Editorial Department. Always include your name, address, age and signature certifying that the work you are submitting is your own. Sample copies available for $5 each. Magazine is also available in major bookstores. Look for e-mail and Web site address in the magazine.

Editor's Remarks: "*Teen Voices* publishes the voice of any young woman, regardless of writing ability. You don't have to worry about spelling or grammar. *Teen Voices* believes that what you have to say is important."

Subscription Rates: In U.S., one year $19.99; two years $35.

[**Author's Note:** Many young female writers who have written me to share their experiences have mentioned being published in *Teen Voices*.]

✔ * ▣ ✉ **WHAT'S INSIDE PRESS**, Acquisition Editor, P.O. Box 16965, Beverly Hills, CA 90209. Web site: www.whatsin sidepress.com. Publisher of high-quality, innovative children's and young adult books. Accepts queries from all writers provided they are in regards to fiction work.

Publishes: Always looking for new fictional children's picture books and young adult novels. Does *not* consider poetry, religious themes or nonfiction.

Submission Info: Query first with SASE; do not send manuscript unless asked to. Appreciates typed manuscripts in standard format, but will accept any format. Include SASE if you wish manuscript returned. Responds to queries in 3–4 weeks and to manuscripts in 4–6 weeks. Full guidelines available on Web site.

Editor's Remarks: "We are dedicated to improving the quality and caliber of literature available to children and young adults. We are not interested in experience or résumés. So, if you believe in your writing, take a chance and send it to us."

Subscription Rates: Catalogs may be obtained by sending $3 to address above. Label it: Catalog request.

[**Author's Note:** Here's a book publisher currently willing to consider book-length submissions from young writers. Be sure to study the publisher's catalog to determine how well your manuscript might fit into its line.]

🖌 * ‡ 🖩 ✉ **WIN MAGAZINE**, E-mail: editor@winmagazin e.org. Web site: www.winmagazine.org. Online magazine that welcomes new writers.

Publishes: Seeks articles and short stories on wide variety of subjects of interest to women such as: culture, education, feminism, fiction, family, finance, health, military, mothering, politics, personalities, psychology and sexuality. Manuscripts can be written in the following styles: (1) detailed report, from interviews and observations, on an issue, person or event; author may take a point of view; (2) personal account, written in first person, usually a personal memoir; such an account can be blended with reportage; (3) interview with one or more interesting women, which may be focused on a specific topic; (4) short stories. Note that this is only a partial listing. *Win* is open to specific queries from authors. Will also consider previously printed published submissions provided necessary reprint permissions have been obtained. *Will not accept articles that have appeared in other Internet publications.* Copyright, unless otherwise indicated, will remain with the magazine. Authors may retain the copyright.

Submission Info: Articles and stories should be between 1,000-2,000 words. E-mail submissions as attachments in either MSWord or .txt format. All material submitted on spec only. Pays $100 upon publication. No submission deadlines. Guidelines and magazine available on the Web site.

Editor's Remarks: "We publish articles on a wide variety of subjects of interest to women. Writing style must be accessible to a general, intellectually informed audience. We are not an academic publication. Authors should keep in mind that our readers come from ninety-five countries so all terms that are not universal must be explained."

[**Author's Note:** This is a high-quality online magazine with a global audience. My suggestion is that only older teens seriously interested in writing and sharing their views consider submitting here.]

✔ * ▣ ✉ **WOMENSNEWSLINK.COM**, 5335 Wisconsin Ave. NW, Suite 305, Washington, DC 20015. Web site: www.wo mensnewslink.com. Visit Web site for e-mail addresses of various departments. Online forum focusing on issues important to women with several sections devoted entirely to contributions from young female writers.

Publishes: Has special Literary Corner featuring book reviews, short stories, poetry and photography by women and girls. Young Journalists' Showcase features pieces by girls 9–19. Also seeking reporters, producers and regular contributors.

Submission Info: Text documents should be sent to writers@ womensnewslink.com or faxed to us at (202) 885–5554. Demo tapes should be sent to address above. Responds to submissions as soon as possible. Visit Web site for more information and instructions.

Editor's Remarks: "We are looking for experienced writers and producers to add to our international network of e-lancers. If you are interested in working for us, please submit your résumé, two of your best work samples and the URL for any online portfolios. We are also looking to recruit writers, photographers and producers aged 9–19 from middle schools, high schools and colleges worldwide. If you have experience with nonfiction writing, television, radio or still photography, submit your résumé, two of your best work samples and your area of interest or specialty."

✔ * ▣ ✉ **THE WRITING CHILD**, Editor Angela Giles Klocke, 127 Bishop Rd. NW, Cartersville, GA 30121. E-mail: twchild@klockepresents.com. Web site: www.klockepresents .com/twchild.html. Printed magazine featuring work from writers 15 and under.

Publishes: Creative stories and essays up to 1,200 words, poems, original jokes and riddles. Maximum age for contributors was lowered to writers 15 years old and under. *Does not want* submissions of actual photographs. Stories on death (as in suicide, murder) are not encouraged. Prefers "fun" stories.

Submission Info: Submit *only* one story at a time or up to five poems. Accepts handwritten, typed or e-mail submissions with manuscript in body of message; does not accept e-mail attachments. Prefers standard format. SASE is required with mailed submissions. Responds within two months. Send SASE for free sample copy; address request: Sample Issue. Guidelines available on Web site, in magazine or send SASE. Pays $4 for stories and essays; $2 for poems; $1 for original jokes/riddles.

Editor's Remarks: "You're never too young to be a successful writer. Don't let a single rejection keep you from continuing your writing. If every writer quit from rejection, we wouldn't have any writers! Don't try to write like another writer. We want to hear *your* voice. Pay is small for now. We hope to increase this as *The Writing Child* takes off."

Subscription Rates: One year (6 issues) $10; outside U.S. $12. Payable by check or online by credit card. Next current issue available for $1 plus SASE.

[**Author's Note:** Klocke Publishing also publishes *The Writing Paper, Bright Ink News* and other publications.]

✔ * ▦ ✉ **YOUNG COMPOSERS**, Cyberkids/Cyberteens, c/o Able Minds, Inc., 1750–1 30th St., #170, Boulder, CO 80301. E-mail: editor@youngcomposers.com. Web site: www.youngcom posers.com.

Publishes: Musical compositions from young composers.

Submission Info: Visit Web site for details.

Editor's Remarks: "Young composers accepts musical compositions from any age, but most are from high school and college students."

YOUNG PLAYWRIGHTS ROUNDTABLE, c/o The Coterie, 2450 Grand Ave., Suite 144, Kansas City, MO 64108-2520. Theater staff members help young writers plan and write plays. Membership limited to Kansas City area youth only.

* **YOUNG SALVATIONIST MAGAZINE**, c/o Youth Editor, P.O. Box 269, Alexandria, VA 22313. Published monthly except summer for high school/early college–aged youth by The Salvation Army.

Publishes: Nonfiction articles that deal with real-life issues teenagers face and that present a Christian perspective on those issues. Fiction along same lines as nonfiction. Rarely uses fillers or poetry.

Submission Info: Use standard format. SASE required for return of material. Pays 10¢ a word on acceptance. Reports in one month on unsolicited manuscripts. Sample issue, guidelines and theme list available for 8½"×11" SASE with three first-class stamps.

Editor's Remarks: "Before sending your manuscript, please take time to request sample copy and theme lists. We like to work with new writers, but all material must fit our guidelines."

Subscription Rates: One year $14 (U.S. funds).

✔* ✉ **YOUR OWN WORLD USA**, www.yowusa.com. Issues-oriented Web site.

Publishes: Articles that investigate current events. Example: Article on global warming that focuses on the possibilities of catastrophic life-changing events.

Submission Info: Acceptable formats for text submissions are .html, .txt, and .rtf. Please do not send .doc files. Use the "Save as" feature in MSWord to save using the Rich Text Format (.rtf) file format. You must use your real name on submissions; no pen names. Be sure to include your name, address and telephone number. Use .jpg or .gif formats for artwork. Review Web site for a sample of the topics published.

Editor's Remarks: "Please note that YOWUSA is an all-volunteer Web site. We do not pay for submissions. All material submitted is viewed as a gift by the author to the public domain. We offer a Special Interest Group (SIGs) program. We have several thousand members in these groups and they are a fertile source of information for our articles."

‡ * **YOUTH UPDATE**, 1615 Republic St., Cincinnati, OH 45210-1298. Monthly publication from St. Anthony Messenger Press to support the growth of teenagers (ages 14–18) in a life of faith through the application of Catholic principles to topics of timely interest.

Publishes: One 2,300-word article per issue. No poetry, fiction or sermons accepted.

Submission Info: *Query first*; include SASE. Send SASE for writer's guidelines and sample. Pays 15¢ per word.

Editor's Remarks: "*Youth Update* has published adult-teen collaborations before with great success."

Subscription Rates: One year $13.

[**Author's Note:** Note that this market uses only one article per issue and you *must* query first.]

Chapter Nine

The Contest List

There are many different types of contests listed in this guide. Some are sponsored through various publishers, some by individual writing groups and others by for-profit companies and not-for-profit associations. Contests are listed alphabetically, including those accessed through the Internet and online computer services.

Each listing contains three individual sections of information to help you understand (1) general information about the contest and its sponsor, (2) how entering the contest might benefit you, and (3) prizes awarded. There are also two optional sections. "Sponsor's Remarks" provides extra insight into the history or goals of the contest and/or advice for producing a winning entry. "Subscription Rates" have been included as an extra service for those interested in receiving a sponsor's publication on a regular basis.

New additions to this edition's contest listings are preceded by a checkmark (✔). Contests that are of special interest to young people are preceded by an asterisk (*). Contests that require an entry fee are marked with a dollar sign ($). Canadian markets are identified with a maple leaf (✹). Listings based outside the United States and Canada or that are especially global in nature are preceded by a globe icon (▣). As in the market listings, look for an envelope icon (✉) for online-only writing contest opportunities as well as those that accept e-mailed submissions.

A few listings are also marked with a double cross (‡). This indicates that this contest should be considered only by serious teen writers, as competition is likely to be with adults and/or very difficult. To help you remember how to interpret the codes and listing information, author's notes have been placed at the bottom of some listings.

Contest listings were researched and chosen using the same criteria as that used for market listings. See details on page 4.

The following chart and sample contest listing will help explain the information contained within each section. Review the sections "What's New in This Edition" and "More About the Listings" in chapter one, plus the advice in chapter three, "Studying and Comparing Opportunities," before reviewing these listings.

CONTEST LISTING CHART

SEC.	YOU WILL FIND	PAY SPECIAL ATTENTION TO
1	Name of Contest. Mailing address for entries, forms, and complete list of rules. Brief description including who is eligible, frequency of contest. Name of sponsor.	Who sponsors this contest and the general theme of each contest. The goal of the contest.
2	General information about the contest. Deadlines for entries. Eligibility requirements. Entry fees, if any. How the contest is judged. Availability of rules and samples.	Any contest designed specifically for young people. Note any age limits. How to enter. Any restrictions.
3	Prizes awarded including cash, certificates, merchandise, and publication and display of winning entries.	The number of prizes awarded. How entries may be published or displayed. How often and how many times you may enter.
4	History of the contest, plus advice and tips for entering and winning, quoted directly from the sponsor or entry form.	Advice to help you submit a winning entry.
5	Subscription rates if sponsored by a publication. Subscription mailing address when it differs from contest entry address.	Included as an extra service for young people, parents and teachers.

SAMPLE CONTEST LISTING

1 _____ **AMERICA & ME ESSAY CONTEST**, Farm Bureau Insurance, Lisa Fedewa, Contest Coordinator, P.O. Box 30400, Lansing, MI 48909. Web site: www.farmbureauinsurance-mi.com. Yearly contest that encourages Michigan young people to explore their roles in America's future.

2 _____ **General Info:** Open to any eighth-grade student in any Michigan school. Students must participate through their school systems. Interested students and schools should contact the main office or a Farm Bureau insurance agent in their area for complete information and requirements. Each school may submit up to ten essays for judging. A 1st-, 2nd- and 3rd-place winner will be selected from each school. Each 1st-place essay is automatically entered into the statewide competition, from which the top essays are selected. Essays must relate to yearly theme and may be up to 500 words long. (Topic examples from recent years: "America & Me—How We Will Work Together"; "Why My Education Is Important to the Future of America.") Schools must preregister.

3 _____ **Prizes:** First- through 3rd-place winners in each school receive certificates. First-place winner's name also appears on plaque that hangs permanently in his or her school. The top ten statewide winners each receive a plaque, plus they share $5,500 in savings bonds. Individual prizes range from $500 to $250 in savings bonds and $500 to $250 in cash. In addition, the top ten essays plus selected excerpts from other essays are compiled into a booklet and distributed to schools, government leaders and the general public.

4 _____ **Sponsor's Remarks:** "This (2000–2001) is the contest's thirty-second year. Since it was started in 1968, more than 300,000 students have participated. Average participation each year is now more than 10,000 students. The final ranking of the top ten winners is made by a panel of VIP judges that in the past has included Governors Engler, Blanchard and Milliken, and former President Gerald Ford."

5 _____ **Subscription Rates:** Samples of the compiled essays are available through Farm Bureau at the above address.

6 _____ **[Author's Note:** This contest is restricted to Michigan youth.]

✓ * 🖾 ⊠ **ACEKIDS POETRY CONTEST**, www.acekids .com/contests.html. Sponsors online writing and other contests for kids.

General Info: Sponsors a variety of story, poem and other contests for kids throughout the year. Check Web site for details of current contests. All entries should be e-mailed as message text. Do not use file attachments. No entry fee to enter. Judges include children of various ages and two adults.

Prizes: All poetry winners receive an ACEKids T-shirt. Other prizes offered from time to time, including a new computer for grand prize winner of the SuperContest. May publish any and all submissions including those that do not win.

Sponsor's Remarks: "ACEKids.com has been providing a safe place for kids to publish their work online since 1995. Kids of all ages can enter any and all of our contests, including the original SuperContest, where you can win prizes just for getting good grades in school. We publish lots of stories and poems from young authors and we constantly add new ones. If you want to see your work published online right alongside writing from kids from all over the world, just send us your short stories and poems."

* **AMERICA & ME ESSAY CONTEST**, Farm Bureau Insurance, Lisa Fedewa, Contest Coordinator, P.O. Box 30400, Lansing, MI 48909. Web site: www.farmbureauinsurance-mi.c om. Yearly contest that encourages Michigan young people to explore their roles in America's future.

General Info: Open to any eighth-grade student in any Michigan school. Students must participate through their school systems. Interested students and schools should contact the main office or a Farm Bureau insurance agent in their area for complete information and requirements. Each school may submit up to ten essays for judging. A 1st-, 2nd- and 3rd-place winner will be selected from each school. Each 1st-place essay is automatically entered into the statewide competition, from which the top essays are selected. Essays must relate to yearly theme and may be up to 500 words long. (Topic examples from recent years: "America & Me—How We Will Work Together"; "Why My

Education Is Important to the Future of America.") Schools must preregister.

Prizes: 1st- through 3rd-place winners in each school receive certificates. 1st-place winner's name also appears on plaque that hangs permanently in his or her school. The top ten statewide winners each receive a plaque, plus they share $5,500 in savings bonds. Individual prizes range from $500 to $250 in savings bonds and $500 to $250 in cash. In addition, the top ten essays plus selected excerpts from other essays are compiled into a booklet and distributed to schools, government leaders and the general public.

Sponsor's Remarks: "This (2000–2001) is the contest's thirty-second year. Since it was started in 1968, more than 300,000 students have participated. Average participation each year is now more than 10,000 students. The final ranking of the top ten winners is made by a panel of VIP judges that in the past has included Governors Engler, Blanchard and Milliken, and former President Gerald Ford."

Subscription Rates: Samples of the compiled essays are available through Farm Bureau at the above address.

[**Author's Note:** This contest is restricted to Michigan youth.]

* THE AMERICAN BEEKEEPING FEDERATION ESSAY CONTEST, P.O. Box 1038, Jesup, GA 31545. Annual contest coordinated between the American Beekeeping Federation and state 4-H offices.

General Info: Contest is open to *active* 4-H club members only. Essays must be 750–1,000 words long, written on the designated subject only. All factual statements must be referenced; failure to do so will result in disqualification. Essays should be submitted to the state 4-H office. *Do not submit essays directly to the American Beekeeping Federation office.* Each state 4-H office is responsible for selecting the state's winner. State winners will be forwarded to the national level. Essays will be judged on accuracy, creativity, conciseness, logical development of the year's topic argument and scope of research. Contact your local or state 4-H office for details, topic for current contest and state deadlines. Contest information is also available from the ABF at the above address.

Prizes: Cash awards to top national winners: 1st place $250; 2nd place $100; 3rd place $50. Each state winner receives an appropriate book about honeybees, beekeeping or honey. All national entries become the property of the ABF and may be published. No essays will be returned.

Sponsor's Remarks: "This national essay contest has been established to stimulate interest among our nation's youth in honeybees and the vital contributions they make to mankind's well-being."

↙ * **AMERICAN GIRL MAGAZINE**, 8400 Fairway Pl., Middleton, WI 53562. Web site: www.americangirl.com. Bimonthly magazine for girls ages 8 and up. Mission is to celebrate girls, yesterday and today. *American Girl* recognizes girls' achievements, inspires their creativity and nurtures their hopes and dreams.

General Info: Each issue contains information on current contests. Contests include various art or photography contests as well as writing contests, including at least one short story contest each year. See details in magazine.

Prizes: See details in magazine.

Sponsor's Remarks: "For your best shot at being published, read a current issue of *American Girl* and respond to the requests for specific types of stories. Generally, entering our contests is the best way to get your work published in *American Girl*."

Subscription Rates: One year (6 issues) $19.95; single issue $3.95.

* $ **ARTS RECOGNITION AND TALENT SEARCH**, National Foundation for Advancement in the Arts, 800 Brickell Ave., Suite 500, Miami, FL 33131. Web site: www.ARTSawards.org. Scholarship opportunities for high school students interested in dance, film and video, jazz, music, photography, theater, visual arts, voice and writing.

General Info: Contact your teacher, guidance counselor or principal for complete registration packet. Call 1 (800) 970-

ARTS, or apply online at our Web site. ARTS is designed for high school seniors, or 17- or 18-year-olds. ARTS is open to American citizens and legal residents except for the Jazz category, which also seeks international students. The early deadline of June 1 carries a processing fee of $25. The final deadline of October 1 carries a processing fee of $35.

Prizes: As a result of ARTS Week activities, winners will earn cash awards of $3,000, $1,500, $1,000, $500 or $100 each. Approximately 300 artists who do not participate in ARTS Week, but are worthy of recognition, will earn $100 honorable mention awards and approximately 500 will receive merit recognition.

Sponsor's Remarks: "The artists are not judged against one another, but by a standard of excellence for their age and art form, therefore ARTS does not have a limit on the number of awards granted in each dollar category."

✔ $ AURAND HARRIS MEMORIAL PLAYWRITING AWARD, The New England Theatre Conference, Northeastern University, 360 Huntington Ave., Boston, MA 02115. Web site: www.NETConline.org. Contest for new full-length plays for young audiences. No entry fee for current NETC members.

General Info: Open to all playwrights who are New England residents and to any NETC member. Playwrights living outside New England may participate by joining NETC. Contest for new full-length plays for young audiences only. No musicals or plays targeted at adult audiences. Entries must *not* have been (1) previously published; (2) submitted to NETC's Gassner Playwriting Contest; (3) previously produced by a professional or Equity company. Handling (entry) fee of $20 must accompany entry unless you are a current NETC member. Entrants may submit only one play to contest each year. Format is one legibly typed and firmly bound copy that includes playwright's name and address on a separate page and the play title on the outside cover; a brief plot synopsis, cast list and brief description of each character; a statement that the play has not previously been published or professionally produced, and is not and will not be under option for publication or professional production prior to September 1 of contest year. Send SAE for acknowledgment of receipt of entry. No scripts returned. Only winners will be notified by mail. Deadline is May 1. Send SASE for full details and deadlines.

Prizes: Two cash prizes awarded: 1st prize $1,000; 2nd prize $500. Judges may withhold prizes if in their opinion no play merits the award. A staged reading of the prize-winning scripts may be given, followed by critique and discussion.

Sponsor's Remarks: "This award was created in 1997 to honor the late Aurand Harris (1915–1996) for his lifetime dedication to all aspects of professional theater for young audiences."

✔ * $ **THE BRANT POINT PRIZE**, P.O. Box 18203, Beverly Hills, CA 90209. Web site: www.brantpointprize.com. Annual themed literary book contest that awards excellence in children's and young adult literature.

General Info: Open to both unpublished and published writers. Entries must be accompanied by $10 entry fee. Contest details available in late October. Deadline is end of February. Entries judged on originality and execution of theme. Visit Web site (after October 20) for full details, rules and regulations and current contest theme. Send SASE for entry application.

Prizes: Winner receives standard book publishing contract plus cash prize. Second and third-place prizes also awarded. Early entrants receive free T-shirt.

Sponsor's Remarks: "100 percent of entry fees used to benefit Penny Lane, an organization that helps abused and neglected children."

* $ **BYLINE STUDENT CONTESTS**, P.O. Box 130596, Edmond, OK 73013. Web site: http://www.bylinemag.com/contests.htm. Special contests for students during school year sponsored by *ByLine* magazine, which is aimed at writers of all ages.

General Info: Variety of monthly writing contests for students 18 years and younger, beginning with September issue and continuing through May each year. Prefers typewritten entries on white bond paper 8½″×11″. Most contests have a small entry fee, which provides cash awards to winners as well as publication. Send SASE for details of upcoming contests. Sample copy $4.

Prizes: Cash prizes and possible publication.

Sponsor's Remarks: "The only student work we publish comes from entries in our contest."

Subscription Rates: One year (11 issues) $22.

[**Author's Note:** Good contest for eager young writers. See profile of editor Marcia Preston in the 2nd edition or on my Web site: www.youngwriternetwork.com.]

✔ * ✉ **A CELEBRATION OF YOUNG POETS**, Young Poets Contest, Creative Communication, 90 N. 100 East, Logan, UT 84321. Web site: www.poeticpower.com. Company's goal is to promote language arts in the United States and Canada. Sponsored poetry contests for students since 1993.

General Info: No entry fee. Open to students in grades 4–12. Poems may be on any topic or in any style. Please do *not* type in all caps. Only one entry per poet for each contest. Poems are limited to 21 lines of text. Must be original creation of submitting poet. Additional information to be submitted with entry: poet's first and last name, grade, school name, school mailing address including city, state and zip code, poet's home mailing address, teacher's name (optional but helpful), title of poem. Check Web site for complete contest details and online entry form. If you have trouble entering contest online, poems and required information can be e-mailed to entry@youngpoets.org or mailed to above address. Deadlines for U.S. students are: December 1 for fall contest; April 17 for spring contest. Deadline for Canadian students is February 1.

Prizes: Winners share almost $40,000 in prizes and receive a complimentary copy of the anthology featuring their poem.

Sponsor's Remarks: "The purpose of the poetry contest is to bring recognition to young writers. In each state or region there are 30 winners in each contest with over 750 winners in the United States and Canada. With each contest regionally based, students are competing against their peers in both grade and location. In addition to the winning poems, other poems of high merit are accepted to be published in our hardbound anthology. Within the guidelines of accepting less than 50 percent of the poems that are entered in each contest, the contest is selective so that it is an honor to be accepted, yet not so exclusive that it is discouraging to enter. Unlike many other organizations who sponsor poetry contests, there is no entry fee and no required purchase in order to become published. We take pride in the fact that our staff is comprised of teachers, professors and poets."

Subscription Rates: Publishes and distributes free to teachers a biannual newsletter (*Poetic Power*) full of tips from other teachers on how to promote poetry in the classroom. Subscribe online at www.poeticpower.com.

✔ $ * ❀ THE CLAREMONT REVIEW POETRY CONTEST, 4980 Wesley Rd., Victoria, British Columbia V8Y 1Y9 Canada. E-mail: aurora@home.com. Web site: www.member s.home.net/review. Publishes fiction and poetry by young adult writers in North America (in English language only).

General Info: Sponsors annual poetry contest. Contestants must be ages 13–19. Maximum three poems per entry. Entry fee of $12 (Canadian). (Send check or money order payable to *The Claremont Review*.) Entry fee includes a one-year subscription. Use standard format. All work should be neatly typed and carefully edited. Put name of author at top of each page. One poem to a page. All entries judged anonymously. Deadline usually March 15 each year. Check current issue or Web site, or send for guidelines for updated contest information.

Prizes: 1st prize $300; 2nd $200; 3rd $100 (plus one-year subscription).

Sponsor's Remarks: "Remember to continue to submit short fiction, short plays and graphic art, but keep them separate from Poetry Contest entries. Good luck and keep writing!"

Subscription Rates: One year (2 issues) $12; two years $20; back issues $5.

‡ ✔ ▦ $ CONTEMPORARY POETRY SERIES, University of Georgia Press, 3300 Research Dr., Athens, GA 30602-4901. Annual poetry collection competition; two divisions.

General Info: Poets who have never had a full-length book of poems published may submit manuscripts during the month of September each year. Chapbook publication does not disqualify a writer from this round, nor does publication of the book in some other genre. Poets with at least one full-length (poetry) book publication with any press including University of Georgia Press should submit entry during January each year. Competition is open to writers of English, whether or not they are U.S. citizens. Poems included in manuscripts may have been published in journals or anthologies. Collected or selected poems will also be considered in the January selection period. Single-spaced manuscripts are $15. Nonwinning manuscripts are discarded after competition. Authors may submit manuscripts to other publishers during judging; however, you must notify University of Georgia Press immediately if a collection submitted elsewhere is accepted for publication. Send SASE for complete details.

Prizes: Four entries selected for publication in the University of Georgia Press's Contemporary Poetry Series. Two winners selected from "emerging talent" and two from poets in "midcareer."

Sponsor's Remarks: "Because the press is interested in both encouraging emerging talent and in helping to maintain poets in midcareer, two separate rounds of manuscript selection are held each year."

[**Author's Note:** Even though this contest judges work by "emerging talent" separately, it is still a very tough competition. It would be wise to read past winning collections before deciding to enter.]

* CRICKET LEAGUE CONTESTS, P.O. Box 300, Peru, IL 61354. Web site: www.cricketmag.com. Monthly contests for young people sponsored by *Cricket* magazine.

General Info: Contest themes vary from month to month. Refer to a current issue of the magazine. Throughout the year, contests are sponsored in four categories: art, poetry, short story and photography. There are two age groups for each contest: 10 and under and 11 and up. All contest rules must be followed. Rules are listed in each issue and on the Web site. If you are 14 years old or younger, you must have your parent's or guardian's permission to send your entry. Each entry must be signed by your parent or guardian saying it is your own original work and that no help was given. If you're older than 14, you must sign your own work verifying that it is original. Deadlines are the 25th of each month.

Prizes: Winners receive prizes and certificates, and most place-winners' entries are published in the magazine.

Sponsor's Remarks: "The *Cricket* League has sponsored contests since the magazine's inception in September 1973. Through these contests, children have an opportunity to express their creativity in writing and the visual arts."

Subscription Rates: Single copy $4. One year $36.

✔ * ▦ ✉ **CYBERKIDS**, Cyberkids/Cyberteens, c/o Able Minds, Inc., 1750–1 30th St., #170, Boulder, CO 80301. E-mail: editor@cyberkids.com. Web site: www.cyberkids.com. Publishes creative work from kids 7–12 on the Web site.

General Info: Sponsors a variety of fiction, nonfiction, poetry and artwork contests. Check Web site or send SASE for current writing contests and full details. Entries may be e-mailed or sent by regular mail.

Prizes: Prizes vary. In past have included both cash (in U.S. dollars), software and other products. Both winners' and nonwinners' work may be published online.

Sponsor's Remarks: "We get a lot of angst-ridden poetry; thus poems in the lighter vein are more likely to get noticed by our editors."

[**Author's Note:** This is a dynamite, well-organized Web site featuring quality creative work by young people. You should really check it out in person before submitting your work.]

✔ * ▦ ✉ **CYBERTEENS**, Cyberkids/Cyberteens, c/o Able Minds, Inc., 1750–1 30th St., #170, Boulder, CO 80301. E-mail: editor@cyberteens.com. Web site: www.cyberteens.com. Publishes creative work from teens 13–17 on Web site.

General Info: Sponsors a variety of fiction, nonfiction, poetry and artwork contests. Check Web site or send SASE for current writing contests and full details. Entries may be e-mailed or sent by regular mail.

Prizes: Prizes vary. In past have included both cash (in U.S.

dollars), software and other products. Both winners' and nonwinners' work may be published online.

Sponsor's Remarks: "We get a lot of angst-ridden poetry; thus poems in the lighter vein are more likely to get noticed by our editors. We also publish a site for young composers: www.youngcomposers.com."

[**Author's Note:** This is a dynamite, well-organized Web site featuring quality creative work by young people. You should really check it out in person before submitting your work.]

‡ DELACORTE PRESS CONTEST FOR FIRST YOUNG ADULT NOVEL, Delacorte Press, 1540 Broadway, New York, NY 10036. Web site: www.randomhouse.com/kids/submit. Annual book contest to encourage the writing of contemporary young adult fiction.

General Info: Annual contest for American and Canadian writers who have not previously published a young adult novel. Submissions should consist of a book-length manuscript with a *contemporary* setting that will be suitable for readers ages 12–18. Manuscripts should be no shorter than 100 typed pages and no longer than 224 typed pages. Include a brief plot summary with your cover letter. See additional format requirements and deadlines on guidelines sheet. Each manuscript must be accompanied by SASE large enough to accommodate manuscript; otherwise the manuscript cannot be returned. Manuscript entries may not be submitted to other publishers while under consideration for the prize. Authors may not submit more than two manuscripts to the competition; each must meet all eligibility requirements. Foreign language manuscripts and translations are not eligible. Judges are the editors of Delacorte Press Books for Young Readers. Judges reserve the right not to award a prize. Send SASE anytime to receive complete guidelines or view on Web site.

Prizes: Winner receives book contract (publisher's standard form) for world rights to a hardcover and a paperback edition, including a $1,500 cash prize and $6,000 advance against royalties.

Sponsor's Remarks: "Our YA novel contest is not primarily for *young* writers. It is for anyone who has never published a YA novel."

[**Author's Note:** Suitable but tough contest for teens with novel-length manuscripts.]

‡ $ **FLANNERY O'CONNOR AWARD FOR SHORT FICTION**, University of Georgia Press, 330 Research Dr., Athens, GA 30602-4901. Annual short story competition.

General Info: Competition is open to writers in English, whether published or unpublished. Stories that have previously appeared in magazines or anthologies may be included. Stories previously published in book-length collection of author's own work may not be included. Collections that include long stories or novellas are acceptable; estimated length of novella 50–150 pages. Novels or single novellas will not be considered. Use standard format; author's name should appear only on the cover sheet. Fee $15. Authors may submit more than one manuscript as long as each is accompanied by a $15 check, meets all eligibility requirements and does not duplicate material submitted to us in another manuscript. Manuscripts must be submitted between April 1–May 31. Those postmarked after May 31 are returned unopened. Authors may submit manuscripts to other publishers during judging; however, you must notify University of Georgia Press immediately if a collection submitted elsewhere has been accepted for publication. Send SASE for complete details.

Prizes: Two winners each receive cash awards of $1,000, and their collections are subsequently published by The University of Georgia Press under a standard book contract. The Press may occasionally select more than two winners.

Sponsor's Remarks: "Young writers need to be aware that this contest attracts entries from both new talent as well as seasoned, published professionals."

[**Author's Note:** Beware. This is a very tough competition that attracts a large number of entries each year.]

* **GANNON UNIVERSITY'S TRI-STATE HIGH SCHOOL POETRY CONTEST**, c/o Berwyn Moore, Assoc. Prof. of English, Gannon University, University Square, Erie, PA 16541. E-mail: moore001@mail1.gannon.edu.

General Info: Open to high school students in Pennsylvania,

New York and Ohio. Each student may submit two poems. No restrictions of forum or content. Entries must be typed. In upper left corner, put name, address, home phone and grade. In upper right corner, put teacher's name, school name, address and phone number. Deadline February 1. No fee to enter. Poems judged by Gannon's English Department faculty. Each poem is read by three judges to determine finalists. Judges look for originality of subject, free verse or traditional forms that *complement* subject and precision of language and imagery.

Prizes: 1st place $50; 2nd place $35; 3rd place $20. Top three winners also receive signed book by famous poet plus publication in program book. Up to as many honorable mention awards given as poems warrant; recipient receives certificate and has name listed in program book. All winners receive complimentary copies of program books and posters.

Sponsor's Remarks: "Contest is part of Gannon's Annual Awards Night held in April. Judges' goal is to reward quality. Gannon University students also receive recognition for their poetry, journalism and research writing. The awards night features a famous poet to present a reading. Past poets have included Gwendolyn Brooks, Donald Hill, Galway Kinnell, Lucille Clifton, W.D. Snodgrass, William Matthews and David Citino."

✔ * ▦ ✉ **GIRL ZONE**, www.girlzone.com. Online magazine and community for girls ages 12–16 where every girl is cool.

General Info: Features a wide variety of monthly articles, poetry and other nonwriting contests. Example topic from September 2000 contest: "Who taught you by (bad) example what you definitely did not want to act like or be like? What did she or he teach you?" See Web site for current contests and complete details.

Prizes: Variety of prizes (often in form of free products).

Sponsor's Remarks: "*Girl Zone* is an online magazine and community for girls age 12–16 where every girl is cool. Girls can come share what's on their minds in our bulletin boards and contests."

‡ $ **GLIMMER TRAIN'S SHORT-STORY AWARD FOR NEW WRITERS**, 710 SW Madison St., Suite 504, Portland, OR 97205. Sponsored by Glimmer Train Press, Inc. Web site: www.glimmertrain.com.

General Info: Held twice yearly. Open to any writer whose fiction hasn't appeared in a nationally distributed publication with a circulation over 5,000. No theme. Length: 1,200—8,000 words. Entry fee $12. Include name, address and phone number on first page of story. *Staple* (rather than paper clip) manuscript pages together. Write "Short-Story Award for New Writers" on outside of envelope. No SASE needed; materials will not be returned. Entries must be postmarked during the months of February/March or August/September. Detailed guidelines available on Web site.

Prizes: Winner receives $1,200 and publication in *Glimmer Train Stories*. First and second runners-up receive $500 and $300, respectively, and honorable mention. Winners telephoned by July 1 for February/March entries and January 1 for August/September entries.

Sponsor's Remarks: "Please, children's stories. We tend to choose stories for their ability to move us emotionally and for their absolute clarity in storytelling."

Subscription Rates: Single issues available for $9.95 in most bookshops or directly from address above.

✔ * 🖥 ✉ **GUIDEPOSTS FOR KIDS**, P.O. Box 638, Chesterton, IN 46304. Web site: www.gp4k.com. Annual contest for kids ages 7–12.

General Info: First person essay contest. In 2000, essay contest theme was "Laws of Life" supporting your own "cool rule." Entries may be handwritten, typed, MSWord or e-mailed in text format. Contest details in September/October issue or look for contest announcement on Web site.

Prizes: 1st place $5,000; 2nd place $3,000; 3rd place $2,000.

Sponsor's Remarks: "It's best to become familiar with our magazine before entering."

✔ * 🖥 🍁 ✉ **INCREDIBLE STORY STUDIO**, ISS Story

Studio Submission Department, P.O. Box 470, Regina, Saskatchewan S4P 3A2 Canada. Web site: www.storystudio.com. Story-
writing contest sponsored in connection with the Incredible Story
Studio Canadian-based television series.

General Info: Stories must be totally original. Submit story
online in the Fan Club section on the Web site, or by mail. If
Incredible Story Studio selects your story, you and your mom,
dad or legal guardian must sign a release form before we can
proceed with your story. The release form isn't required when
you submit a story online in our Fan Club, but it is required
should your story be selected. You must submit the release form
with mailed entries. Complete contest details, as well as additional writing and storytelling tips available on the Web site. Special ISS Writing Workshop kits are available in a number of formats. (For instance, one for parents and legal guardians to use
with young writers at home, another course for use by teachers
in a classroom setting.)

Prizes: Selected stories are produced on the television show.
Every story properly submitted is read and considered for the
show.

Sponsor's Remarks: "We recommend that you ask your
teacher to put your school's name (Canadian schools only) on the
Incredible School Hit List. Each year Incredible Story Studio
visits a limited number of classrooms where we run a mini writing
workshop. Every kid involved will have their story read and considered for the show. The ISS writing courses will teach you the
writing process successful kids have used to write an Incredible
Story. You can work the course at home with help from mom,
dad or guardian. See details on our Web site."

✔ * 圖 ✉ **INKSPOT FOR YOUNG WRITERS,** www.ink
spot.com/young. Online writer's Web site with special section,
Young Writers Room, for writers 18 and under.

General Info: Variety of monthly contests held throughout
year. Sometimes, contests are random draw, sometimes they're
based on "50 words or less" essays that the young writer submits
in answering questions such as "What is a writer?" and "Why do

stories need to be told?" Complete details for current contests available on the Web site.

Prizes: Usual prize for all contests is a writing-related book. (*Market Guide for Young Writers* has been one of the books given away.)

Sponsor's Remarks: "If you are under 18, use the Young Writers Room and *not* the main chat area. Once logged in, click Other Rooms, then Young Writers."

Subscription Rates: Free opt-in e-newsletter. See Web site to sign up.

[**Author's Note:** Inkspot is one of the oldest and most respected Web sites devoted specifically to writers and writing. You'll find updated market and contest information here, as well as tons of other useful information about writing and getting published.]

✔ $ JOHN GASSNER MEMORIAL PLAYWRITING AWARD, The New England Theatre Conference, Northeastern University, 360 Huntington Ave., Boston, MA 02115. Web site: www.NETConline.org. Contest for new full-length plays. No entry fee for current NETC members.

General Info: Open to all playwrights who are New England residents and to any NETC member. Playwrights living outside New England may participate by joining NETC. Handling (entry) fee of $10 must accompany entry unless you are a current NETC member. Contest for new full-length plays only. No musicals. Entries must *not* have been previously published (including by a professional or Equity company). Plays submitted that have had workshop productions or staged readings are eligible and encouraged. Also eligible are plays that have been submitted to other playwriting contests, including winning entries. However, such plays must not have been published or professionally produced and must not be under option for publication or professional production. Entrants may submit only one play to the contest each year. Format is one legibly typed and firmly bound copy that includes playwright's name and address on a separate page and the play title on the outside cover; a brief plot synopsis, cast list and brief description of each character; a statement that the

play has not previously been published or professionally produced and is not and will not be under option for publication or
professional production prior to September 1 of contest year.
Send SAE for acknowledgment of receipt of entry. No scripts
returned. Only winners will be notified by mail. Deadline is April
15, 2001. Check Web site or send SASE for full details and current deadline. Winners announced in September.

Prizes: Two cash prizes awarded: 1st prize $1,000; 2nd prize
$500. Judges may withhold prizes if in their opinion no play mer-
its the award. A staged reading of the prize-winning scripts, or of
selected scenes from those scripts followed by a discussion, may
be given at the annual NETC convention in November or on
another occasion.

Sponsor's Remarks: "This award was created in 1967 to
honor the late John Gassner (1903–1967) for his lifetime dedication to all aspects of professional theater and academic theater."

✔ $ * ▦ ✉ KIDS' HIGHWAY FICTION CONTESTS,
P.O. Box 6275, Bryan, TX 77805-6275. E-mail: kidshighway@att
.net. Web site: http://home.att.net/~kidshighway. Sponsored by
Kids' Highway magazine and Web site.

General Info: Sponsors variety of writing contests. Entry fee
$2. Entry must be 900 words or less. See Web site for current
contest guidelines and submission tips. Put your name, address
and word count on everything you submit. Students should include their age. Entries must be mailed with fee(s); include SASE
if you wish to be notified of contest results.

Prizes: First place $10, plus publication with your byline in
our printed magazine and publication on our Web site with your
own page and link, if desired. Also receive free copy of issue in
which your work appears.

Sponsor's Remarks: "Material should be entertaining and
leave our readers with a smile. Please read guidelines carefully,
and check your envelope for everything you need. Failure to
comply with contest rules may lead to disqualification."

Subscription Rates: See Web site.

✔ ▦ ✉ L. RON HUBBARD WRITERS OF THE FU-

TURE CONTEST, P.O. Box 1630, Los Angeles, CA 90078. Web site: www.writersofthefuture.com. Contest especially for writers of science fiction or fantasy novelettes or short stories.

General Info: Open to unpublished novelists (candidates may have previously published three short stories or a novelette). All entries must be original works of science fiction or fantasy in English. Short stories are under 10,000 words; novelettes are under 17,000 words. Use standard format plus special instructions detailed on contest guidelines sheet available on the Web site or send SASE. Entries must include SASE. See Web site or contest sheet for complete details and current deadlines.

Prizes: Cash prizes plus publication.

Sponsor's Remarks: "Established in 1983 expressly for the unpublished novelist, Writers of the Future has subsequently become the most respected and significant forum for new talent in the whole of the fantasy and science fiction realm. Accordingly, judges are drawn from among the most celebrated names of the genre. In addition to cash awards, winning entries are annually published in L. Ron Hubbard Presents Writers of the Future anthology—the best-selling new fiction anthology of its kind and a proven springboard for the future publication of contributors."

✔ * ⊠ LIVE POETS SOCIETY NATIONAL HIGH SCHOOL POETRY CONTEST, DIET-Live Poets Society, P.O. Box 8841, Turnersville, NJ 08012. Web site: http://geocities .com/diet-lps. Third annual contest sponsored by Dimensions in Education Today in 2000–2001 school year.

General Info: All U.S. high school students (based on status as of fall of the year of entry) are eligible to enter. Poems must be no more than 20 lines, unpublished and the sole work of the entrant. Only one poem per poet may be entered into each qualifying contest. There is no entry fee, and no purchase of any kind is required to enter or win the contest. See Web site or send SASE for complete contest guidelines and current deadlines for each of three qualifying contests held during school year. National winner announced in July. You may enter a different poem in each contest. Type your one poem entry on 8½″ × 11″ paper. Include your name, full mailing address, graduating year, and name of school in the top right-hand corner of each page. Mail your entry to above address. Entries will be judged on creativity, originality, imagery and artistic quality. Form and rhyme are not required or encouraged, unless you are able to do so artistically. *All entries must include SASE.* Winners will be notified by mail.

Prizes: Grand prize for year 2000–2001 contest $1,500 college scholarship. There are also numerous other prizes including five 2nd prizes, ten 3rd prizes, plus hundreds of regional winners.

Sponsor's Remarks: "The Live Poets Society (NJ) teen poets club was originated and is maintained by some of the previous winners of our contests. We have allowed them to use our name and to link up to our site because we admire their initiative, are convinced of their high ethical standards and are in line with their feelings that sharing poetry is the ultimate goal of writing poetry. We also feel that individuals involved with this club understand that encouragement is necessary to the growth of young poets. We hope that you will make yourself at home here and join in the conversation [on the Web site]."

✔ * ✉ **LONGMEADOW JOURNAL LITERARY COMPETITION,** c/o Robert and Rita Morton, 6750 Longmeadow Ave., Lincolnwood, IL 60712. Open to young writers.

General Info: Open to short story writers between the ages of 10–19. Manuscript must be typed, double-spaced, less than 3,000 words and submitted with SASE before April 30, 2001. Send SASE for updated guidelines and deadlines. Editors will be the final judges of all submissions and reserve the right of first publication.

Prizes: Annually publishes 20 short stories. Awards the following cash prizes: 1st place $175; 2nd place $100; and five prizes of $50.

Sponsor's Remarks: "If you mention a teacher, librarian, dean or advisor (with mailing address) who encouraged you to enter your short story, and win a cash prize, we will recognize that person with a special award of $50."

‡ **MARGUERITE DE ANGELI PRIZE CONTEST,** Delacorte Press, Random House Children's Books, 1540 Broad-

way, New York, NY 10036. Annual first book for middle-grade readers competition to encourage the writing of fiction that examines the diversity of the American experience in the same spirit as the works of Marguerite de Angeli.

General Info: Open to U.S. and Canadian writers who have not previously published a novel for middle-grade readers. Submissions should consist of a fiction manuscript, suitable for readers 7–10 years of age, that concerns the diversity of the American experience, either contemporary or historical. Do *not* submit art with your manuscript unless you have illustrated the work yourself. If you do submit artwork, do not send the originals. If you submit a dummy, also submit the text separately using standard format. Manuscripts should be no shorter than 40 typed pages and no more than 96 typed pages. Include a brief plot summary with your cover letter. Send SASE for notification. Authors may not submit more than two manuscripts; each must meet all eligibility requirements. Title should also appear on each manuscript page. Entries must be postmarked no earlier than March 31 and no later than June 30. Send SASE for complete rules sheet. Contest results announced in October. Manuscripts sent to Doubleday may not be submitted to other publishers while under consideration for the prize.

Prizes: One hardcover and paperback book contract, in addition to a cash award advance of $1,500 and a $3,500 advance against royalties.

Sponsor's Remarks: "Marguerite de Angeli told simple stories about the lives and dreams of active, impulsive and inquisitive children, whose adventures often brought them into contact with persons of other races and cultures. With books such as *Thee, Hannah!; Elin's Amerika; Bright April; Up the Hill; Henner's Lydia; Petite Suzanne; Jared's Island;* and *Yonie Wondernose,* de Angeli helped children of many cultures to understand and appreciate each other and showed all children that they were important parts of a diverse, larger society."

✔ * ▦ ✉ MARY ROBERTS RINEHART AWARD,
English Dept., MSN 3E4, George Mason University, 4400 Uni-

versity Dr., Fairfax, VA 22030-4444. Writing grant awards for aspiring authors; established by the Rinehart family.

General Info: Grants are made only for unpublished works
by writers who have not yet published a book or whose writing
is not regularly appearing in nationally circulated commercial or
literary magazines. An unpublished work is defined as one that
has not appeared in any venue generally accessible to the public,
either in printed or electronic form. Grant recipients are not required to be U.S. citizens, but only works in English will be read,
and awards are made only in U.S. dollars. There are other specific
eligibility and submission guidelines that need to be followed.
Send SASE or e-mail: bgompert@osf1.gmu.edu for complete
guidelines.

Prizes: Three grants of $2,000 each are awarded in spring for
the best nominated manuscript in fiction, nonfiction, and poetry.

Sponsor's Remarks: "To help aspiring authors, the family
of the late Mary Roberts Rinehart began a number of years ago
awarding small grants to writers whose work showed particular
promise. These grants were given to honor Ms. Rinehart, a writer
of fiction and nonfiction whose work was popular in the earlier
decades of the 1900s. In 1983, the Rinehart family established
[the fund and award] at George Mason University to finance annual grants to promising writers."

* MERLYN'S PEN SHORT STORY CONTEST, P.O.
Box 910, East Greenwich, RI 02818. (401) 885–5175, (800) 247–
2027. E-mail: merlynspen@aol.com. Web site: www.merlynspen
.com. Sponsored by *MERLYN'S PEN: Fiction, Poetry, and Essays
by America's Teens*. Open to middle school and high school students, grades 6–12.

General Info: Publication and prizes are offered in two categories: Middle Division (grades 6–9) and Senior Division (grades
10–12). Story length must be between 600 and 7,500 words. All
topics and story genres, including personal narratives and "true"
stories, are welcome. Students submitting work for the contest
must use the *Merlyn's Pen* cover sheet, printed in every current
issue, in our catalog and on our Web site. To enter, staple a
Merlyn's Pen cover sheet to each story. Follow directions on the

cover sheet. Select the Response Only or the Response and Comprehensive Critique option. Do not send a self-addressed, stamped envelope: the $1 fee includes one. There is no additional fee to enter the contest. Multiple entries by the same author are welcome; each entry must be stapled to its own cover sheet. Mail all entries to: *Merlyn's Pen* Story Contest, P.O. Box 910, East Greenwich, RI 02818-0910. Entries must be postmarked by March 1.

Prizes: One 1st prize of $500 will be awarded in each division: Middle (grades 6–9) and Senior (grades 10–12). Up to two 2nd prizes of $250 may be awarded in each division. Winners will be notified by July 1. Prize-winning stories will appear in *Merlyn's Pen*, published every November, at the magazine's Web site and in the teen area at the Barnes & Noble Web site: www.bn.com. Stories not selected as winners may still be considered for publication.

Sponsor's Remarks: *"Merlyn's Pen* receives up to 12,000 submissions per year and publishes approximately 50. Short story contest winners are selected from the works we accept for publication. We do not favor any one particular 'type' of story. Our only preference is for excellent writing and a great story. We welcome work on challenging topics and writing that takes risks. It's a good idea to read any issue of the magazine or check out our Web site to read past winners."

Subscription Rates: Published annually. Current issue $19.95. Back issues $17.95. Discounts available for classroom sets (15 or more copies). Issues available through www.merlynspen .com and online booksellers.

[**Author's Note:** See profile of editor Jim Stahl in the 4th edition on my Web site: www.youngwriternetwork.com. *Merlyn's Pen* is one of the premier opportunities for young writers. This listing has changed dramatically from previous listings and for the first time includes the nominal $1 submission fee. Because this fee replaces enclosing a standard SASE with a submission, I have decided not to include the $ (dollar sign) code in its listing.]

✔ * ⊞ ✉ MIDLINK MAGAZINE, THE DIGITAL MAGAZINE FOR KIDS BY KIDS. E-mail: midlink@sas.c

om. Web site: http://longwood.cs.udf.edu/~Midlink/. Award-winning online magazine, established in 1994, is a nonprofit educational project sponsored by SAS inSchool, NCSU and UCF. Open to kids ages 8–18.

General Info: Teachers should read details on Web site.

Prizes: Publication on Web site that is accessed by students worldwide.

Sponsor's Remarks: "Feel free to enter your project in any gobal competitions. We welcome new ideas. Our goal is to share creative work taking place in classrooms around the world."

✔ * ▦ ✉ **MY LITTLE MAGAZINE**, P.O. Box 2120, Channelview, TX 77530. Online and printed versions. See page 182 for Web site. Quarterly magazine dedicated to helping young writers ages 8–18 improve their skills and have fun doing so.

General Info: Each issue features a Finish This Story contest. See current issue or Web site details, or sign up for email notifications of current contests. Open to students ages 8–18. Separate set of guidelines available for adult contributors.

Prizes: Varies with contest, including publication of winning entry.

Sponsor's Remarks: "Our mission is dedicated to helping young writers ages 8–18 improve their skills and have fun doing so. Our goals are to provide the tools young writers need to bring their work to its best form, stimulate creativity, give information on where and how to get published and to foster determination."

Subscription Rates: One year $16.95 (Canada and foreign higher). Single issue $3.95. Sample copy $2.50 and will count toward purchase of subscription.

$ * **NPT YOUNG WRITER'S COMPETITION**, 214 Fifth Ave., Lehigh Acres, FL 33972. Annual contest sponsored by NPT Corporation, Member Lehigh Acres Chamber of Commerce. E-mail: MNPT2000@aol.com.

General Info: Entrants may enter up to two short stories and two poems. Junior division ages 8–10; Senior division ages 11–13. Short stories $25 fee per submission. (Special rates for schools with multiple entries.) Story must have a young person as a major character, a plot in which problem or situation must be resolved and resolution resulting from main character's action or decision. See Writers' INTERNATIONAL Forum Web site for manuscript guidelines. Story length should be between 500–2,000 words. Fee for poem is $10 per submission. Maximum length of 20 lines. Submit two copies of each entry; late entries automatically placed in next year's contest. Send SASE for complete details. Final judging by Writers' International Forum.

Prizes: Three U.S. savings bonds (worth $50–$200) awarded in short story contest. Winning entries may be e-published on Writers' International Forum Web site at www.bristolservicesintl .com. First-place poetry winners in each division receive $50 savings bond; certificates awarded to top three in each poetry division.

Sponsor's Remarks: "We encourage young people to begin and/or continue to express themselves with thoughts and words. To give them the opportunity to achieve their dreams of using the written word to expand their own creativity. As always, write what you know . . . what you feel and tell it well."

$ NWA NONFICTION CONTEST, National Writer's Association, 3140 S. Peoria #295, Aurora, CO 80014. Annual contest open to all writers. Web site: www.nationalwriters.com.

General Info: Any nonfiction article or essay is eligible, provided it does not exceed 5,000 words. Submissions must be in standard typed format. You may enter as many manuscripts as you wish, but each must be accompanied by an entry form, $18 entry fee and SASE with sufficient return postage. Judging based on originality, freshness of style, significance and marketability. Send SASE for complete details and entry form. Forms also available on Web site; click Contests. Critiques available for additional fee. Deadline is December 31. Judging sheets are included if SASE accompanies entry.

Prizes: 1st place $200; 2nd $100; 3rd $50; 4th-10th choice of books; 11th–20th place honorable mention certificate.

Sponsor's Remarks: "Our purpose is to encourage writers in this creative form and to recognize those who excel in nonfiction writing."

Subscription Rates: See *Authorship* market listing on page 165.

[**Author's Note:** NWA contests allow writers to submit their manuscript entries to a publisher. If you do, tell the publisher so in a cover letter.]

$ NWA NOVEL CONTEST, National Writers Association, 3140 S. Peoria #295, Aurora, CO 80014. Web site: www.natio nalwriters.com. Annual contest open to all writers.

General Info: Any genre or category of novel manuscript may be entered. Only *unpublished, unbound* manuscripts eligible. Use standard typed format. English only. Maximum length is 100,000 words. Send appropriate SASE if you wish your manuscript returned. Entry fee for each novel is $35. Contest opens December 1. All materials, complete with entry form and fees, must be postmarked no later than April 1. Entries may be submitted to publishers while contest is in progress. Top three entries offered to NWA's literary agents for consideration. Send SASE for complete details and entry form. Critiques available for additional fee. Judging sheets available for SASE. Entry forms available on Web site.

Prizes: 1st place $500; 2nd $250; 3rd $150; plus other awards for 4th-20th places.

Sponsor's Remarks: "Our purpose is to help develop creative skills, to recognize and reward outstanding ability and to increase the opportunity for the marketing and subsequent publication of novel manuscripts."

[**Author's Note:** See profile of NWA Executive Director Sandy Whelchel in fifth edition or on my Web site: www.youngwriternetwork.com.]

$ NWA POETRY CONTEST, National Writers Association, 3140 S. Peoria #295, Aurora, CO 80014. Annual contest open to all writers. Web site: www.nationalwriters.com.

General Info: All poems are eligible; lyric, ballad, free verse, experimental and traditional. Entry must be accompanied by entry fee, entry form and SASE. Your name and address must appear on the first page of your poems. Only unpublished poems are eligible. Authors retain all rights and may submit their entries to publishers while contest is in progress. Judging based on originality, technique, significance and emotional values. Entry fee for poems 40 lines or shorter is $10; see details regarding longer poems. Awards given an annual conference. Send SASE for complete details and entry form. Forms also available on Web site; click Contests. Critiques available for additional fee. Opens July 1; closes September 30.

Prizes: 1st place $200; 2nd $100; 3rd $50; plus other awards through 20th place. Winning poem published in *Authorship*, Winter issue.

Sponsor's Remarks: "Our purpose is to encourage the writing of poetry, an important form of individual expression, but with a limited commercial market."

Subscription Rates: See *Authorship* market listing.

$ NWA SHORT STORY CONTEST, National Writers Association, 3140 S. Peoria #295, Aurora, CO 80014. Annual contest open to all writers. Web site: www.nationalwriters.com.

General Info: Any type of fiction is eligible, provided it does not exceed 5,000 words. Any nonfiction article or essay is eligible, provided it does not exceed 5,000 words. Submissions must be in standard typed format. You may enter as many manuscripts as you wish, but each must be accompanied by an entry form, $15 entry fee and SASE with sufficient return postage. Although only unpublished short stories are eligible, authors retain all rights and may submit their entries to publishers while contest is in progress. Judging based on originality, imagination, freshness of style, significance, emotional value and marketability. Send SASE for complete details and entry form. Forms also available on Web site; click Contests. Critiques available for additional fee. Opens April 1; closes July 1.

Prizes: 1st place $200; 2nd $100; 3rd $50; plus other awards through 20th place. Winning entry published in *Authorship*.

Sponsor's Remarks: "Our purpose is to encourage writers in this creative form and to recognize those who excel in short story writing."

Subscription Rates: See *Authorship* market listing.

🖊 * 🖼 $ ✤ **ONTARIO POETRY SOCIETY CON-TEST**, c/o I.B. Iskov, 31 Marisa Ct., Thornhill, Ontario L4J 6H9 Canada.

General Info: Theme for year 2001 contest is "Much Ado About Poetry." Categories include best haiku, best free verse poem (maximum length 50 lines) and best rhyming poem (maximum length 50 lines). Poems must be unpublished and not sent elsewhere. Contest fee is $2 per poem or three poems for $5 (Canadian funds). Blind judging format: No names of authors to appear on the same page as the poem. Include a separate sheet with title (or first line) of poem along with author's name, address, phone number and e-mail (if possible). Deadline for 2001 contest is June 15. Send SASE for current and detailed contest information.

Prizes: Winner in each category receives $50 (Canadian funds) plus publication in the Fall/Winter issue of "We Are T.O.P.S." Newsletter.

* **PAUL A. WITTY OUTSTANDING LITERA-TURE AWARD**, c/o Cathy Collins Block, Ph.D., Professor of Education, Texas Christian University, P.O. Box 32925, Fort Worth, TX 76129. Sponsored by Special Interest Group, Reading for Gifted and Creative Students, International Reading Association.

General Info: Entries from elementary, junior high and high school judged separately. Two categories: prose and poetry. Elementary prose limited to 1,000 words. Entries from secondary students must be typed and may exceed 1,000 words, if necessary. Set of five poems required. Entries judged on creativity, originality and beauty of expression. Entry blanks and more information sent to teachers for SASE.

Prizes: National awards, $25 and plaques; also certificates of merit.

Sponsor's Remarks: "Begun in 1979 to honor Dr. Paul Witty, between 500 and 1,000 entries are received yearly. Our goal is to encourage gifted writers and their teachers by recognizing and rewarding their achievements. We grant awards as deserved, from one to six in past years, although two different years, no entry was deemed to award quality. From contact with winners, I learned that most of them write continuously and go to their folios to select entries."

🖊 * $ 🖥 ✉ **PLOT LINE FOYER CONTESTS**, G.S. & S., 3601 Owens, Bryan, TX 77808-0969. E-mail: PlotLineFoyer@ att.net. Web site: http://home.att.net/~plotlinefoyer. Short story contest.

General Info: Length for short stories is 1,500–3,500 words. Stories can be on any subject, except no sexual content, occult, graphic violence or ethnic hatred. If submitting by regular mail, entry must be typed with your name, address, phone number and word count on the top right-hand corner of the first page of your manuscript. If submitting by e-mail, embed that same information and story in the body of the e-mail message. *Attachments will not be opened.* Submissions will only be read after the $10 per story fee has been received. Include SASE or an e-mail address for notification purposes only. Manuscripts will not be returned. Deadline for year 2000 was September 1. See Web site or send SASE for complete and current contest information.

Prizes: In year 2000, winner received $100, publication at the Plotline Foyer Web site, plus a complimentary issue of *Kids' Highway* in which the winning entry appeared.

Sponsor's Remarks: "By special arrangement with the editors of *Kids' Highway*, the 1st-place winner will also be published in their December 2000 issue."

[**Author's Note:** Be sure to check for most current contest information.]

$ * **POETS AT WORK CONTESTS**, Jessee Poet, VAMC 325 New Castle Rd., Box 113, Butler, PA 16001. Sponsored by *Poets at Work* magazine for poets of all ages. Some contests require entry fee.

General Info: Current contest flyer offers 31 contests with various themes and money prizes. Entry fees vary from $1 per poem to two entries for $1. Accepts typed and legible handwritten entries. Simultaneous submissions accepted. No specific line length limits, but poets are asked to "be reasonable—no epics, please." Send SASE to request flyer containing all themes and deadlines. New flyer mailed quarterly to all who enter and send SASE. You do *not* need to subscribe to the magazine in order to enter contests.

Prizes: Judges are well-known poets, many of whom judge for state or national contests. For monthly contests—one-half the entry fees; six monthly contests on each flyer. Previously published poetry and previous prize-winning poetry limited to winning $25 maximum. Each of the twenty-five special contests pays $15 each. Each winner of the ten "easy" contests receives $10. Prizes are awarded promptly.

Sponsor's Remarks: "To understand the future of our country, we need only to understand the youth of today, for they will be the leaders of tomorrow. As I get to see more and more of what young people are writing, I am optimistic that the future of our nation will be in good hands. What they write is frequently inspiring, uplifting, and often I can read between the lines and sense some of their anxieties. I get glimpses of their humor, their love of nature and their interest in protecting and preserving our planet. I welcome all of you to *Poets at Work*. My publication and I, as its editor, am in step with the way you think. Many of the things that are important to you are also important to me, and many of your goals are my goals too. Among the pages of *Poets at Work* you will encounter all age poets, and we blend well, and we learn from each other. I'll look for you in Box 113."

Subscription Rates: One year (6 issues) $20.

[**Author's Note:** *Poets at Work* magazine and *Poets at Work* contests are handled separately by the same publisher. Be sure to follow the specific guidelines for submitting to each one.]

* ❀ $ THE PRISM AWARDS, 90 Venice Crescent, Thornhill, Ontario L4J 7T1 Canada. Contest sponsored by The Kids Network, Canada Post Corporation. The Kids Network works directly with winners to produce professionally written and published books. Open to Canadian children only.

General Info: Restricted to Canadian children ages 7–14. Entry fee of $2 required. Each story must be between 4 and 18 pages and in one of the story categories listed on the official entry form. Entry form must be signed by the child writer and parent attesting that the story is the original work of the child. The same story may not be submitted to The Prism Awards more than once. Children may submit one manuscript each year. Manuscripts cannot be coauthored but must be the original work of one child and not edited or changed by an adult. Over twenty judges review manuscripts according to preset criteria that emphasize conceptual thinking. Judges appreciate manuscripts that are double-spaced. Official entry form is required; available in October of every year. Strict January deadline. No late entries accepted.

Prizes: There is one winner in 7–10 age group, one in the 11–14 age group for *each* story category listed on entry form. Winners receive a $500 cash award and a crystal prism trophy. They also join The Kids Network Training Program, work with a team of professional editors and have the possibility of being published as part of The Kids Network series of books. Child authors whose books are published received royalties.

Sponsor's Remarks: "Understanding is the purpose of The Prism Awards Program. If you think you have something you'd like to write about and you love to write, we encourage you to enter the program. Only a few of The Prism Award winners ever thought they would win! We see it as a way for kids to share with other kids their talents, interests, wildest imaginings and innermost feelings."

Subscription Rates: Write to above address to be placed on mailing list to receive official entry form, or fax your request to (905) 881-7558.

* $ QUILL AND SCROLL INTERNATIONAL WRITING/PHOTOGRAPHY CONTEST, Quill and Scroll Society, School of Journalism, University of Iowa, Iowa City, IA 52242-1528. Contest open to grades 9–12.

General Info: Competition open to all high school students. Each school may submit up to four entries in ten categories: editorial, editorial cartoon, investigative reporting (individual and team), news story, features story, sports story, advertisement and photography (news feature and sports). Entries must have been published in school paper or professional paper. Entries must be tearsheet form. Two-dollar entry fee must accompany each entry. Contest rules are sent, in late December, to all schools on mailing list. Guidelines and entry form also appear in the December/ January issue of *Quill and Scroll* magazine. If your school does not receive information about this contest, request information from the above address. Materials will be sent to the journalism adviser, principal or counselors at your school. See contest guideline sheet for formatting information for each category. Deadline is February 5. Note: Senior national winners are automatically eligible for the Edward J. Neel Memorial Scholarship in Journalism.

Prizes: National winners will be notified by mail through their advisers and receive the Gold Key Award and will be listed in the April/May issue of *Quill and Scroll* magazine. Senior winners intending to major in journalism at a college or university that offers a major in journalism are eligible for $500 scholarships. All winners are published in *Quill and Scroll*.

Sponsor's Remarks: "Currently enrolled high school students are invited to enter the National Writing/Photo Contest. Awards are made in each of the ten divisions."

Subscription Rates: One year $14.

* $ QUILL AND SCROLL YEARBOOK EXCEL-LENCE CONTEST, Quill and Scroll Society, School of Journalism, University of Iowa, Iowa City, IA 52242-1528.

General Info: Contest evaluates yearbook spreads in ten different categories and overall theme development. Photo categories must include original photo as well as yearbook spread. Contest is open to students in grades 9–12. Students must attend a high school that is chartered by *Quill and Scroll* (more than 13,000 schools are chartered). Each school may submit four spread sheet entries in each of the categories. These are student life, academics, sports action photo, academic photo, feature photo, graphic and index. Only one entry may be submitted for the theme development division. Submit $2 entry fee for each entry. Entry applications will be sent to each member school in late August. Request applications or membership information from the above address. Deadline is November 1.

Prizes: Winners received a Gold Key Award and are eligible to apply for the Edward J. Nell scholarship during their senior year. Winners are published in *Quill and Scroll* magazine.

Subscription Rates: One year $14.

✒ * ▦ **RALPH WALDO EMERSON PRIZE**, Will Fitzhugh, Editor, *The Concord Review*, P.O. Box 661, Concord, MA 01742. E-mail: fitzhugh@tcr.org. Web site: www.tcr.org. Open to secondary history students.

General Info: Essays by secondary students of history from around the world. See Web site, a current issue or write for details.

Prizes: In 2000, each Emerson Prize laureate received check for $2,000 and a copy of David McCullough's Pulitzer Prize-winning biography *Truman*, along with the letter of award.

Sponsor's Remarks: "Past awards have gone to students from several U.S. states and Czechoslovakia, New Zealand, Japan and Moscow. Founded in 1987, *TCR*, the first and only journal in the world for the academic work of secondary students, has published 41 issues with 451 essays (average 5,000 words) by students of history in 38 states and 25 countries."

Subscription Rates: See *The Concord Review* listing on page 168.

* ▦ $ **SKIPPING STONES YOUTH HONOR AWARDS**, P.O. Box 3939, Eugene, OR 97403. E-mail: skippin g@efn.org. Web site: www.efn.org/~skipping. Annual awards program sponsored by *Skipping Stones*, an international nonprofit magazine featuring writing and art by children ages 7–18. Annual theme. Contest open to youth 17 and under.

General Info: Entries accepted written in English and other languages. Open to writings and artwork by youth ages 7–18 that promote multicultural awareness, nature and ecology, social issues, peace and nonviolence. Deadline June 20. Prose entries (essays, short stories, etc.) limited to 750 words; poems less than 30 lines; original artwork (drawings, cartoons, paintings or photo essays with captions) limited to eight pieces. Include name, age, school and home address on each page. Send entry with a cover letter, a certificate of originality (from a parent or teacher), SASE and a $3 entry fee. Youth organizations also invited to enter by telling how their club or group works locally to (1) enhance the quality of life for low-income, minority or disabled people; (2) preserve nature and ecology; or (3) improve racial or cultural harmony in a school or community. Send SASE for complete information.

Prizes: Ten awards are given to student groups and youth 17 years old and under. Everyone entering contest will receive the Autumn issue containing the ten winning entries.

Sponsor's Remarks: "The goal of *Skipping Stones* is to reach children around the world, in economically disadvantaged as well as privileged families, including underrepresented and special populations within North America. *Skipping Stones* encourages cooperation, creativity and celebration of cultural and environmental richness. It provides a playful forum for sharing ideas and experiences among children from different lands and backgrounds."

Subscription Rates: In the United States: one year $25; institutions $35; foreign $30 in U.S. funds. Third World libraries and schools or low-income U.S. families may purchase one-year subscription for $15. Airmail $10 extra.

[**Author's Note:** Low-income entrants and subscribers are eligible for one free entry to contest. Contact *Skipping Stones* editorial office by e-mail for information. See profile of Executive Editor Arun Toké in the fourth edition or on my Web site: www.youngwriternetwork.com.]

✔ * $ ▦ ✉ **SOUL-MAKING LITERARY PRIZE**, Webhallow House, 1544 Sweetwood Dr., Colma, CA 95015-2029. Annual contests open to everyone, everywhere. Web site: http://members.aol.com/PenNobHill. Sponsored by the National League of American Pen Women. Includes special youth categories for writers between ages 12–17.

General Info: Several contest categories sponsored including two special ones for young writers: Stephen Eisen Memorial Youth Prize, featuring a poetry category (three poems per entry) and a short story category (up to 3,000 words). All youth entrants must be between ages of 12–17 (7th through 12th grade) or equivalent. Important: Be sure to indicate Youth Entry on envelope, manuscript and card. Entry fee is $5 per entry payable to NLAPW, Nob Hill Branch (checks or money order for U.S. dollars only). Do not put your name on your manuscript; instead enclose one 3″×5″ card typed with your name, address, phone number, fax, e-mail, category and title(s) of work. Manuscripts must be typed. Use standard format. Enclose SASE for competition results. See Web site or send SASE for complete details on current contests.

Prizes: In Youth categories: 1st place $50; 2nd $25; 3rd $10. All winners will be invited to read at the awards ceremony held annually in the Koret Auditorium of the San Francisco Main Public Library, Civic Center.

Sponsor's Remarks: "The National League of American Pen Women, a nonprofit organization headquartered in Washington, DC, was established in 1897 and has a membership of more than 6,000 professional writers, artists and composers. The Nob Hill, San Francisco Bay Area Branch sponsors literary and visual art competitions, offers a biannual Nourishing the Creative Woman Conference, a monthly Pen Women Presents television show (interviews with Pen Women and others who support, inspire, teach and mentor their creative efforts) on CTC's cable access Channel 29 (every fourth Sunday at 5:00 P.M.). We also award an annual scholarship to a mature woman currently enrolled in City College of San Francisco."

✔ * 🍁 ✉ **STUDENT AND CHAPBOOK WRITING COMPETITIONS**, Web site: http://www3.sympatico.ca/susanio/WWCcomp.html.

General Info: Visit the above Web site for access to a number of excellent writing contests for students across Canada. Web site includes general information about writing for and submitting to competitions. Example of the listings include:

- The League of Canadian Poets, which now invites high school and postsecondary students to be part of the poetry community
- A story and poem contest sponsored by Hazel Hutchins, a

widely published Canadian children's novelist
- Write2000, a contest sponsored by IBM Printing Systems for writers under age 18
- The Newfoundland and Labrador Arts and Letters Competition with special categories for young writers
- Cavendish Tourist Association Creative Writing Award for Young People
- *The Tree House* Poetry Contest for poets ages 6–18.
- The "Writers of Tomorrow Short Story Contest," sponsored by Cochran Entertainment, producers of the prime-time television series *Pit Pony*
- And many, many others

Prizes: Lots of the contests listed offer substantial cash awards plus publication.

[**Author's Note:** This is an excellent resource Web site for young writers based in Canada.]

✔ * **S.W.T.A. NATIONAL NEW PLAY CONTEST**, Andrew Gaupp & Dennis Maher, Cochairs, S.W.T.A. New Plays Committee, c/o The University of Texas at Arlington, Theatre Arts Program, Box 19103, Arlington, TX 76019-0103. Annual contest open to all writers residing in the United States, sponsored by the Southwest Theatre Association.

General Info: Open to all writers of original one-act or full-length plays that have not previously been fully produced or published. Musicals, translations or adaptations of previously produced or published works, and plays for young audiences are not eligible. Writers must reside in the United States. The postmark deadline for submission in year 2001 is March 15. Only one play may be submitted by a writer (this includes plays that are cowritten) each contest year. Send SASE to receive contest submission guidelines. Send submissions by U.S. mail only. See guidelines for submissions start date.

Prizes: Winner (in 2001) will receive $200 honorarium; an award plaque, a public reading at the annual combined conference; a one-year membership in S.W.T.A.; complimentary registration for the year 2001 conference; and the possibility of excerpt publication in *Theatre Southwest*, the professional journal of the S.W.T.A. (pending editorial acceptance).

Sponsor's Remarks: "S.W.T.A. offers a separate contest for plays for young audiences through the S.W.T.A. Children's Theatre Division. Call the S.W.T.A. Executive Director's office at (405) 946–9380 for more information, or e-mail at swtajimmyv@aol.com."

* THE VEGETARIAN RESOURCE GROUP ESSAY CONTEST, P.O. Box 1436, Baltimore, MD 21203. Open to children 18 and under.

General Info: Separate contest categories for students ages 14–18, ages 9–13 and ages 8 and under. Entrants should base their 2- to 3-page essays on interviewing, research and/or personal opinion. You do not need to be a vegetarian to enter. Essays can be on any aspect of vegetarianism. All essays become property of The Vegetarian Resource Group. Each essay must include the author's name, age, grade, school and teacher's name. Entries must be postmarked by May 1 of contest year. Send SASE for contest guidelines.

Prizes: A $50 savings bond is awarded in each category. Plus winning entries are published in *The Vegetarian Journal*.

Sponsor's Remarks: "Vegetarianism is not eating meat, fish and birds (for example, chicken or duck). Among the many reasons for being a vegetarian are beliefs about ethics, culture, health, aesthetics, religion, world peace, economics, world hunger and the environment."

Subscription Rates: Membership includes subscription. Student rate for one year $14.40.

* VOICE OF DEMOCRACY AUDIO ESSAY SCHOLARSHIP COMPETITION. Contact the local VFW post in your community or your state VFW headquarters. U.S. high school students in grades 10–12 eligible. Program began in 1946 and was originally sponsored by the National Association of Broadcasters with assistance from the Veterans of Foreign Wars of the United States.

General Info: Eligible students must be in grades 10–12 and properly enrolled in a public, private or parochial high school in the United States, its territories and possessions, or enrolled in an overseas school as a dependent of U.S. military or U.S. civilian personnel. (Foreign exchange students are excluded.) Entries are submitted in both typed and audio recorded forms (not less than 3 minutes or more than 5 minutes in length). Check with your school counselor or local VFW post for details, application forms and deadlines. Local winners advance to next competition level; state winners compete at national level.

Prizes: Scholarships at national level include: 1st place $20,000; 2nd place $15,000; 3rd place $10,000; 4th place $6,000; 5th place $5,000; 6th place $4,000; 7th place $3,000; 8th place $2,500; 9th place $2,000; 10th–16th place $1,500; all additional scholarships $1,000. State winners are required to attend the National Finals Program in its entirety in Washington, DC, as the guest of the VFW National Organization.

Sponsor's Remarks: "The Veterans of Foreign Wars of the United States and its Ladies Auxiliary hope that every high school in the country will provide the opportunity for its students to take part in this program. Through classroom study projects and special assignments, students will be motivated, while writing and speaking, to express their opinion about their personal responsibilities and understanding of the rights and responsibilities of being an American."

✔ * ❀ **WRITE 'EM COWBOY SHORT STORY COMPETITION,** c/o The Western Heritage Centre, Box 1477, Cochrane, Alberta T0L 0W0 Canada. Web site: www.westernherit age.net/shortstory.html. Third annual junior division competition held in year 2000.

General Info: Open to students in Canada in grades 5–9. Short stories should be about the people of the west; cowboys (or cowgirls), farmers, rodeo riders, pioneers or anyone else who might have lived in the Canadian West. Material may be drawn from fact, fiction or a combination of both. Story length is 2,000–3,000 words. No entry fee. Entrants must submit complete story, double-spaced and preferably typed. All submission must have a title and be accompanied by a cover page containing name, address, name of school attended and contact phone number.

Prizes: Up to six prize winners notified by mid-October of contest year. **Prizes:** 1st place $500; 2nd place $250; 3rd place $125; others $50. Prize winners and parents invited to awards banquet. See Web site for detailed information and guidelines.

Sponsor's Remarks: "Our purpose is to encourage young writers to test their talents by writing a story set in Western Canada. We're grateful for our many sponsors."

✔ * ▥ ✉ **WRITE YOUR OWN ADVENTURE CONTEST**, Real Kids, Real Adventures, P.O. Box 461572, Garland, TX 75046-1572. Web site: www.realkids.com. Sponsored by Deborah Morris, author of the *Real Kids, Real Adventures* series, for kids worldwide between the ages of 8–17.

General Info: Variety of contests open to kids ages 8–17. All entries must be in English. *No electronic (e-mail) submissions.* See Web site for complete details, topic and deadlines for current contests. Winners are notified by phone. No entries returned, so save a copy for yourself. Entries must be typed or neatly printed, double-spaced, black ink on clean white paper. Entries must include name, age, address, phone number (include area code), parent/guardian's name and a school name. Example of past contest: Write an essay on the subject: "A 'Real Kid' Is . . . ," making sure to include the following elements: first person point of view, creativity and passion in your approach to the subject, organized presentation of your opinion, persuasive summary at the end. Length limit was 2,500 words. Samples of past winners available on the Web site.

Prizes: May vary. Past prizes included: 1st place $50 (U.S. check) and an autographed copy of a *Real Kids, Real Adventures* book, plus the 1st place winner's school (or community group if homeschooled) received a personal visit in May 2000 from author Deborah Morris. (Personal author visits apply in United States and provincial Canada; if 1st place winner lives outside United States or Canada, Deborah Morris will provide a virtual author visit online.) 2nd place $50 check and certificate; 3rd place $25 check and certificate. Honorable mentions receive award certificate.

Sponsor's Remarks: See the profile of Deborah Morris on page 151.

✔ * $ ▣ ✉ **YOUNG NATURALIST AWARDS**, Alliance for Young Artists & Writers, Inc., 555 Broadway, 4th Floor, New York, NY 10012-3999. Web site: www.amnh.org/youngnaturalistawards. National program supported and judged by scientists at the American Museum of Natural History.

General Info: Select one of the projects detailed in contest brochure or on Web site. Length of final draft differs depending on grade student is in. Open to students in grades 7–12 who are currently enrolled in a public or nonpublic school in the United States, Canada, the U.S. territories, or in a U.S.-sponsored school abroad. For complete details, guidelines and entry form, see Web site, call (212) 343–6493 or e-mail: A&WgeneralInfo@Scholastic.com. Entry fee of $3.

Prizes: There are 12 Young Naturalist Scholarships available, 2 from each grade. Cash awards include: grade 12, $2,500; grade 11, $2,000; grade 10, $1,500; grade 9, $1,000; grade 8, $750; grade 7, $500. Plus winning entries will be published in a special nationally distributed catalog and on the museum's web site. Excerpts from selected entries will be published in *Natural History* magazine. The top 12 award-winning students will be invited to a celebration at the museum. Finalists (36 authors) will receive a cash award of $50 each; semifinalists (up to 300) will receive a non-cash award and a certificate of recognition. Teachers of award-winning students will receive a collection of books and resources for their school.

Sponsor's Remarks: "For more than 230 years, the American Museum of Natural History has been a leader in scientific research, conservation and education. See our Web site for more information of this year's program and winning entries from previous years. Helpful tips and resources for students and teachers are also available on the Web site."

* $ **YOUNG SALVATIONIST MAGAZINE-CONTEST**, c/o Youth Editor, P.O. Box 269, Alexandria, VA

22313. Published monthly except summer for high school/early college-aged youth by The Salvation Army.

General Info: Open only to young members of The Salvation Army under the age of 23. Send SASE to above address for further details.

Subscription Rates: One year $14 (U.S. funds).

✔ * ▣ ✉ **YOUNG WRITER'S GUIDE TO GETTING PUBLISHED ESSAY CONTEST**, c/o Kathy Henderson, Writer's Digest Books, 1507 Dana Ave., Cincinnati, OH 45207. E-mail: essay@youngwriternetwork.com. Web site: www.youngw riternetwork.com. Personal experience essay contest for young writers ages 5–18.

General Info: Open to young writers ages 5–18. Entries must be in English or accompanied by an English translation. Essays must be about experiences the writer had writing and submitting to markets and contests. You do *not* need to have been previously published or have won a contest before entering. *Important:* Entries must be the original work of the entrant. Adults may help by transcribing essays or retyping. It must include some advice or words of inspiration and motivation from the writer's point of view about writing, editing or getting published. *Tip:* Read the essays of young writers previously profiled in the current or past editions of this book. Will accept handwritten entries. Prefers typed entries in standard format. Entries may be mailed, e-mailed or submitted directly on the Young Writer Network Web site. If e-mailed, include essay in the body of the message; do not send as an attachment. This will be an ongoing contest. See Web site or send SASE for complete details. Enclose SAE if you wish verification that your mailed entry has been received. You may include a photo of yourself (such as a school picture), but please do not send résumés or examples of your other writing, published or unpublished, unless it is a part of your actual essay. Entrants are free to submit their essays elsewhere. Be sure to include your name, age, grade, school, your full mailing address and e-mail address if available.

Prizes: Winning entries, or portions of winning entries, may be published in future editions of *The Young Writer's Guide to Get-*

ting Published. Those published will also receive a free copy of the next edition. Other prizes to entrants may also be awarded.

Sponsor's Remarks: "Many of the young writers featured in my book first introduced themselves to me in a letter. This contest is an opportunity for readers to write and submit something specifically for consideration for future editions of *The Young Writer's Guide to Getting Published.*"

INDEX